THE ULTIMATE S

The Jersey islanders who died in German prisons and concentration camps during the Occupation 1940 - 1945

Paul Sanders

COVER IMAGE

'In the Camp' (1940), by Felix Nussbaum. Nussbaum was born in Osnabrueck, Germany, in 1904, and studied in Hamburg, Berlin and Rome. He settled in Belgium in 1935. After the German invasion of May 1940, he was arrested and sent to the camps of Saint Cyprien and Gurs ('The camps of shame'), in southern France. Nussbaum escaped and then went into hiding in Brussels. He was denounced in 1944 and transported to Auschwitz where he perished, on August 2, 1944.

Completely revised and updated second edition 2004

First published in Jersey in 1998
by Jersey Heritage Trust

ISBN 0-9538858-4-4

Typeset and layout, Jersey Heritage Trust

Printed in Great Britain by Biddles Limited

Jersey Heritage Trust
Jersey Museum
The Weighbridge
St Helier
Jersey JE2 3NF

Tel 01534-633300
Fax 01534-633301

DEDICATION

To Joe Mière

Without whose decades of persistent groundwork the story of the twenty two Jersey prisoners would have remained untold

To Peter Hassall

Jersey's 'Night and Fog' survivor who shared with the author the pain of his story of courage, compassion and endurance

ILLUSTRATIONS

Portraits of Clifford Cohu, Joseph Tierney, John Nicolle, Arthur Dimmery, William Marsh, George Fox, Clifford Querée, Frederick Page, Clarence Painter, Peter Painter, Dorothy Painter, John Painter, Jean Painter, Ivy Forster, Dora Hacquoil, Alice Gavey, Frank Le Villio, Marcel Rossi, Walter Dauny taken from Occupation Registration cards (Jersey Archives Service, D/S/A), *Gloucester Street Prison, Jersey* (Société Jersiaise Photographic Archive), *Feldgendarmerie headquarters in Bagatelle Road* (Paul Sanders), *Secret Field Police headquarters at Silvertide, Havre des Pas* (Paul Sanders), *The scene of a memorable 'wireless case' in occupied Jersey: St Saviour's Church and Parish Hall* (Paul Sanders), *Portrait of Emile Paisnel* (Birdie Paisnel), *Portrait of Maurice Gould* (Jersey Archives Service, L/C/26/1), *The beach at Green Island, Jersey* (Paul Sanders), *Pomme d'Or Hotel, the seat of the German Harbour Police in Jersey* (Société Jersiaise Photographic Archive), *Portraits of Peter Hassall and Dennis Audrain* (Peter Hassall), *Fresnes Prison near Paris* (Paul Sanders), *SS-Special Camp Hinzert in 1946* (Peter Hassall), *Wittlich Prison* (Peter Hassall), *'Work' in the Concentration Camp: Hundreds of prisoners perished hauling blocks of granite up the notorious 'staircase' leading from the Mauthausen quarry* (Centre de Documentation Juive Contemporaine, CCXLV - 350), *Maurice Gould's grave in Howard Davis Park, St Helier* (Paul Sanders), *Peter and Clarence Painter in happier days* (John Painter), *Portraits of James Houillebecq and Louisa Gould* (Joe Mière), *Harold Le Druillenec MBE after the war* (Jersey Archives Service), *Commemorative plaque at La Fontaine Millais, St Ouen* (Rex Forster), *Portrait of Frank Le Villio 1945/46, Portrait of Advocate Ogier* (Joe Mière), *Young Advocate Ogier; Ogier's younger son Richard at the time of the Occupation; Ogier's wife Emma; The Ogier children Kenneth, Barbara and Richard in 1951* (Helen Ogier), *Biberach town in 1945* (Société Jersiaise Photographic Archive), *Biberach Internment Camp* (Société Jersiaise Photographic Archive), *June Sinclair* (Joe Mière), *Wireless confiscation notice* (Société Jersiaise Photographic Archive), *Major General Müller, Commander of 319th Infantry Division and Head of overall command in the Channel Islands from May 1941 to September 1943* (Société Jersiaise Photographic Archive), *Major General Graf von Schmettow in 1944* (Société Jersiaise Photographic Archive), *German sailor with Police Constable, The Duchess of Kent meeting escapees after the Occupation, Colonel Knackfuss* (Société Jersiaise Photographic Archive), *The Memorial to the Jersey Twenty in St Helier* (Paul Sanders).*

CONTENTS

PART ONE

'Offences against the Occupying Authorities'
The Case Histories

PART TWO

'Impressions of an Occupation'

FOREWORD

There is nothing noble about a military occupation. From the viewpoint of the occupied it is a period of continuing humiliation. For the occupier it is often a corrosive and corrupting experience. For Channel Islanders, the small size of the islands and the vast scale of the fortifications inflicted upon them, made the five years of German occupation between 1940 and 1945 a time of suffocation, intrusion and social paralysis. Moral ambiguities abounded. Where was the line to be drawn between submission and collaboration, between intransigence and resistance?

In this important contribution to the expanding literature of the German occupation of the Channel Islands, Paul Sanders examines the histories of twenty individuals who were deported from Jersey for trivial offences against the occupying authorities, and who never returned. It is a fitting adjunct to the memorial on the New North Quay unveiled in 1996.

But of equal importance is the analysis which follows of the meaning of defiance in the context of small communities largely bereft of their menfolk of fighting age, and swamped by superior force. Taken in the round, Channel Islanders who endured the German occupation have little of which to be ashamed. This was no model occupation. We owe a debt to the author for sweeping aside many misconceptions and for helping to lay the foundations for more detailed and objective historical study of documentation now available than has yet seen the light of day.

Philip Bailhache

Sir Philip Bailhache, Bailiff of Jersey

ACKNOWLEDGEMENTS

Five and a half years have passed since this book first went public and almost seven years since I first started research, a period that has seen many an interesting turn: two new names, Jack Soyer and Edward Muels, were added to the Lighthouse Memorial on New North Quay, bringing the total number of Jersey offenders who died during the Occupation to twenty-two; the Jersey Archives Service, my place of work during several months in 1997, moved to a *branché* and wonderfully light and spacious building in 2000. I am afraid to say that it wasn't the sweet words of encouragement in my last chapter that lay at the base of this development; one thing, however, I have had a hand in was the fact that there have been few significant sensationalist attempts to exploit the topic of Jersey's wartime record and that, perhaps more importantly, the tone of the discussion is becoming more to the point and matter-of-fact. Openness and transparency, best reflected in the archives' policy, is paying off. It is perhaps no exaggeration to say that this text, despite its modest volume and other limitations, has created a new minimum critical standard for research. For one thing it is based on a variety of previously unpublished material at the Jersey and Guernsey Archives, the Public Record Office, the Bundesarchiv and several other repositories in France and Germany. This brings a breath of fresh air to what has become, over the years, a rather stale diet of popular authors repackaging and reiterating elements found in other publications. Worse, this undiscerning research ethic has led to the inevitable transmission of errors, from one book to the next. Knowing that this publication would be submitted to particularly exacting scrutiny - characterized as it is by the intention to 'de-contaminate' and refocus on the real issue of Jersey offenders - all information has been checked and counterchecked, thereby reducing the error margin to what was humanely and realistically achievable by one man working with finite resources and time. In all those cases where information could not be conclusively evidenced, the deliberate choice was made to discard rather than to peddle 'untruths' and give them a further lease of life. Had we not done so, the narrative flow might have been enhanced at times, but at the price of veracity. And this was a price we were unwilling to pay. As a historian I am also extremely pleased about another development that has seen the light of day, the funding scheme to further professional research into the history of the Channel Islands introduced by the Jersey Heritage Trust.

With the first edition of this book having proven popular enough to sell out in five years, and with demand continuing, I am both pleased and privileged to have been asked to update and rejuvenate this text for a second edition. The result of this effort is, hopefully, an improved text, containing material which only surfaced recently. Prose and narrative style also received a good polishing.

Naturally, no book like this is a 'one-man' effort and I owe a steadily rising debt to many individuals and institutions. The egg was hatched at the Jersey Archives Service, where the first archival research began in May 1997. This included the systematic perusal of the Occupation registration cards. Further clues about the fate of Jersey offenders were found in the Bailiff's war files and the files of the Attorney General. The staff put up with my incessant Oliver Twist style demands for 'extra food' with exemplary patience and professionalism. During the weeks of research and writing, the Jersey Museum became something of a second home, owing to the cordial reception I received from Michael Day and that marvellous group of people who make the Jersey Museum the successful venture it is. After a one day photocopying stint at the Guernsey Archives, my research focus shifted to France and Germany. The reconstruction of the odyssey of the prisoners I have called the 'Frankfurt and Naumburg Seven' was feasible on the basis of prison and court files accessible at the State Archives of Hesse, in Wiesbaden, Germany. The latter are one of the few archives where an entire set of prison records has been safeguarded for posterity. Further details on Canon Cohu and his fellow prisoners were provided through the autobiographical accounts of Frank Falla and Donald Journeaux.

My narrative of offences against the occupying authorities, German security concerns (I call them 'obsessions'), resistance, the memory of the Occupation and other related issues in Part II of the book draws on Bundesarchiv material. This was equally instrumental in unraveling the fate of William Marsh and Walter Dauny. I am particularly grateful to Mr Meentz and Mrs Frischmuth at the Bundesarchiv (Aachen) for their help in cutting through the red tape and letting me access some extremely important files relating to Channel Islands offenders. At the Bundesarchiv (Freiburg) Mr Boehm and the always helpful Mrs Waibl achieved similar marvels in helping me locate sources. I was also fortunate to have been brought in contact with Mess. Koelsch and Le Galle, of the French Ministry of Veterans and War Victims, who demonstrated a forthcoming and unbureaucratic attitude by providing me with a list of Channel Islanders in French prisons, an item that was to become absolutely indispensable. I am also grateful to Mrs Krause and the German Historical Museum in Berlin for their permission to use an image of 'Im Lager' ('In the Camp'), a painting by Felix Nussbaum, a German-Jewish artist who died in Auschwitz in 1944, for the new cover. Likewise Stephen Walton at the Imperial War Museum proved exceptionally kind. It is sad that - almost sixty years after the end of World War II - not all archives were as well-disposed towards my historical research, failing to perceive its significance. Some were what can only be described as downright obstructive. Still, their indifference made the dedicated efforts of the others all the more poignant. In the end, the negative elements were heavily outweighed by the positive.

If the story of Jersey offenders comes alive in the first part of the book, this is thanks largely to the relatives and friends of ex-offenders I had the privilege of meeting, and the interviews they granted me. Many of them were of a certain age, they had suffered and lost loved ones and prompting their memory was painful. The fact that they decided to come forward with their testimonies and bid their lost ones a last symbolic farewell was an altogether humbling experience. Sometimes they perhaps did not realize how crucial their input was toward bestowing upon this project a profound humaneness. They were the essential connector between past and present, and I drew much inspiration and motivation from their taped voices echoing in the quietness of my room when I embarked upon the stage of writing. I trust they will consider this exercise as much their book as that of their deceased relatives and friends. On a sad note, many of them have passed away since the first edition in 1998 and I do have doubts whether it would still be possible to produce this text today. It would be a great consolation to know that this project provided some relief over the fact that the sacrifice of their loved ones had not been in vain, and that they will be remembered.

The vital intermediary to the island community was Joe Mière, former curator of the German Underground Military Hospital and guardian of Jersey Occupation memory, and himself imprisoned by the Germans. He provided essential details in my quest for interviewees and honoured me with his trust. My interviewees were: Madeleine Breslin, Wg-Cd. Vernon Cavey, Rex Forster, Phyllis Le Druillenec, Robert Le Sueur, Raymonde Martel, Roy Mourant, Helen Ogier, John Painter, 'Birdie' Paisnel, George Sty, Daphne Syvret, Douglas Tanguy and Advocate Valpy. A number of other people assisted in the progress of research by furnishing additional information, among them Nancy Aylward (née Houillebecq), Elizabeth Bois, Jim Carter, Dr Wilhelm Casper, Albert (Bert) Chardine, Frederick Cohen, Superintendent Registrar Kerley, Michael Day, Geoffrey Delauney, Peter Hassall, Brian Le Bouthillier, Leslie Le Sueur, Senator Jean Le Maistre, John Noel, J G Messervy Norman, Mrs L J Rossi, David Sarre, Dr Ian Shenkin, Malcolm Sinel of Ogier & Le Masurier, Yvonne Stone (née Rossi) and Leonard Torpy. John Painter and Helen Ogier authorized the use of their family photographs and papers, and the late Peter Hassall shared the pain of his extraordinary story, and his autobiography, with a stranger.

My final thanks go to my proof-readers, Jessica Irons and Bhavana Padiyath, previously of the Times of India, for their suggestions on style and substance; and, of course, to my wife, all the family and friends for their encouragement of my chosen path as a historian.

Oxford, March 2004

NOTE ON TERMINOLOGY

Creating a standard terminology was one of the main concerns when work began on this project. The most difficult nut to crack was to find a generic term defining the type of action taken in contravention of occupation 'law'. It soon became clear that the term 'defiance' registered the common denominator. Therefore the wartime expression 'offences against the occupying authorities' has been retained throughout the text. The dichotomy of 'offences against the occupying authorities' and 'acts of defiance' encapsulates the reality of this crucial episode of the social and political history of the Occupation. Both terms have been used in the relevant contexts because they respect the peculiarity of the situation in the Channel Islands, and because they are more to the point than alternative definitions such as 'petty resistance' and 'passive resistance'. The first has been avoided due to its judgmental connotation. And 'passive resistance' is an outright contradiction in the context of defiance towards the Nazi regime, as there was no scope for a political campaign along the lines of Gandhi or Martin Luther King. Colonialism and institutionalised racism was brought to an end because it was in direct contradiction to the core principles of British and American politics and because this contradiction could no longer be sustained by the system. Core values helping in the march forward were the guarantee of property and individual rights, and the independence of the judiciary. Nothing remotely similar existed in the German example. The term 'resistance' has been avoided where possible as it is too evocative of armed and political combat, which did not play a pre-eminent role in the Channel Islands.

'Political crimes' is another problematic expression, fraught with the potential for distorted interpretation, despite the legitimate definition of some of the protagonists in this account as 'political prisoners'. The reason for this is rather simple: in order to keep control of mounting tension, the Germans chose to issue a growing body of regulations limiting individual freedoms and choice, and turned any infringement of these into an offence. While deliberate protest against these often illegal orders was an inherently political act – and this type of protest existed for example in the case of the wireless confiscation - many of the other myriad of acts the occupier punished were committed out of desperation rather than politics, even politics in its widest sense. As a consequence a duty to sort 'apples from pears' exists, otherwise we might fall accomplice to endorsing the occupier's logic, and the accompanying terminology of these offences as 'political crimes'. Therefore it is vital to make distinctions. The one to be made here is that the reason for turning such action into crimes was entirely the business of the occupier.

More than anything else this illustrates a mechanism, the most powerful description of which exists in George Orwell's novel *Nineteen Eighty-Four*: how the manipulation of language leads to the manipulation of minds and reality. That modern dictatorships criminalise many types of non-conformist, or even perfectly ordinary, behaviour and declare them 'political' follows a pattern already identified by the early theorists of totalitarianism such as Hannah Arendt and Carl J. Friedrich. What constitutes a 'political act' becomes a matter of shifting interpretation, depending on how far the ambit of politics is extended into the individual's private sphere. The objective of the totalitarian ruler being absolute power, the curtailment of individual liberties puts lives and property at his mercy. Regulation requiring yet more regulation, in order to circumscribe rapidly decreasing individual margins of liberty, this politicisation of non-conformist behaviour has a snowball effect, in many instances punishing mere difference of race, religion or ethnicity. Therefore repression in totalitarian dictatorships accedes to the ultimate stage of paranoia, targeting both actual and imagined (potential) enemies. Without the 'checks and balances' of democracy or constitutionalism, it lies in the discretion of the executive to call the shots and to decide what constitutes inimical acts and what does not. This notion served Nazism just as well as Stalinism or, more recently, Saddam Hussein, and the Stalinist purges are a particularly good reminder as to what extremes the notion of 'potential enemy' can go. The tool designed to silence 'potential enemies' is pre-emption; with this almost any measure can be justified and it is employed to encompass a growing number of individuals. As a result trivial occurrences are increasingly categorized as serious 'offences'.

INTRODUCTION

On 9 November 1996 a memorial recording the names of twenty Jersey residents was unveiled by the Bailiff of Jersey, Sir Philip Bailhache, on the New North Quay, opposite the Occupation Tapestry Gallery and the Yacht Marina in St Helier, Jersey. The twenty women and men to whom the memorial is dedicated defied the German authorities during the Occupation of the island in World War II. All of them died as a consequence of ill-treatment and deprivations they suffered in prisons and concentration camps in occupied France and Germany. This publication is the sequel to the new memorial to which it provides the natural complement. The story it tells will, hopefully, encourage reflection on this period of duress in the history of the island and become a source of pride to its people. The book's focus is one topical aspect of Jersey under the Occupation: defiance and repression. It details the diversity of acts of defiance – the patterns of defiance – and the reasons which motivated ordinary people to engage in such action. Finally, it will discuss the response of the occupier to the challenge of his authority and try to unravel some of the mysteries of the Occupation. If this publication serves to commemorate those who suffered, it will have largely accomplished its task. It would, however, be unfortunate to limit oneself to mere biography in the face of as important a topic as defiance and 'offences against the occupying authorities'. This was, after all, *the* critical nexus of Occupation history (concerning, as it did, virtually everyone). Therefore the text also offers a critical appraisal of connected issues, some of which have remained similarly contentious. Desiring above all to provide a genuinely unbiased view - a notoriously difficult undertaking which has seen many a failure - *The Ultimate Sacrifice* should not be deemed 'yet another book' on the Occupation.

The memorial in honour of the 'Jersey Twenty' testifies to the many Channel Islanders who engaged in acts of defiance or disobedience and who had to face similar ordeals as a consequence. Repression was vital in containing pressure on the occupying authority and dissuading people from engaging in hostile acts. Some of the prisoners in this book were prominent members of the island community and their imprisonment and subsequent deportation was intended as a deterrent. If we take this into account, the figure twenty – the number of names put onto the memorial in 1995 - proves to be strikingly representative and significant: while pointing to the absence of a mass basis for openly contestant action, it also illustrates that a sufficiently large number of individuals were willing to take risks and that as a phenomenon of daily life defiance was extraordinarily recurrent and ubiquitous. While twenty Jersey people died for their convictions and actions in German prisons and camps, twenty other Jersey people - in some cases close friends and relatives of the first group - received gold watches in honour of their support for Soviet wartime fugitives on the island, in 1966. Finally, twenty bundles of German prison records giving details of those imprisoned by the occupying authorities were disposed of as waste when the prison in Gloucester Street, St Helier was demolished in the post-war era. Had these documents survived, they would have been a formidable resource in establishing the names and the numbers of Jersey wartime prisoners.

The total number of people known to have been sent from Jersey to the European mainland for imprisonment in penal institutions and concentration camps currently stands at 172[1] - a figure that includes the 'Twenty'. The first part of the book will describe the circumstances of the arrest, trial, deportation and death of each of these prisoners. Their story forms part of the general story of Channel Islands prisoners, meaning that thematical elements and biography have been interwoven. Other themes touched upon in the book include the employment of civilian workers of British nationality on German sites, the sheltering of slave workers and the ravages of Hitler's 'Night and Fog' decree, a key tool in the sowing of terror in Jersey as it was in occupied Europe.

The people commemorated in this book are exemplary cases, as they embodied all varieties of dissident behaviour during the Occupation, coming as they did from diverse layers of island society. Their ranks included labourers, farmers, a shop-keeper, a middle-class entrepreneur, a priest and an advocate of the Royal Court. The limelight of attention is focused on them because they made the ultimate sacrifice of their lives. Contrary to the over-inclusive and erroneous notion of island compliance, offences against the occupying authorities were a standard feature of occupied Jersey and by no means a few isolated incidents, as some authors would want to have us believe. Joe Mière, the former curator of the German Underground Military Hospital in Jersey, estimates the number of sentences for such offences in the Channel Islands at 4,000. Thus five per cent of the population ran into some sort of trouble with the Germans during the

---

[1] Using archival material located in France and Germany, Joe Mière, the former curator of the Underground Hospital in Jersey, estimates the number of Channel Islands prisoners sent to the Continent for 'offences against the occupying authorities' as: Jersey 172, Guernsey 144 and Sark 7. According to his estimates the final number of such prisoners could reach between 350 and 400, s. letter of Joe Mière to author, 20 Apr. 1998.

Occupation; a population depleted of its most combative members - the men serving in the British armed forces. Most of the incidents were of a minor nature; most of these offences should never have been punishable in the first place, even under the special circumstances of military occupation. Though the punishment was often fairly lenient, there was absolutely no guarantee against the Germans striking out hard on some occasions, if only to prove the point that they could do as they please and that, ultimately, nobody could consider himself or herself entirely safe. If things had been left to the *Feldkommandantur* 515, the German civil affairs unit in the Channel Islands, it would have been bad enough; but the undue influence of hardened, jittery combat commanders only made matters worse. They invariably adopted a tough stance in their dealings with the island population. From it emerged the principle of a discretionary and selective rule of law, motivated by the political intention of 'reducing the pressure on the lid', often by using the more high profile cases as a warning to others. Because of the trivial nature of these offences, many commentators have tended to put their assessments on a similarly trivial footing. To them they are 'closet resistance', without substantial risk. Such deductions present a logical fallacy and an anachronism, as the consequences of many of these 'trivial offences' were not trivial at all, but genuinely tragic. Especially in the later phase of the Occupation, the limits of German tolerance were extremely low. And it was entirely up to the Germans which of the myriad of trivial offences they chose to punish in a way more reminiscent of Nazi occupation policy in Eastern Europe, and to which they would turn a blind eye.

There were a number of German courts in the Channel Islands. However, the majority of cases were dealt with by the court of the *Feldkommandantur* 515, headquartered at Victoria College House in Jersey. As far as has been possible to determine, this court sat at the States building. Other islanders were tried by the Jersey branch of the court of the 319th Infantry Division based in Guernsey. The most typical offences tried by German courts during the Occupation included possession of a radio set, spreading BBC news or countering German propaganda, insulting German troops or 'dishonouring the Reich', sheltering escaped slave-labourers or German deserters, stealing German goods (or even receiving these), blackmarketeering, sabotage, 'going slow', escape and weapons possession.[2] Most terms were executed in Jersey, but sentences longer than three months were served in continental

---

[2] Taken from a list partly compiled by Michael Ginns, s. JAS. C/C/L. Occupation and Liberation Committee Files, letter of Michael Ginns to Jean Baird, 6 Nov. 1996.

prisons. These prisoners had to expect the worst and, indeed, many were transferred to concentration camps after completion of sentence.

The second part of the book shifts attention away from the individual stories to the broader historical dimension. It intends to make a modest contribution to the historiography of the Channel Islands war. Surprisingly few attempts have been made to get a solid grip on German policy towards the Channel Islands or to thematize the unfounded security paranoia that had taken root in certain quarters of the German military; many of whom were besieged by the conviction that the islands were swamped by British agents. Nothing, of course, could have been further from the truth. Gaining an understanding of the workings of the German institutions is an important stepping-stone in unravelling the fate of offenders. Virtually undocumented are the rivalry and the differences of opinion thriving among the German occupiers and their impact on the implementation of measures on the civilian population. The *Feldkommandantur* (FK) was an administrative unit that should not be confused with the combat troops in the islands. Although staffed by the military – hence the name *Feldkommandantur* - its principal tasks were not military in character.

In broad terms the FK assumed the rights of the sovereign and was responsible for the civilian population as well as for the maintenance of law and order. In line with the principle of indirect administration – a principle borrowed from British Imperial administration – it was a supervisory authority. This meant that, in practice, the actual number of FK staffers was tiny and that their main tasks consisted in establishing directives, passing them on to the local authorities and double-checking that they had been duly executed. On a large number of issues the island authorities were co-opted. At least in theory the FK should have been the highest German authority in the islands. However, it can be hardly surprising that, with such a strong garrison, the final word in many areas, even on measures concerning the civilian population, lay not with the *Feldkommandant* but with the Commander of the combat troops in the islands, the *Befehlshaber*. Perhaps the most illustrious example of their influence was their suggestion of deporting the entire population, an idea that seems to have stemmed from the beginning of the fortification of the Channel Islands in 1941. In their opinion the presence of civilians was anathema to the smooth running of a fortress. Although the more radical plan never materialised, the basic idea of removing groups of people - if not the entire population - was never entirely abandoned, but partially implemented on several occasions. The Damocles sword of deportation became a tool of totalitarian control of the population. The availability of food and labour, and the demands of fortification served as the rationale underpinning most decisions on whom to deport, and the FK had to strike a balance: while the presence of certain categories of 'essential workers', e.g. those active in food production, was considered beneficial (it reduced the scale of German imports from France), they were less well-disposed toward 'superfluous eaters', with no useful employment in the German sense, or presenting a nuisance. These they had no scruples in removing from the Islands. Offenders, especially repeat offenders, clearly were labelled 'undesirables'.

Steps to deport civilians were also linked to the tightening of security procedures on the fortification project during 1941 and 1942. After this watershed repression was stepped up. The new security scare soon led the German authorities also to differentiate between politically 'reliable' and 'unreliable' elements in the islands. Some civilians, it was thought, were more receptive to outside influences and had a more hostile attitude toward Germany than others.[3] Non-native islanders of mainland origin were the prime targets for such suspicion. Thus the notions of 'undesirable', 'useless eater' and 'potential enemy' provided the basis for the selection of islanders to be deported to internment camps in 1942/43, as well as for the treatment of offenders.

---

[3] German military commanders took the commando raid on Sark in October 1942 for proof that not all 'unreliable elements' had been removed from the islands in the September 1942 deportations; this served as the chief argument for a second round of deportations of islanders in February 1943.

PART ONE

'OFFENCES AGAINST THE OCCUPYING AUTHORITIES'
THE CASE HISTORIES

1. The St Saviour's Wireless Case

The ban and subsequent confiscation of the civilian population's wireless sets in June 1942 was one of the most controversial measures imposed by the German authorities and represented a major intervention in island life. It triggered defiance on a massive scale and is of vital interest to our story, as some of its protagonists fell victim to German action taken against the continued reception of BBC news. Probably the best remembered of the 'wireless cases' in occupied Jersey occurred in the parish of St Saviour in spring 1943. It involved - among many others - four of the people whose names are engraved on the Jersey memorial: Canon Clifford Cohu, John Whitley Nicolle, Joseph Tierney and Arthur Dimmery.[4]

Clifford John Cohu was born in Câtel, Guernsey on December 30, 1883 as the son of Reverend Jean Rougier Cohu and Ada Sophia Orange. In 1884 the family moved to Yorkshire where his father was the Headmaster of Richmond School until 1890. Thereafter the Cohus lived at Aston Clinton in Buckinghamshire. Educated at Elizabeth College, Guernsey, and Keble College, Oxford, Cohu was ordained priest in 1908. In 1912 he went to India where he served as a minister in several communities, including as canon of Allahabad, until 1935. He was highly regarded for his straightforwardness and chivalry, earning the affectionate designation of *pukka sahib* from the local populace. He was a member of the Indian Ecclesiastical Establishment in Lucknow and held the rank of Colonel in the chaplain's department on his decommission in October 1935. He retired to Jersey in 1937 where he lived at Holly Lodge, Five Oaks with his wife Harriet, whom he had met in India, and was nominated as acting rector of St Saviour when the post became vacant in 1940.[5] Despite his eccentricity, Cohu enjoyed widespread popularity and, consequently, became the single

---

[4] The other people who received prison sentences in connection with the St Saviour's wireless case were: Marguerite Alexander, Alfred Henry Coutanche, Harold Alexander Leneghan, Maud Alice Bathe, Arthur William Downer, Donald Journeaux, his wife Irene, Agnes Maria Sarah Newland (Mrs Journeaux's mother), Frederick John Nicolle (John's Nicolle's father), Mabel Rubina Nicolle (John Nicolle's wife), John Whitley Starck, Arthur Stanley Wakeham, Edward John Gideon Mourant, Thomas Philip Mourant, s. JAS. D/Z Law Officer's Department; Journeaux, Donald, *Raise the White Flag - A Life in Occupied Jersey,* Leatherhead (Surrey), 1995, 66.

[5] JAS. D/S/A. Occupation Registration card No 21247; 'Definite News of Canon Cohu', *The Evening Post*, Jersey, 25 Sept. 1945; 'The Late Canon Cohu - An Appreciation', *The Evening Post*, Jersey, 29 Sept. 1945; 'Canon Clifford John Cohu: A Victim of the Occupation' Part One by Alex Glendinning, *Sunday Island Times,* 27 Feb. 1994.

most prominent member of the island community to have died in a German camp.

Twenty-three years spent in India had a profound intercultural influence on this man who was well attuned to the problems of his day. Many islanders still fondly cherish his memory and remember his acts of defiance, most spectacularly the rendering of the news while riding down the Parade, St Helier on his bicycle which has been confirmed for at least one occasion. In his position as chaplain of the General Hospital he further challenged German authority by disseminating information on his visits to the general and maternity wards. Not only did Cohu demonstrate bravado, but also a sense of humour. When, on one occasion, a nurse reprimanded him for his all-too-liberal handling of the forbidden fruit, he is alleged to have replied along the lines of *'Don't worry, God's on my side!'*[6] Not everyone took kindly to Cohu's stance, however. In October 1940 information reached the Attorney General from the Constable of St Helier, C. J. Cumming, (who again had received this information from members of the congregation) that Cohu *'had preached against the Germans'* (whatever that may have meant, n.b.), in his sermon of Sunday, 21 October 1940. Although opinions remained divided – Duret Aubin asked for an alternative opinion from Advocate Bois who challenged the original version - the fact that the authorities followed up on the first information shows that they were concerned and thought that such an eventuality was not unlikely.[7]

Cohu's source of information was the parish cemetery worker Joseph Tierney who wrote out the news he received every morning from John Whitley Nicolle and his father, a St Saviour farmer, who retained a radio set which had been loaned to them by Mrs Bathe. On the basis of this information, news-sheets were produced by Tierney and Arthur Wakeham, which were then carried to Canon Cohu and Henry Coutanche who worked at St Saviour's Parish Hall.[8] While the threat to the Germans from such behaviour was little more than innocuous, Cohu's non-conformism made him a thorn in the Germans' side and catapulted him to the top of the occupier's blacklist of 'undesirables'. Substantiating this is a letter Harriet Cohu wrote to the Attorney General after the Occupation and in which she pointed out that her husband's arrest had entailed no house-searches and no

---

[6] s. Garnier, Val, *Medical History of the Jersey Hospitals and Nursing Homes during the Occupation 1940-1945*, London, 2002.

[7] JAS. D/Z/H5/97. Law Officer's Department. Correspondence concerning Canon Cohu's sermon of 21 Oct. 1940.

[8] Falla, Frank, *The Silent War*, Guernsey, 1991 (reprint), 124-5.

questioning of herself nor of the companion who was living with them, Miss Eleanor Margaret Curtis, but that his *'chief fault in their eyes* [the Germans'] *was that he tried to keep up other people's spirits.'* [9]

Joseph Tierney, who was living at 23, Cheapside in St Helier, was the first member of the network to be seized on March 3, 1943, followed by a number of arrests over the ensuing fortnight. Cohu himself was arrested by the GFP, the German Secret Field Police, and taken to their HQ at Silvertide, Havre des Pas, in a car on Friday, March 12.[10] Surviving documents show that in the end a total of eighteen people were tried - most of them for receiving and disseminating BBC news or assisting this endeavour in one way or the other. However, it appears that the number of people interrogated was higher. Law draftsman Francis de Lisle Bois passed a warning from Cohu to Reverend Matthew Le Marinel, the rector of St Helier, and Curate Preston who were equally involved in the spreading of news.[11] With so many people involved, most of whom had probably never prepared for the eventuality of being arrested, there was plenty of scope for manoeuvre and a gifted interrogator would have had few problems trying to retrieve the type of information needed to indict as many people as possible.

The German authorities were becoming increasingly nervous about popular disobedience to the wireless confiscation order, a measure the FK had never been enthusiastic about, owing to the difficulty of its enforcement and the potential it carried for undermining its own authority. A purportedly harmless activity, when banned, turned overnight into an act of great significance. The continued reception of news now represented an act of defiance which challenged the FK's total authority. Once tarnished, a loss of authority could easily extend into other areas. A go-soft approach to this issue was therefore out of the question. The St Saviour's wireless case was the perfect opportunity to stage a show-trial that could act as a deterrent and persuade the rest of the population to abstain from illegal action. However, the result was forcefully counter-productive, with the challenge to the FK's supremacy spreading into other areas: though islanders became more circumspect, they also became more technically ingenious and developed all kinds of virtually undetectable crystal sets. As is attested in many diaries and memoirs, news invariably found its way around the island. Having

---

[9] Letter of Mrs H Cohu to Duret Aubin 29 Oct. 1945, in: JAS. D/Z Law Officer's Department.

[10] 'Canon Clifford John Cohu: A Victim of the Occupation' Part One by Alex Glendinning, *Sunday Island Times*, 27 Feb. 1994.

[11] 'Canon Clifford John Cohu: A Victim of the Occupation' Part Two by Alex Glendinning, *Sunday Island Times*, 6 Mar. 1994.

handed in one set, many people kept a replica hidden away in a safe place and an impressive number of these contraptions appeared on window-sills on 8 May 1945, ready to blast out Churchill's speech.

The trial took place, barely one month after the arrests, on April 9, 1943, behind closed doors in the Lower Committee Room of the States Building. Eager to give this one occasion a semblance of legality and exploit it for propaganda purposes, the court made a unique provision for Advocate Valpy, Mrs Bathe's lawyer, to act as defence counsel. This is the only documented case where an island lawyer was ever allowed to defend a client in a German court. Not that it made any difference; as in Valpy's view the outcome of the trial was clear from the outset; the court procedures bore no resemblance to the standards required in a fair trial; guilt was assumed and all the defence counsel could do was plead in mitigation. However, unlike other trials, the case enjoyed a great deal of public exposure - something the Germans surely could have avoided had they aimed for more secrecy. Donald Journeaux, one of the defendants, recounts that on leaving the States Building after the trial, large crowds had gathered in the Royal Square, eagerly awaiting the result - a fact substantiated by an entry in Sinel's Occupation diary.[12]

A determination to rid the island of Cohu's presence altogether accounts for the disproportionately harsh sentence he received, in striking contrast to the sentences given to other defendants for very much the same offence. Cohu was sentenced to 18 months imprisonment for *'failing to surrender leaflets and [...] disseminating anti-German news'*, whereas usually sentences for convictions of this category ranged between a mere one to two months. Equally, Tierney's two-year sentence *'for manufacturing and distributing leaflets'* appears as a telling idiosyncrasy in the light of the two months imposed on another defendant, Arthur Stanley Wakeham, for an identical offence. Clearly a hidden agenda was at work seeking to isolate 'troublemakers' and emblematic figures like Cohu.

The second blow was directed at those believed to have demonstrated initiative, as shown in the case of Tierney and Nicolle (the latter being branded as the chief 'criminal' by the German prosecution).[13] The third line of attack targeted those involved who were English-born, as in the case of Arthur Dimmery. He was a gardener whose crime constituted having dug

---

[12] Journeaux, op. cit., 66; s. corresponding entry in: Sinel, Leslie, *The German Occupation of Jersey: A Complete Diary of Events, June 1940-June 1945*, Jersey, 1984.
[13] Journeaux, op. cit., 65.

up Mrs Bathe's wireless set which, afterwards, was handed over to Mr Nicolle. Dimmery's relatively low sentence of three months and two weeks was to be served on the Continent, whence he never returned.[14] He left Jersey for an unknown destination together with Nicolle, on May 5, 1943. After completing his term he probably found himself in the hands of the Gestapo and was sent to Neuengamme concentration camp, outside Hamburg.[15] How Dimmery came to be admitted to Laufen, one of the internment camps for Channel Islanders, remains a mystery. He died there on April 4, 1944 and lies buried at Salzach Municipal Cemetery.[16]

Five days after the verdict, on April 14, 1943, Cohu was transferred from the military (German) to the civilian side of Gloucester Street prison where life was easier.[17] The Germans had taken over two blocks of the prison for their own purposes. The larger building was reserved for German servicemen and the smaller for civilian offenders against the occupying authority. The civilians remained in the German part of the prison until the time of their trial; however, once the German court had reached a verdict, prisoners were transferred to the civilian side under the Jersey authorities. Cohu spent three months in the civilian side before being shipped to the Continent on July 13. In a letter written the same day to Jurat Baudains and the Public Health Committee, he correctly predicted his first way-station, Fort d'Hauteville,[18] near Dijon:

> I am leaving tonight for somewhere in France - probably Dijon - and I want to thank you for all your kindness to my wife and myself. I shall be so grateful if you will, on my behalf, thank the Matron and all the members of the staff for the delicious suppers they have sent over to me every evening. You can scarcely imagine what a lot it has meant to me.
>
> The hearty greetings from the windows I shall greatly miss, but I trust to be permitted to return some day, then I hope to

---

[14] JAS. D/Z Law Officer's Department; Journeaux, op. cit., 46-71

[15] JAS. L/C/24/A/5. Joe Mière Collection, List of political prisoners in the Channel Islands 1940-1945.

[16] JAS. B/A/W/85/5. Bailiff's War Files, War graves.

[17] 'Canon Clifford John Cohu: A Victim of the Occupation' Part Two by Alex Glendinning, *Sunday Island Times*, 6 Mar. 1994.

[18] JAS. B/A/L/15. Bailiff's Liberation Files. Inquiries for Relatives, letter of Mrs Cohu to Lt-Col. J W Taylor, British Military Authority, Mil HQ, Jersey, 18 May 1945.

show you all that I do not forget all your kindness and sympathy.
Till then, with kindest regards, yours very sincerely,
Clifford J Cohu[19]

Tierney, who in the meantime had been allowed to attend the christening ceremony of his new-born daughter, followed him there on September 18, 1943. The relocation of prisoners to Dijon was necessitated by the pressures of accommodating a growing torrent of prisoners at the French central prison of Villeneuve St Georges. Henceforth the Fort of Hauteville started to share the functions of the central prison and became a collecting point for all those selected to serve their sentences in Germany.[20]

Five of the seven Jersey prisoners we will meet in chapter Three ('The Frankfurt and Naumburg Seven') were regrouped at Hauteville before being sent to prisons in Germany, first Frankfurt and then, six months later, to Naumburg. They were Canon Cohu, Joseph Tierney, Frederick Page, Clifford Querée and George Fox. The final transfer from Fort d'Hauteville was on December 21, 1943, taking them first to Saarbrücken prison in Germany where they stayed for two weeks[21] and then, on January 6, 1944, to the prison of Frankfurt-Preungesheim.

As the 'chief culprit', John Nicolle did not join the rest of the Jersey prisoners on their journey to Frankfurt, although he had been transferred with them from Fort d'Hauteville and had spent Christmas with them at Saarbrücken. Immediately after the holidays, however, on December 27, 1943, he was transported to an altogether different destination: Zweibrücken, where he was detained together with Alfred Connor, another Jerseyman arrested for possession of explosives.[22] Three and half months

---

[19] s. Garnier, Val, *Medical History of the Jersey Hospitals and Nursing Homes during the Occupation 1940-1945*, London, 2002, appendix VI.

[20] The relocation of prisoners from Villeneuve St Georges to Hauteville was officially sanctioned in May 1944. At this stage it became the practice to send all prisoners with sentences running over three months to Germany, s. BA-R 22. Reich Ministry of Justice. 1341. Note of the Militärbefehlshaber in France to Section Ib (Kommandostab), Group 3, 10 May 1944.

[21] List provided by the French Ministry of Veterans and War Victims, 31 July 1997; file on George Fox at Prosecutor's Office at Frankfurt District Court, State Archives of Hesse, Wiesbaden, Ref. 46, 18893/5.

[22] Connor and another man, Norman Dexter from Guernsey, had also been in the party of Hauteville prisoners sent to Saarbrücken on 23 Dec. 1943. Dexter joined the 'Frankfurt group' and survived Preungesheim and Naumburg, s. list provided by the French Ministry of Veterans and Victims of War, 31 July 1997.

later both men were sent to Bochum where they arrived on April 17, 1944.[23] The fact that Nicolle had been sentenced to three years' simple prison and that prison terms over two years were executed at Bochum prison, accounted for his separation from the other prisoners.[24] A few days later Nicolle was sent on to Dortmund where he arrived on April 21.[25] This prison was particularly vile as is recounted by one survivor, according to whom Bochum was already *'bad, but it was a palace compared to Dortmund'*. John Nicolle's journey ended at Dortmund where he perished from starvation and overwork, at an unknown date.[26]

---

[23] List provided by the French Ministry of Veterans and Victims of War, 31 July 1997.

[24] BA-R 22. RMJ. 1341. Army Notification Bulletins 1944, 10th edition, 18 May 1944.

[25] List provided by the French Ministry of Veterans and Victims of War, 31 July 1997.

[26] According to a letter written by Mr Verbene Amart to Ruby Nicolle after the war and cited by J H L'Amy in his unpublished memoirs *The German Occupation of Jersey* (in custody of the Société Jersiaise).

2. William Marsh's Fatal Breach of the Nazi Work Ethic

William Marsh was born in St Helier on November 28, 1920. A motor mechanic by profession, he worked as a bread roundsman in the beginning of the Occupation.[27] Described as a recluse who spent his free-time repairing and riding his bicycle, he took up employment with the Germans.[28] First at the Grand Hotel and then, one year later - on the promise of better pay - with the Organisation Todt (OT), the German labour organisation, at Bel Royal Garages. Another five months later he was on the payroll of the most active German contractor in Jersey, Elsche & Co., where he stayed for a year before joining the *Inselwaffenmeisterei* (island armouries) in November 1943. In all save the first case he was sacked because of his rebelliousness and his adoption of a 'go-slow' work ethic. His confrontational attitude had much to do with Marsh's own temperament, but it was also influenced by the fact that one of his closest relatives, his grandfather Samuel Selig Simon, was one of the registered Jews in Jersey. Unlike most other islanders who, on a personal level, were little affected and could almost ignore this reality of occupation, the Marsh family faced the daily experience of racial discrimination. The tightening grip of the anti-Semitic measures greatly affected them as Marsh's grandparents lived in constant fear of deportation. The Marshes moved from Le Geyt Street to Elston, Langley Park on May 11, 1942, to be closer to Samuel and his wife who had been given consent to take up residence in Vallée des Vaux, a five-minute-walk away, one month earlier.[29] Samuel was ill and the Marshes' move clearly bore a relation to the restrictions which severely immobilised and isolated Jews. Later Samuel moved to Elston, the Marsh home, where he eventually died on November 7, 1943, a short time before William's arrest.

Marsh's pattern of unruliness did not change when he arrived at the *Inselwaffenmeisterei* that same month: every morning, on arrival at the worksite, he spread BBC news among the other 15 British civilians who started imitating his example. To keep the workers happy the Germans then introduced a supplementary breakfast pause which at times became rather extended, again due to Marsh's influence. These incidents, one surmises - though a cause of irritation - would have probably been dismissed as a

---

[27] JAS. D/S/A. Occupation Registration Cards (form attached to card; signed 17 Jan. 1941).
[28] Information provided by an anonymous relative.
[29] Cohen, Frederick, *The Jews in the Channel Islands during the German Occupation 1940-1945*, Jersey, 2000, 19.

hazard of having to rely on naturally reluctant British civilian workers, had Marsh not started to offer his own opinions. What caused German irritation was his tendency to discuss the political situation and get into arguments with the Germans, who did not take kindly to being contradicted. Clearly, Marsh was too outspoken, perhaps also naïve. He later conceded that:

> It was never my intention to talk bad about the Germans, but through the conversations on war and politics at the *Inselwaffenmeisterei* it often happened that in the course of a dialogue, sometimes out of fun sometimes out of anger, things were said that otherwise wouldn't have been said.[30]

Marsh had clearly misjudged German sensitivities. Moreover, as a worker on a military project he was not exempt from military discipline. Therefore, when he was reported for misconduct in February 1944, he could not expect to get off with a simple dismissal from his workplace. In any case not after having repeatedly worn his true sentiments on his sleeve. Subsequently he was interrogated by the *Feldgendarmerie* and put on trial. The outcome of this trial was far from obvious, as the search of Marsh's room had produced no results: the Germans could unearth neither a radio set nor any incriminating print matter. Significantly, the German non-commissioned officer who had nicknamed Marsh 'minister of propaganda' tried to downplay the affair when he was questioned by the *Feldgendarmerie*. He stated that he *'did not regard Marsh's behaviour as sabotage, he simply wanted to impress his work mates with his alleged knowledge of the news'.*[31] It is therefore reasonable to presume that a less assertive stance and a more unassuming tone in the courtroom plus a willingness to belittle the import of his actions might have shortened Marsh's impending sentence. However, left to fend for himself and in the absence of a defence counsel, Marsh failed to take advantage of the slim margin. Sensing the noose tightening around his neck, he made a last ditch attempt to retract himself from the deadly embrace: thus, he claimed that it had not been his intention to brand the German news as 'propaganda' - as the two German witnesses claimed he had done – simply to point out that in times of war *'propaganda comes from both sides'.*[32]

---

[30] Interrogation of William Marsh, 3 Feb. 1944, in: BA-ZNA. Z 726. Court of the 319th I.D., Jersey Branch. Investigations into the case against William Marsh.

[31] Examination of the witness NCO Joseph H., 4 Feb. 1944, in BA-ZNA. Z 726. Court of the 319th I.D., Jersey Branch. Investigations into the case against William Marsh.

[32] Trial report, 19 Feb. 1944, in BA-ZNA. Z 726. Court of the 319th I.D., Jersey Branch. Investigations into the case against William Marsh.

Subconsciously, however, his mind was bent on not letting the Germans have it 'their own way'. Despite his pleas, the court remained sceptical, as their belief in his subversive and dangerous role was reinforced by his occasional outbursts during the proceedings. And the curtain fell when he commented on the absence of fair trial procedures by alleging that the soldiers [who acted as witnesses] had received orders regarding their testimonies. This was a direct reference to the fact that they had not been sworn in. It proved to be a suicidal slip of the tongue, as the court deemed it a grave *'insult to the German forces which exposed Marsh's dangerous attitude'*, and they decided to include it in the verdict. Marsh then desperately tried to retract this statement, only to find his offer rejected by the presiding judge. Harmless actions, which ordinarily would have been simply a matter of reprimand, had become - in the words of the court - the motivated handiwork of a *'fanatical enemy [...] who had to be eliminated for a longer period of time'.*[33]

On 19 February 1944 Marsh was sentenced by the court of the 319th Infantry Division, at King's Cliff House, St Helier, to one year and three months' imprisonment for *'insulting the German forces, disturbing the working peace and disseminating anti-German information.'* [34] He was deported to Germany where he shared the fate of several other jailed Channel-Islanders.

---

[33] Verdict of court of 319th I.D., Jersey, 19 Feb. 1944, in BA-ZNA. Z 726. Court of the 319th I.D., Jersey Branch. Investigations into the case against William Marsh.

[34] BA-ZNA. Z 726. Court of the 319th I.D., Jersey Branch. Investigations into the case against William Marsh; JAS. D/Z. Law Officer's Department.

3. The Frankfurt and Naumburg Seven

... to get away from the body and reside with the Lord (St Paul, 2 Cor, v.8)

In 1944 the prison in the Frankfurt borough of Preungesheim became one of the principal detention centres for Channel Islands offenders in Germany.[35] A rule enacted in 1942 decreed that residents of the Western occupied territories sentenced by German courts to prison terms exceeding three years were to be transferred to penitentiaries in Germany. However, whether prisoners were deported to Germany or not depended heavily upon the discretion of the competent court.[36] At that time men sentenced to simple prison could be sent to Saarbrücken and Wolfenbüttel (via Freiburg and Karlsruhe), and women to Cologne.[37] In December 1943 Saarbrücken was replaced by Frankfurt[38] as the detention centre for those with sentences of up to two years.[39] Finally, when Saarbrücken suffered heavy bomb damage in 1944,[40] many Frankfurt prisoners were sent to Naumburg, in order to provide prison space for new arrivals from the Western occupied territories.[41] The practice changed over the years and it appears that in the latter part of the war all sentences longer than nine months were carried out in Germany.[42]

It was a grim sojourn for Frank Falla, a Guernsey journalist, and his colleagues Charles Machon, Cyril Duquemin, Joseph Gillingham and Ernest Legg, all sent to prison in Germany for the publication and distribution of news-sheets containing the BBC news, the Guernsey Underground News Service (GUNS). Arriving at Preungesheim in June 1944, he found fifteen Channel Islanders serving their sentences there. Seven of the Jersey people

---

[35] BA-R 22. RMJ. 1341. Army Notification Bulletins 1944, 10th edition, 18 May 1944.
[36] BA-R 22. RMJ. 1342 (Microfilms). OKW Memo, 13 May 1942, re. transfer of Belgians and French to German penitentiaries.
[37] BA-R 22. RMJ. 1341. Army Notification Bulletins 1944, 10th edition, 18 May 1944. Execution of sentences in area of military government in France.
[38] BA-R 22.RMJ. 1341, Military government in France, Sec. Ib (Kommandostab)-Group 3, 1 Dec. 1943, re. Order concerning the execution of sentences, 21 Oct. 1943.
[39] Sentences over two years were executed at Bochum prison, in: BA-R 22. RMJ. 1341. Army Notification Bulletins 1944, 10th edition, 18 May 1944.
[40] BA-1342. RMJ to Mess. Public Prosecutors, 24 June 1944.
[41] Letter of Chief Prosecutor in Frankfurt to the Prosecutor at Frankfurt District Court re. Order of the RMJ of 8 Oct. 1943 , 4 Jan. 1944, s. Preungesheim prison records at State Archives Hesse, Wiesbaden (Reference: 409/4, file 2).
[42] BA-R 22. RMJ. 1341. Army Notification Bulletins 1944, 10th edition, 18 May 1944.

commemorated in this study were regrouped at Preungesheim after having transferred from prisons on the Western border of Germany.

George James Fox and Clifford Bond Querée were born a decade apart in St Helier, the former on May 22, 1896, the latter on September 27, 1906. They were also living there at the time of their arrest. Fox, originally a cabinet-maker, was employed as a kitchen-helper during the Occupation. Querée was employed as a labourer and storeman.[43] The men were tried together by decree of the Court of Field Command 515 on June 23, 1943 and received two-year sentences: Fox for 'continual larceny', Querée for his 'continual receiving of stolen articles'.[44] As the case was taken over by the German court it can be assumed that their property offence had concerned goods belonging to the Germans, most likely bread or other foodstuffs.[45] After their trial both men were transported to Fort d'Hauteville, Dijon, together with Canon Cohu, on July 13, 1943.[46]

Around the same time Frederick William Page was facing charges with four other men - James Davey, Davey's brother Isaac, Owen Dore and George Louis Sty – for a 'wireless offence' committed at Le Coin Bungalow, James Davey's home, at Route des Pres, St Saviour. Sty, the only member of this group still alive today, testified that three groups of radio listeners took turns in the loft of the house, but he never knew who the members of the other two groups were. Besides their social function, the main aim of the get–togethers was to by-pass the firm German control on information. Sty recounts that Page, an agricultural labourer born in Portsmouth, on November 20, 1900, was an unassuming and calm man, practically indistinguishable from the other listeners. As in the St Saviour's Wireless Case, the listeners were not caught in the act, but hauled out of their beds, one morning at 6 a.m., and taken to *Feldgendarmerie* HQ at 'Tudor House', Bagatelle Road where each one was interrogated separately for three hours. The Germans had, no doubt, been observing the premises and their aim consisted in hunting down all of Davey's flock. On July 19, 1943 the group, together with nine other people, was summoned before the court. Sty remembers that the prosecutor was ebullient and, in a fierce move,

---

[43] JAS, D/Z Law Officer's Department; State Archives Saxony-Anhalt in Merseburg, Rep. C 131 II, 3463, 808.

[44] JAS. D/Z Law Officer's Department.

[45] Harris, Roger E., *Islanders Deported. Part 1: The Complete History of those British subjects who were deported from the Channel Islands during the German Occupation of 1940-45 and imprisoned in Europe,* Illford, 1980, *157.*

[46] Harris, op. cit., 157/58.

demanded that all the defendants be deported to Germany. If things took a different turn for most of the men involved it was due to their consciously low profile during the hearings. With the sole exception of Page who disregarded all caution and displayed an extraordinarily temperamental attitude: from the beginning he made no secret of the fact that he was English-born, boasting that he had fought the 'Hun' as a Guardsman during the First World War. As in the case against William Marsh, the German judge saw a particular danger in his defiant attitude and there was little hesitation about removing Page, who had already been exempted once from the 1942 deportation, from the island. Page and Davey faced tough sentences of 21 and 18 months respectively for *'failing to surrender a wireless set'*. The other three men were fined between 100 and 150 RM each, for having *'listened to wireless broadcasts in company with others'*.[47] Page was sent to Fort d'Hauteville on September 18, 1943, along with Joe Tierney.[48]

Further details on the exact circumstances of this case became available through the recent discovery of a bundle of Occupation files from the Attorney General's office. The case itself is one of the most important to have emerged, for there is proof that this offence was not first discovered by the Germans, but during a routine search of the Jersey police. This occurrence makes it extremely compelling and instructive, providing an excellent case study on the ethical dilemmas of cooperation and how the authorities dealt with these.

The Jersey police stumbled across the case while investigating a robbery in the vicinity of Davey's home in late May 1943. During their interrogations of neighbours they were told that Davey had a wireless set at his residence. Following up this lead, the police questioned Mrs Davey who pointed out a loose panel in the ceiling which gave access to the roof space where three wireless sets and spare wireless parts were hidden. One of these belonged to Davey, the other two to Page.[49] As was customary, the Attorney General was informed about the discovery on 2 June 1943, and the next day he forwarded this information to Germans. A straightforward case of collaboration, one might be tempted to think. But things were not quite that simple: a German order of 18 December 1942, in fact, instructed all officials to submit all information to the occupier which bore a relation to

---

[47] JAS. D/Z Law Officer's Department.
[48] List provided by the French Ministry of Veterans and War Victims, 31 July 1997.
[49] JAS. D/Z/1943/19. Police Report. Centenier Garden to Attorney General, 2 June 1943.

infractions against German orders. The Attorney General explained the dilemma of the situation, when the case was investigated by the British:

> Three days before I received the report in question from Centenier Garden, he called upon me and told me that he was gravely disturbed in his own mind as to what action he should take in consequence of the discovery by him during the course of a police investigation and the possession, contrary to a German Order, by a civilian of one or more sets of wireless receiving apparatus. Centenier Garden informed me that the police investigations which he had been making emerged from a neighbour's quarrel and that he was afraid that his discovery of the wireless sets in question was known to and being generally talked about by several people who were hostile to one another and that, therefore, there was a grave risk that knowledge of the police discovery of the wireless sets in question would soon reach the ears of the German police. In these circumstances, he was in doubt, he told me, where his duty lay; whether to report the facts, as was his legal obligation, and thus expose a civilian to prosecution or to conceal the facts and thus run the risk, in the event of the Germans discovering the facts, of the police of St Saviour being suppressed and, consequently, the whole of the police administration of the parish of St Saviour being taken over by the Germans, a situation which it had, throughout the occupation, been the settled policy of the insular administration to avoid. I told Centenier Garden that I was not disposed to give him an order one way or the other in a matter into which considerations of conscience entered so strongly, and that he must decide with his own conscience where his duty lay. I added that if I did receive a formal police report from him I would have no alternative but to forward it to the occupying authority. Centenier Garden subsequently informed me that he had put the matter to his colleagues at a meeting at the St Saviour police and that their unanimous opinion was that the duty of the police was

to the community rather than to the individual and that he should therefore report.[50]

This outcome of the ballot was more or less inevitable. The risk of a denunciation to the German police being no invention, the policemen could not be expected to shoulder such a risk. What is more intriguing is the propagation, by the authorities, of a utilitarian 'greater number' argument. This principle itself is frequently applied in battlefield or other crisis situations. Accordingly, in theory, there is nothing wrong about applying it in an emergency such as military occupation. Also the act of reporting an offence to the Germans as such was not contentious. By the time the Jersey police discovered Davey's radio, the island authorities had already missed their opportunity to put up resistance to German orders in connection with 'wireless offences'. Resisting at this point would have been a futile gesture. Not reporting the offence would have also sent out the wrong type of signal to the remainder of the population. There is no doubt that word of non-pursuance by the island police would have spread like a bush-fire, triggering a movement of mass defiance. This, in turn, would have led to some very uncomfortable questions from the Germans, with unforeseeable consequences.

What was disingenuous about the Attorney General's use of the 'greater good' argument, however, was to present the entire case as *force majeure*; passing under a veil of silence the part of the island authorities in turning an activity, which should have never been an offence in the first place, into a punishable offence. While the confiscation of the radios was something the island population had to accept, the prosecution of 'radio offenders' had no basis in international law. This was the principle the island authorities had not contested, neither before nor after the Germans issued their order of 18 December 1942, when the trap closed. The devil had crept up behind them and they had either failed to notice or turned a blind eye. This is where more could have been expected from the authorities, who liked to bask in paternalism, but clearly did not always measure up to their calling of providing a buffer. In order to provide a more effective buffer, their attitude would have required less risk-averseness. In addition, it would warrant further examination whether the 'sacred cow' of preventing a German take-over of the police administration of the parish of St Saviour was a goal worth the deliberate sacrifice of individuals, i.e. whether it was ethically sound to apply the 'greater good principle' in this situation. Exactly the

---

[50] JAS. D/Z/1943/19. Memorandum, Attorney General, 4 Aug. 1945.

35

same idea - the safeguard of as much French sovereignty as possible - induced Vichy to round up one-fourth of the Jews of France and hand them over to their executioners.

Emile Paisnel, born on April 9, 1883 in St Clement, was a farmer living at Boulivot de Bas. His case, like Marsh's, was taken over by the court martial of the 319th Infantry Division (I.D.). This court had jurisdiction over all the cases affecting the direct interests of this combat unit. Most of the transgressions under the scrutiny of its court involved breaches of discipline and misappropriation of military supplies, whereas the general interests of the occupying authority were represented by the court of FK 515. The cases taken over by the court of 319th ID were predominantly against German soldiers and foreign workers, but occasionally also involved British civilians. Paisnel was tried for 'receiving stolen articles' on February 19, 1944. His granddaughter 'Birdie' Paisnel believes that he was denounced for the recovery of goods later discovered by the Germans, most probably a lot of coal. Paisnel bartered wheat for coal and his purveyors were two men, a British driver for the German military and a Dutch OT worker, who siphoned off the fuel from German stocks. Both were sentenced together with Paisnel, to five and four-month terms respectively, on the grounds of 'military larceny'.[51] For reasons unknown to us Paisnel received a stiffer, ten months' imprisonment. This was one of the rare occasions where a island dignitary, Jurat Bree, is known to have intervened on behalf of an offender - pleading for Paisnel's sentence to be executed in Jersey - the appeal was rejected on March 24, 1944, on the grounds that his sentence was too long.[52] Anticipating the worst, Paisnel tried to take precautions: he left the island with a large amount of cash stitched in the handle of his suitcase. Deported to St Lô prison, where he arrived on May 5, he was later despatched to Fresnes.[53]

Tierney, Cohu, Page, Querée and Fox arrived at Frankfurt-Preungesheim from Saarbrücken prison on January 6, 1944. William Marsh and Emile Paisnel who were both tried in February 1944, arrived at Frankfurt on April 18 and May 23 respectively, after a short sojourn at Karlsruhe prison. Preungesheim had four five-floor blocks, filled with 850 prisoners of all European nationalities. The blocks led onto a central building which Frank Falla described as '*a kind of platform and enclosed cabin in which worked*

---

[51] JAS. D/Z Law Officer's Department; interview of author with 'Birdie' Paisnel, July 1997.
[52] ibid.
[53] State Archives Hesse, Wiesbaden. Files of Prosecutor's Office, Frankfurt District Court (Reference 461, Nr 18893/11).

the prison administrators, complete with Nazi uniform, Iron Cross, other medals, sword and all the trappings that were supposed to impress us. ' [54] Conditions in Frankfurt were severe, but up to the D-Day landings inmates could communicate with their relatives in Jersey once a month, and both Cohu and Tierney took steps for obtaining an early release after serving two-thirds of their time. Mrs Cohu remained equally active from her side and repeatedly went to College House to appeal for her husband's release. The last time she heard from him was in July 1944. After the war she testified that he had remained in solitary confinement at Preungesheim, spending ten and a half hours a day inserting hooks into cardboard frames. Although the German judge in Jersey had assured Mrs Cohu that parcels could be sent, these were confiscated on arrival. Unequipped to supplement the wholly deficient diet which consisted of a weekly bread ration of four and a half pounds,[55] emaciation soon took its toll and Cohu's weight dropped from 10 stone 3 lb. when he left the island to 7 stone in May 1944.[56] In his letters to his wife he frequently referred to the gruelling conditions in prison, particularly the cold and the hunger. Prisoners frequently had to join work-parties clearing rubble or removing unexploded bombs from the devastated streets of Frankfurt. Preungesheim also served as place of execution for all civilians - both Germans and foreigners - tried by special Nazi courts in the districts of Frankfurt, Kassel and Darmstadt and by the 'People's Court'.[57] In mid-1944 executions were taking place at a weekly rate of 30.[58] The eyewitness account of one unknown prisoner makes for macabre reading:

> In the beginning they were beheaded with a hatchet, opposite the chapel. Later they [the prison authorities, n.b.] added a hall where they set up a guillotine. Mostly, the executions took place very early in the morning. The executioner and his assistants would arrive the night before at the prison, where a nice room had been prepared for them; cigarettes and alcohol were plentiful and they drank

---

[54] Falla, op. cit., 114.

[55] Falla, op. cit., 122.

[56] JAS. B/A/L15. Bailiff's Liberation Files. Inquiries for relatives, letter of Mrs Cohu to Lt-Col. J W Taylor, British Military Authority, Military HQ, Jersey, 18 May 1945.

[57] Falla, op. cit., 122. This special jurisdiction under the Nazi judge Roland Freisler was responsible for high treason cases such as the trials against the members of the failed plot to assassinate Hitler on July 20, 1944.

[58] Falla, op. cit., 116; SPD Preungesheim, *8. Mai 1945 - 8. Mai 1985. Preungesheim 40 Jahre danach - erinnern oder vergessen?*, 29.

and made noise throughout the night until the executions commenced at 6:30 a.m. Heads were chopped at intervals of five minutes.[59]

No air-raid shelters existed for prisoners and the frequent air bombardments on Frankfurt sent waves of terror and anguish through the prisoners who were confined to their crowded and claustrophobic cells. One particularly heavy attack scored many direct hits in the immediate vicinity of Preungesheim prison on February 4, 1944, at a time when five of the seven Jersey prisoners were incarcerated there.[60] Worse was to come: in July 1944, the Channel Islands prisoners were transferred to Naumburg-on-Saale, where conditions for 350 prisoners were even worse than in Preungesheim. Typically, rations would consist of a mere six ounces of bread and a litre bowl of 'soup' a day. Cells measured 16 cubic metres and conditions were even more cramped than in Frankfurt. Dysentery and dropsy, for which no medication was available, were rampant. According to Falla, they *were not allowed to smoke, talk, sing, hum or smile - it was starkly grim, but at no time were our spirits dampened, our hopes shattered, for we knew and had explicit faith that one day our torturers would be conquered.'* [61] Frank Falla also recalled that Cohu's two most heartfelt, but unsatisfied, wishes were to be reunited with his wife and to be allowed to bury the Englishmen who died in prison. Prison deaths occurred at a rate of 18 men a week,[62] and after exchanging half a bread ration against a one-inch-stub of pencil, Falla recorded the names and dates of his companions as they perished in quick succession.[63] Of the Jerseymen, Paisnel was the first to die on August 29, 1944, four weeks after his arrival at Naumburg prison.[64] Of his last days Frank Falla wrote: *'Like Percy Miller (a fellow prisoner at Preungesheim, n.b.) he was too far gone, mentally and*

---

[59] SPD Preungesheim, *8. Mai 1945 - 8. Mai 1985. Preungesheim 40 Jahre danach - erinnern oder vergessen?,* 31.

[60] Eyewitness account by Emil Schmidt, a political prisoner in Preungesheim, in: SPD Preungesheim, *8. Mai 1945, 8. Mai 1985. Preungesheim 40 Jahre danach - erinnern oder vergessen?,* 6.

[61] According to information provided by Frank Falla, in: L'Amy, op. cit., 10.

[62] Ibid.

[63] Falla, op. cit., 123.

[64] State Archives Saxony-Anhalt in Merseburg. Naumburg Death Register, Rep. C 131 II, Nr 3461, 574; State Archives Hesse, Wiesbaden. Files of Prosecutor's Office, Frankfurt District Court (Reference 461, Nr 18893/11).

physically, to care, and towards his end refused to eat the paltry food put before him.' [65]

In spite of their state of advanced emaciation Page, Fox and Quérée lived through one more miserable winter in prison, but died soon afterwards: first Page. For a long time the prison administration had been aware that he was hovering between life and death, but refrained from taking any steps to ameliorate the situation. Finally, two weeks before his death, they sent a note marked 'urgent' to the Chief Prosecutor's Office in Frankfurt. It consisted of an authenticated copy of a recommendation by Dr Weissgerber, head of the Office of Public Health in Naumburg, and it wistfully noted that Page was suffering from *'heavy circulation disorders and extensive infections of cell tissue. He is no longer fit to be kept in prison. It is required that he be released as soon as possible.'* [66] The request was transmitted on from Frankfurt to the court of FK 515, the deciding authority. On January 4, 1945 the prosecutor was notified of the court's consent and on that day (or the next) a telegram was sent from Frankfurt to Naumburg, authorising the administration to proceed with Page's immediate release.[67] By this time, Page was on his death-bed and he passed away on January 5, 1945, at 6 a.m.[68] The belated action on Page's behalf, corroborates that the prison authorities were never genuinely concerned about the prisoners in their custody. It stands out that the general disposition of the prison staff towards the prisoners was negligent and often brutal, a point also expounded in Frank Falla's account of conditions in Naumburg.[69] An innocuous little note found at the Hesse State Archives in Wiesbaden offers a further hint on why the prison authorities could have been interested in releasing Page. This note, scripted by the Prosecutor's Office, informed the mayor of Naumburg that his claim for reimbursement of the costs of Paisnel's funeral has been rejected. It continues: *'According to regulations such costs cannot be covered by funds of the department of Justice [...]'* [70] From this it seems

---

[65] PRO. FO 950 765. Letter of Frank Falla to Foreign Office, 13 Apr. 1965.

[66] Medical certificate re. Frederick Page, sent to the Chief Prosecutor's Office in Frankfurt, 22 Dec. 1943, s. State Archives Hesse, Wiesbaden. Files of Prosecutor's Office, Frankfurt District Court (Ref. 461, Nr 18894/2).

[67] Ibid.

[68] Ibid.; State Archives Saxony-Anhalt in Merseburg. Naumburg Death Register, Rep. C 131 II, Nr 3462/25.

[69] One of the numerous differences between detention in a prison and a concentration camp. Clearly, the latter had removed most bureaucratic barriers and even the minimal accountancy of death was eventually disposed of.

[70] State Archives Hesse, Wiesbaden. Files of Prosecutor's Office, Frankfurt District Court (Ref. 461, Nr. 18894/11).

highly likely that the prison and, for that matter, the city authorities were trying to discard their moral and financial liability toward prisoners who died in their custody, by obtaining early releases. George Fox was the next prisoner to die, on March 11, 1945, leaving behind four children.[71] Two days later, on March 13, 1945, a query reached the Chief Prosecutor's Office in Frankfurt inviting objections to a proposed early release of the last remaining Jersey prisoner, Clifford Querée. Such an eventuality would have mattered little to Querée who was on the brink of death. Naturally, the underlying motive was not altruism, but rather the wish to avoid accountability for the appalling conditions at Naumburg and, in particular, the deaths by neglect of British civilian prisoners.[72] The overwhelming impulse to evade responsibility found further expression in the burning of the prison records in the same month of March 1945. After having almost completely lacked this amenity during the cold winter months, those who had survived so far were now in for their hottest showers ever![73] On April 16, 1945 the prison was finally liberated by the Allied forces and Querée was admitted to hospital. Strenuous efforts of Frank Falla and the American doctors failed to improve Querée's sinking health and he died two weeks later of pneumonia, on May 1, 1945.[74] The four Jerseymen who died in Naumburg lie buried at the British Cemetery in Heerstrasse, Berlin [75]

Cohu, Tierney and Marsh, all initially part of this group, had been discharged from Naumburg and transported to unknown destinations. Their gruelling fate did not come to light until after the war: Canon Cohu's sentence officially ended on September 24, 1944, Tierney's on March 25, 1945. During their imprisonment in Frankfurt both men had laid the groundwork for an early release.[76] On August 16, 1944, two weeks before he was handed over to the SS, Cohu made one last appeal to the court of FK

[71]State Archives Saxony-Anhalt in Merseburg. Naumburg Death Register, Rep. C 131 II, Naumburg, Nr. 3462/25.
[72]State Archives Hesse, Wiesbaden. Files of Prosecutor's Office, Frankfurt District Court (Reference 461, Nr 18894/2).
[73]Falla, op. cit., 122.
[74]JAS. D/Z Law Officer's Department; State Archives Saxony-Anhalt in Merseburg. Naumburg Death Register, Rep. C 131 II, Nr. 3463/808.
[75]JAS. Bailiff's War Files. BA W85/5. War Graves-Civilians in enemy and enemy occupied territory.
[76]On October 11, 1944, Tierney sent a plea for clemency to the court of FK 515, s. State Archives Hesse, Wiesbaden. Files of Prosecutor's Office, Frankfurt District Court (Reference 461, Nr 18894/2).

515 in Jersey.[77] This may have influenced the treatment he received after he was taken from Naumburg. Walter Lainé, a Guernseyman convicted for radio possession, was kept in solitary confinement at Frankfurt after his 15 month-sentence ended on October 25, 1944. In a post-war communication with the War Office, Lainé attributed this to the fact that he did not volunteer to work for the Germans. Norman Dexter, who was imprisoned on the same charge, received the same treatment and both prisoners were later transferred to Straubing prison, in Bavaria.[78] Similarly, neither Cohu nor Tierney had displayed any enthusiasm for the German war effort. They considered their departure from Naumburg would be a transit arrangement leading to an internment camp. The prison records relate that on August 30, 1944 Cohu was released from Naumburg prison on the grounds of a 'suspension of sentence'.[79] This bureaucratic jargon was tailor-made for keeping up legalistic pretences.[80] As soon as both men's sentences had been 'suspended' they left the tutelage of the Reich Ministry of Justice and were taken over by the Gestapo which sent them to camps under SS authority. Cohu was put in a 'work education camp' in Zöschen, 22 miles from Naumburg and halfway between the two cities of Halle and Leipzig. He arrived there with a group of 50 prisoners, on September 13, 1944, at a time when the camp population had swollen to 500.[81] Conditions in 'work education camps' were primitive and reputedly worse than those in most concentration camps. Typically, 30 men were cramped into small round paper tents (16 x 16 foot), with nothing but straw spread out on the bare soil. Cohu attracted attention and became a prime target for abuse, the minute he set foot in the camp. His position could not have been less enviable: being the only British prisoner was exposure enough; in addition, he was also a priest, which provoked the guards' perverse ingenuity. Feeble and thin, he was unable to lift a shovel, which earned him the direst of abuse (*'You English swine, you want to bomb us, we will bloody show you, you cripple'*) and continual beatings. The camp SS were bent on bringing about one guard's ominous prognosis that he would not last longer than

---

[77]State Archives Hesse, Wiesbaden. Files of Prosecutor's Office, Frankfurt District Court (Reference 461, Nr 18894/1).

[78]PRO. WO 311/677. War crimes in the Channel Islands-Evidence and investigations, letter by W H Lainé to the War Office, 25 Oct. 1945.

[79]State Archives Hesse, Wiesbaden. Preungesheim prison records (Reference 409/4, Nr 2).

[80]As we will see in other parts of this book, Nazism had hardly ever to grapple with the challenge of modifying the legal environment, as the rule of law was slowly superseded by arbitrary administrative measures.

[81]PRO. FO 950/766. 'Index to names of British subjects in enemy concentration camps and statistical survey of camps'.

seven days, and their brutality prevailed on September 20, 1944. That day Cohu finally succumbed to the privations of his 18-month ordeal. When preparing his body, Przemysl Polacek - the Czech survivor who broke the story of Cohu's death - found a small bible tightly pressed against his breast.[82] Such was Cohu's conviction that he had managed to hide this most valuable possession, against all conceivable odds, in defiance of body searches and despite the infernal treatment and terminal exhaustion of his final days. The last act of defiance of an extraordinary man, whose body was abused and broken, but whose faith remained intact. Doubt lingers about what happened to Cohu's remains: an official document created after the war lists Cohu as having been buried at Zöschen, but a French survivor told Mrs Cohu that her husband's body was more likely to have been incinerated in Halle.[83] Cohu's tragic disappearance was painfully felt in the island and it was not long after the war that a commemorative plaque was set up in his honour in St Saviour's church.

Next to no information has survived on Joe Tierney's movements following his discharge from Naumburg prison: except that he died in Celle in April 1945, following his recapture after a failed escape attempt.[84] Even less is known of Marsh's final fate. Documents provided to the Foreign Office by Frank Falla in 1965 show that he was removed from Naumburg and died near the town of Zeitz on March 12, 1945.[85]

---

[82]For an account of Cohu's seven days at Zöschen, s. Przemysl Polacek's letter to the British Embassy in Prague, 25 Oct. 1945, in: JAS. D/Z Law Officer's Department.

[83]State Archives Merseburg, Saxony-Anhalt, Rep. C 131 II, 982, 34; Rep. K, 662, 146.

[84]After the war a letter from a Belgian prisoner, René Vandenterghen, told Eileen, Tierney's wife, of the circumstances of her husband's death, s. L'Amy, J.H., *The German occupation of Jersey*, unpublished memoirs.

[85]PRO. FO 950/765, letter of Frank Falla to Foreign Office, 13 Apr. 1965.

4. Into the Night and Fog

On May 3, 1997, St Luke's Church in Jersey was the scene of great emotional poignancy, the experience of which promises to remain long engraved in the collective consciousness, as the Lieutenant Governor, the Bailiff and members of the public attended a service which was followed by a short ceremony at the War Cemetery in Howard Davis Park. The congregation had gathered in order to bid a final adieu to and honour a remarkable youth, Maurice Jay Gould. As they stood in solemn silence, watching his remains being laid to rest in Jersey soil, those whose living memory stretched back fifty-five years recalled the fateful day of May 3, 1942, when Maurice Gould, Peter Hassall and Dennis Audrain had failed dramatically in an attempt to escape the island. The outcome could not have been more harrowing: Dennis paid with his life and the two surviving youngsters were deported to Germany where Maurice died in 1943. Only Peter survived the cataclysm, and the ceremony marked the end of his fifty-year struggle to fulfil Maurice's last wish: '*bring me back home.*' Many Jersey folk lie buried in foreign soil, but Maurice suffered a rather peculiar fate, for his remains had lain alongside German military personnel and members of the Waffen-SS in a war cemetery. The inauguration of Jersey's memorial to the 'Twenty' made it a fitting moment to remedy this unsavoury state of affairs, which a more sensitised public opinion could no longer admit. For the first time in fifty years serious efforts were made to find a suitable resting-place for Maurice's remains. Help came from many quarters, with the Jersey Branch of the Royal British Legion playing a major part in the logistics of the operation and the States of Jersey endorsing the proposed action by a vote of funds. Finally when Maurice's next-of-kin gave their approval, appropriate steps were taken which culminated in the ceremony in Howard Davis Park.

Measured against similar occasions, which are often protocol-driven events lacking a certain intimacy, the commemoration of this small, yet important foot-note of the Occupation brought back to the public memory the tale of the three teenagers. This story was a perfect epitomy of Jersey's wartime plight, not least because it involved youngsters. The gesture was instinctively endorsed by everyone, for it transcended controversy and struck an emotional chord which left nobody untouched. The three teenage boys, whose venture ended in tragedy, bear a lasting testimony to the capacity of individuals to defy oppression and engage in authentic resistance. Ultimately, they have left a reverberating legacy worthy of emulation by future generations.

Peter was the only member of the trio to survive the war and the memories of his dead companions and of his own mental and physical suffering continued to haunt him for many years. He only started coming to terms with his past by putting himself through the painful process of resummoning the traumatic experiences, casting them into words and immortalising the voices of his friends in a biographical account. Accompanying this was an obligation he felt towards Dennis and Maurice, namely to dispel misinterpretations they were subject to and protect their memory against all allegations that their action had risked 'rocking the boat', i.e. that it may have provoked the Germans into countering with harsh reprisals. Such claims were, of course, absurd, as nobody had ever suggested that the successful escapees of 1944/45 had provoked such a thing; on the contrary, they secured a permanent place in the Pantheon of Jersey folk heroes.

Maurice Jay Gould was born on May 31, 1924 in Leicester. He came to Jersey at the early age of two and a half to live with his grandfather, 'Pop' Trueblood, the proprietor of the 'Australian Herbalist shop' in St Helier. In 1941 he worked as an apprentice mechanic-blacksmith.[86] Over six feet tall, Maurice was not a person who went unnoticed: a *'gentle giant'*, he was adorned by nature with *'a mass of chestnut coloured hair'* and sported *'even, white teeth [...] always in evidence, because of a built-in grin.'*[87] Unfortunately, his singularity did not escape his future tormentors at SS-Special Camp Hinzert whose favoured object of abuse he became.

Maurice's character was impeccable. During the preparations the boys often had to make use of a certain amount of deviousness and cunning and Maurice took little part in this. Peter Hassall later explained that *'Maurice had very strong principles, and disliked any form of deceit [...].'*[88] Although their personal motives varied - Peter had strong personal reasons to put the island behind him, whereas Maurice had an extremely harmonious relationship with his grandfather - the three escapees shared a common repudiation of all things Nazi. They suffered from the moral dilemmas of accommodation with the enemy and were desperate to free themselves of the iron grip that was suffocating the island, and them. As the rest of Europe, Jersey was exposed to racist infamy, with the Germans launching the propaganda film 'Jew Süss', an insidious anti-Semitic diatribe

---

[86] Hassall, Peter, *Night and Fog Prisoners*, 26, at
<http://www.jerseyheritagetrust.org/occupation_memorial/pdfs/hassallbookcomplete.pdf.>
[87] Hassall, op. cit., 13.
[88] Ibid., 43.

commissioned by Goebbels, which was on show at West's Cinema in 1941. Dennis and Peter went to see 'Jew Süss' and on leaving the cinema they were more disgusted by the effect the film had had on some of the viewers than by the film itself. In any case this only reinforced their conviction that they had to escape.

The experience of war, destruction and brutality has profound effects on the young; the Occupation was no exception and would have been the cause not only of frustration, but also of psychological strain to sensitive and perceptive youngsters. They were ill-equipped for coping with anything as difficult as the Occupation, an event which placed them at a distinct disadvantage to adults who had more experience of confronting complex situations. While adults knew that there was a thin line between 'confronting' and 'compromising', young people tended to see things in black-and-white, thus depriving themselves of options.

Their preparations display a great deal of thoroughness as they tried to calculate every eventuality. They were equally determined not to arrive empty-handed in England and had therefore prepared a detailed map of German fortifications and photographs of state-of-the-art war material. Peter was in an excellent position to provide such material, as his father held a virtual monopoly on the development of the snapshots taken and brought to his officially licensed film processing workshop by the unsuspecting German troops. Without his father's knowledge Peter and his brother Bernard duplicated photographs from these negatives.

On the other hand, there was also an element of amateurism and hot-headedness, as they disregarded the warnings of Captain Sowden and Jersey policeman Albert Chardine, who told them that their boat was too small. They certainly lacked the expertise of Dennis Vibert whose feat they were bent on emulating. Vibert was 22 years old at the time of his successful escape in 1941 and he had learnt the basics of sea faring and navigation as a trainee in the merchant navy, from 1934 to 1937. Had they stuck it out two more years, until the summer following the D-Day landings, their chances of being aboard one of the many successful craft that were sneaking across to France would have been better. How much the boys were inspired by Vibert's example is clearly shown by Peter himself, in a synopsis of the preparations leading to the escape:

In October 1941, Peter learned of Dennis Vibert's brave escape to England. [89] This gave him and his friend, Dennis Audrain,[90] ideas of their own, and after talking things over, the two decided to follow Vibert's course to England. Later into their planning, they enlisted the help of another youth, Maurice Gould, who was 17 at the time. In order to obtain the money to buy a boat and motor, Peter temporarily left school to work at his father's shop [...] When sufficient money was on hand, a twelve-foot dinghy and outboard motor were purchased. It was transported across town in plain view of the Germans, then stored in an uncle's back-yard, where it was caulked, painted and made ready for the voyage.

By April 1942, the trio had assembled all the necessary equipment for their escape, then taking into consideration the tides and curfew, the boys decided to leave on Sunday 3 May, 1942 [...] A few days before the escape, the dinghy was loaded onto a horse-drawn cart, then brazenly driven along the German occupied streets of St Helier. It was off-loaded at Green Island, on the island's South East coast, where a party of young German soldiers helped the youths get it off the cart.[91]

The boys knew the risks and the fate that awaited anyone caught trying to escape. The consequences of such action had been well demonstrated in 1941 when the German military meted out a death sentence to Frenchman François Scornet who was shot in the grounds of St Ouen's Manor, and jailed 15 other French would-be escapees stranded in Jersey which they had mistaken for the Isle of Wight. But they firmly believed that it was worth the risk and also that there was only one form of resistance à la Jerriaise - escape. And there was some justification for their reasoning: if one accepts

---

[89] Dennis Vibert displayed a tremendous amount of sang-froid and a wonderful determination when, after returning from a failed attempt in November 1940, he repeated his feat ten months later in the 'Ragamuffin', an 8ft boat. His fabulous coup was one of the few known escapes from the Channel Islands between the onset of Occupation in 1940 and summer 1944, s. Thomas, Roy, *Lest we forget. Escapes and attempted Escapes from Jersey during the German Occupation 1940-1945*, Jersey, 1992, 2; Mayne, Richard, 'People who escaped from Jersey during the Occupation', in: *Channel Islands Occupation Review* 1975, 22-4.

[90] Dennis Désiré Audrain (*1925) was Hassall's closest friend at De la Salle College ('The Beeches'), a private Catholic boy's school in St Helier, s. Hassall, op. cit., 8.

[91] Hassall, synopsis of his memoirs, 5-6.

the metaphor of Jersey as a prison, the great act of defiance was not to revolt against the warder, but to surmount the walls of the prison. This was the only way of creating genuine frustration in the enemy camp. An option that was, however, an exclusive prerogative of the young, the fit, the courageous and the most imaginative. The boys had these qualities in abundance, but on the fateful evening of their escape they ran out of what they probably needed more than anything else - luck:

> When time came to launch the boat at 10:00 p.m., the winds had risen, and the ebb tide was very rough, therefore the launch was postponed. As time was running out, the dinghy was finally launched at 10:45 p.m., despite the rough seas. Unfortunately, when the boat was but a few hundred yards from shore, a combination of starting the motor, a large wave and heavy swells threw it against a rock, and caused it to capsize. Maurice was swept out to sea, as Peter struggled to save his friend, Dennis.[92]

Dennis, a non-swimmer, drowned in the attempt to reach the shore. When Maurice and Peter reached safety they were arrested almost immediately by the German Harbour Police and taken to their HQ at the Pomme d'Or Hotel. The next day they were picked up by the *Feldgendarmerie* and placed in the German wing of Gloucester Street prison where they were treated as alleged 'terrorists' and manhandled. The Secret Field Police had found the trio's nautical chart on Dennis's body and the photographs in a suitcase. As they believed that adults were behind the escape, the two boys underwent rigorous interrogations during the following ten days. Meanwhile Gestapo headquarters in France had grown interested in the case, demanding that the two youngsters be transported to Paris for further questioning. In France they were to experience to an even fuller extent what had become the hallmark of Nazi brutality all over Europe.

At the time of their escape, the German Nacht und Nebel decree had just entered into effect. This measure was designed to curb the rising tide of resistance activities in many parts of occupied Europe. The Nacht und Nebel (NN)[93] decree was issued on December 7, 1941 by the Chief-of-Staff of the Wehrmacht High Command (the highest military authority in Nazi Germany), Field Marshal Keitel, on instructions from Hitler. It followed increased resistance activity in France and in other parts of Western and

---

[92] Hassall, synopsis, 7.
[93] The English translation is 'Night and Fog'.

Northern Europe after the launch of 'Barbarossa', the German invasion of the Soviet Union in June 1941. France, in particular, had become the stage for several assassinations of Germans and throughout the summer of 1941 military courts had stepped up their repressive stance. Perceiving their failure to cope with the deluge of court proceedings, while the tide of resistance was continuing to grow, Hitler decreed the need for special expeditious methods designed to deter. Their implementation was entrusted to bodies Hitler trusted: the Ministry of Justice, the Central Office of Reich Security[94] and the Special and People's Courts. The provisions made by the decree were to cover 'punishable offences against the German Reich or the occupying power', a term that could be interpreted more widely than the terms set out by the martial and penal law then in force. It was applied in all those cases where a speedy death sentence - pronounced by a military trial within a period of eight days - could not be guaranteed by the military authorities. NN prisoners were tried by Special and People's Courts and the main purpose of the decree was to introduce a new dimension of fear and increase the deterrence factor. The NN decree was to sound the bell for a new phase in psychological warfare, expressly targeting civilians. The second set of underlying themes responsible for this decree was Hitler's disdain for 'lawyers' in particular and for regular legal procedures. It was the Führer's long-standing opinion that the lawyers serving in the military courts were superfluous. One of his favourite lines, and an often reiterated theme for that matter, was that 'soldiers should keep away from things they don't understand', meaning by this that all matters of 'security' should be handed over to his most devoted acolytes, the SS.[95] The general direction since 1933 had been to replace the independent judiciary of the Weimar Republic by a justice system drawn along Nazi lines. With the outbreak of war this tendency made a major leap forward, to the point where the judiciary's former independence was in total eclipse.

---

[94] In German: Reichssicherheitshauptamt (RSHA); the most important institutional merger of SS and State Police services and 'umbrella' for Reich Security, comprising:
1.   Geheime Staatspolizei, short: Gestapo (Secret State Police),
2.   Kriminalpolizei, short: Kripo (Criminal Police).
These two services were merged in 1936, to become the Sicherheitspolizei (SIPO), Security Police.
3.   Sicherheitsdienst, short: SD (Security Service of the SS).
The common acronym for the three services was SIPO-SD. The term 'Gestapo' was, and is, often used *pars pro toto,* which can lead to confusion.
[95] The notion of 'security' was extremely elastic and could be abused at will.

Another well-cherished, but erroneous, concept was the idea to prevent resistance fighters from becoming 'martyrs' in the public mind; Hitler claimed that the exposure of lengthy court procedures achieved exactly that. Here again his prejudice (and not empirically based hard facts) came into play. Trials, it was thought, reinforced the capabilities of resistance and acted as an inspiration to others.[96] Field Marshal Keitel, a man with no opinion of his own, acquiesced to Hitler's demands and claimed that the NN procedure was a step designed to save the face of military justice. In fact, it contributed to the creeping erosion of military pre-eminence in the Third Reich, for the expedience of the procedure made it an extremely handy tool of repression, soon monopolised by the SS.

The NN procedure was set in motion in all cases which had an element of resistance: attempts on the lives of Germans or collaborators, espionage, sabotage, communist activities, creating unrest, aiding and abetting the enemy by being a member of an escape network, attempting to join the Allies or giving support to enemy military personnel, and illegal possession of firearms. NN prisoners were held incommunicado, with the prisoners cut off from all outside contacts or sources of information. This provision was rigorously enforced: no news was given to their families or governments, their whereabouts were kept secret, they received no letters, no food parcels and they were strictly separated from other categories of prisoners.[97] NN trials had all the characteristics of a travesty of justice. They involved rapid proceedings, no pre-trial procedures and pronounced disequilibria which worked in favour of the prosecution. Neither did they make provision for witnesses or a defence counsel. Translators, when provided, were incompetent. These trials often ended in summary death sentences, and those who received prison sentences or were acquitted, found the Gestapo outside the prison offering them a ride, most commonly to a concentration camp.

In accordance with the implementation of the Night and Fog Decree, Maurice Gould and Peter Hassall disappeared shortly after their escape attempt, only to re-surface at Fresnes prison, just outside Paris. Fresnes was a detention centre for political prisoners, controlled by the military, and the 3000-strong jail was used as a clearing-house for both Allied escapees and French resistance members. The Gestapo did not believe the boys' version

---

[96] Father de la Martinière, a former NN prisoner, also described the procedure as 'a variation of hostage taking', concealed behind *pro forma* legality, s. Martinière, Joseph (de la), *Nuit et brouillard à Hinzert. Les déportés NN en camp spécial SS, n.d.*
[97] Hassall, op. cit., 55.

of a self-supported escape and continued to assume that they had received logistical and financial support from British agents in the Island. Interrogations therefore continued at Gestapo HQ (rue des Saussaies in Central Paris) where the boys endured a method of abuse that had acquired notoriety in French resistance circles as *le supplice du bagnoire* - the bathtub torture. This standard Gestapo implement involved plunging prisoners into a bathtub full of cold water and forcing their heads under water until their lungs felt like bursting. Hassall and Gould survived this ordeal and were sent to Trier on June 12, in a convoy, along with fifty-two French prisoners. Their final destination was SS Special Camp Hinzert, situated a short distance from Trier in the hillsides of the Hunsrück region.[98] The idyllic setting of the surrounding countryside, which tricked many new arrivals into developing false hopes, painfully contrasted with the horrors perpetrated behind the barbed-wire fence.

In October 1939 this camp was opened as a detention centre for unruly OT labourers employed on the *Westwall,* a fortification project on Germany's Western border. From summer 1941 the camp started receiving a large number of Luxembourgers who opposed the Germanisation of their homecountry. Other prisoners included Italians, French Foreign Legionaries of German nationality and, increasingly, French NN prisoners. Altogether, 41 convoys of NN prisoners arrived at Hinzert, the first on May 29, 1942 and the last in September 1943.[99] Hassall described Hinzert as a '*brutal little camp*' where the prisoners were like '*fish in a small glass bowl*', never out of the '*sadists' sight*' [100] and gaped at by the civilian population who did not hesitate to approach the camp perimeter on their Sunday outings.

Hassall established a minimal modus vivendi necessary to maximise his chances of survival, which in any case were dim. As an example, he soon learnt how to avoid beatings. Maurice on the other hand, proved less able to adapt, most of all because of his all-pervading gentleness from which his shell of physical sturdiness failed to divert attention for long. Maurice attracted unwelcome attention because of his physical stature; while his lack of knowledge of the camp's official languages - German and French -

---

[98] Fighting to lay the past to rest', in: *JEP*, 9 Dec. 1996, 18-19; Note of Gestapo HQ to the administration of Fresnes prison, re. prisoner transfer, 5 June 1942 (by courtesy of Peter Hassall).

[99] From November 1943 Natzweiler became *the* camp of the French NN, s. Martinière, Joseph (de la), *Le décret et la procédure Nacht und Nebel (Nuit et Brouillard)*, Orleans, 1981; Martiniére, Joseph (de la), *Nuit et Brouillard à Hinzert. Les déportés NN en camp spécial SS*, n.d.

[100] Hassall, op. cit., 106

magnified his isolation. Maurice had no chance of ever letting his British credentials work to his advantage; in his case it increased his vulnerability. His inability to make any sense of the madness of the concentration camp microcosm was misunderstood as a special form of perfidiousness, inviting the nickname of 'Churchill'. He became a favourite target for the vicious attacks of an anglophobe kapo named André Callaux. Hassall reckoned that 'of all the young prisoners in Hinzert, Maurice had been the most brutally abused.'[101] He suffered his worst beating at the hands of Callaux when it was his (and Hassall's) turn for one of the several bone-crunching work parties, the infamous *Kohlenkommando* (coal work party). The Hinzert *Kohlenkommando* had all the characteristics of the worst type of 'work' in other concentration camps whose main function was 'Extermination through Work' (*Vernichtung durch Arbeit*).

The word 'work' in the context of the concentration camp differed drastically from its customary connotation. The idea of 'work' in the latter is embodied in a whole web of beliefs centred on human progress; it is a symbol of modern human self-determination, nearly always associated with constructive action.[102] The Kohlenkommando was a parody of this: its basic rationale was to assign to a party of about a dozen (or more) youths a job normally done by horses. The aim to degrade human beings by placing them on par with four-legged equestrians was achieved through a gruelling rigorous regimen. Once the prisoners had loaded a cart with two tons of coal, it had to be drawn over a distance of several miles, past rugged hilltops. After unloading, the same procedure was repeated again, from dawn to dusk. For want of alternative footwear, most prisoners performed this type of back-breaking work wearing wooden clogs and Maurice earned a vicious beating for having tried to recover his which he had lost in a downhill stumble.

Another camp routine was the practice of rushing and parading naked, emaciated, undernourished prisoners up and down the camp, a practice cynically termed 'exercises', 'gymnastics' or, simply, 'sports'. Every movement in the camp was accompanied by continuous beatings. Severely

---

[101] Ibid., 104

[102] Concentration camp 'work' was 'anti-work'. To illustrate this notion further it may be useful to take a look at the situation in Mauthausen, one of the most brutal camps. A particularly distinctive feature of this camp were the infamous 'stairs', chiselled into the rock and descending from the camp to a nearby quarry. The heavy blocks of stone that were transported uphill by undernourished and beaten prisoners caused a heavy death toll that was in no way a matter of accident, but of callous and calculated premeditation.

traumatised and unable to bear the incomprehensible onslaught, Maurice's condition degraded rapidly. In place of a survival strategy grew frustration, born out of the failure to comprehend the reason for the cruelty of his fate, and his condition was soon worsened by premonitions that he would not be able to survive. Peter writes:

> I was very concerned for Maurice, because one needed a cast iron will to live, and it seemed that Callaux had beaten him to the point of giving up. I was aware, and I am sure Maurice was, that he would not live unless his will to fight back was restored [...]. I do not think that a cross word had ever been spoken in his home and neither had he witnessed any violence, and from such a warm and loving home he had been thrown in the Nazi arena to be re-educated by Hitler's sadists. [...] He had not learned to hate as I had.[103]

The two Jersey youngsters' worst suffering ended on July 24, 1942, six weeks after their arrival at Hinzert when the prisoners were transferred to nearby Wittlich prison, a way-station for NN-prisoners destined for trial. Wittlich was *an 'oasis' in the centre of Germany's wartime morass of concentration camps and prisons* and when the prisoners arrived, Dr Bitthorn, the prison director, was overheard saying *'that he had never seen such emaciated and badly treated men'.[104]*

Despite the limitations of their means, the prison director and a few other well-intended civilians tried to make life bearable for the prisoners by banning beatings and supplementing the meagre rations allocated by the Gestapo in Trier with food grown on prison-owned lands. However, this had little effect on the death toll taken by the main NN killer at Wittlich, TB, which spread easily under conditions of dampness, lack of heating and food deficiencies. There was nothing that could save Maurice whose health had been irreparably damaged at Hinzert: when he arrived at Wittlich he had already lost 50 pounds[105] and by November 1942 it became rapidly clear that, seriously ill with TB, he was doomed. As an NN prisoner he stood no chance of being sent to a sanatorium and, with no adequate medical treatment available, the only relief to his suffering lay in sparing no efforts to make the last months of his cruelly shortened life as bearable as possible. Eventually, he was transferred to a special sick ward set up by a

---

[103] Hassall, op. cit., 106

[104] 'Fighting to lay the past to rest', in: *JEP*, 9 Dec. 1996, 18-19.

[105] Hassall, op. cit., 110.

French doctor. In September 1943 he virtually stopped eating and he was completely skeletal when he died on October 1, 1943, in Peter's arms. Again, it was due to the efforts of Dr Bitthorn and Father Barz, the prison priest, that he was afforded a Christian burial in Wittlich's old cemetery; in defiance of explicit orders from the Gestapo who kept a watchful eye on 'enemies of the Reich'. Unfortunately, the good intentions demonstrated in this noble gesture were frustrated in 1973, when West Germany's Federal reburial unit displayed their disturbing lack of sensitivity by relocating his body to a military cemetery.[106]

Hassall's odyssey through the horror of the Third Reich's prisons continued and like for his native island, liberation was not to come to him before May 1945. In March 1944, at a time when he had rebuilt some of his lost inner reserves, the Gestapo's order to transfer prisoner Hassall could no longer be resisted by Dr Bitthorn and he was sent to Breslau (today Wroclaw, Poland) in Silesia, where he was to await his trial. Breslau had become the seat of the 'Special Tribunal' assigned to try NN prisoners, after Cologne (and its prison) had been heavily wrecked by bomb damage in July 1943. Peter Hassall was tried on June 1, 1944 and a combination of favourable circumstances, i.e. his age, nationality, ability to defend himself in German and clever defence tactics helped him to avoid the death sentence. Instead he received a four-year prison sentence and was able to avoid the common destination of so many other NN - the vicious concentration camp of nearby Gross-Rosen - being sent, instead, to Schweidnitz, a filthy but more 'survivable' prison. When the Russian advance closed in on Schweidnitz, he was moved one more time to Hirschberg prison. With the front-line having by-passed Hirschberg, his liberation on 9 May 1945 was undramatic: the door of his cell was unlocked and he was commanded to pick up his few belongings and leave.

The Painters

Two other NN prisoners from Jersey who died in Nazi concentration camps were the Painters, father and son.[107]

Clarence Claude Painter was born in Abingdon, Berkshire on November 2, 1893. He had served in the forces and worked in the office of a railway company before his marriage, in Jersey, to Dorothy Mary Smith on his

---

[106] 'Fighting to lay the past to rest', in: *JEP*, 9 Dec. 1996, 18-19.
[107] Musée de la résistance et de la déportation, Besançon, de la Martinière files concerning NN prisoners.

twenty-eighth birthday. Miss Smith was the daughter of a well-known Jersey ice cream and mineral water manufacturer and had taught in England during the First World War. After their marriage Clarence took up a managerial post in his father-in-law's firm and at the time of the latter's death in 1936 he was responsible for the mineral water side of the business, with premises in Cannon Street.

When evacuation procedures for the Channel Islands started in June 1940 it was initially decided that Clarence would stay in order to ensure the continuity of the business and that the rest of family would go to England. In the end, however, it was only the family of Mrs Painter's brother who seized the opportunity, while the Painters remained in Jersey.

Peter Edward, the Painters' eldest son, was born on April 11, 1924 in St Helier.[108] Various people described him as a 'generous and unassuming' young man, 'wise beyond his years' and destined 'to succeed in life'.[109] At the time of his arrest in 1943 he had already completed his schooling at Victoria College where he had been popular both with the teaching staff and his fellow pupils. He had distinguished himself as a first-class sportsman, demonstrated his leadership qualities as a scout troop leader before the war and later joined the OTC (Officer Training Corps). Despite a German ban, conspiratorial Boy Scout activities were maintained throughout the Occupation by some dedicated and astute individuals, among them Sidney Guy. The Painter house was used for Scouts' meetings on a regular basis, right until the time of the arrest. A photograph at the German Underground Hospital in Jersey shows Peter in the company of students at Captain Sowden's 'Nautical College', of which he was a member, in June 1943. Sowden, a sea captain who retired to Jersey before the war, founded this institution after he was discharged from the command of the SS Normand, a freighter plying the Jersey-Normandy route, in 1941. The discharge followed his refusal to contravene the clauses of the Hague Convention by transporting German ammunitions aboard his ship. While many of his students at the Nautical College envisaged a naval career or wanted to join the merchant navy once the war was over, others, like the 1944 escapees and would-be escapees who acquired their navigation skills from Sowden, had less mundane ideas.

Peter belonged to that *'crowd of cheerful, though frustrated, youngsters'* who saw the best times of their life wasted under the constraints of military

---

[108] JAS. D/S/A. Occupation Registration card No 23351.
[109] Quotations taken from letters sent to Mrs Painter, s. Painter Papers.

occupation.[110] Like many others, Peter tried to ignore the presence of the occupying forces as much as possible, through the pragmatic policy of *'carrying on as though they weren't here'*. This however did not keep him from defying the authority of the occupier. For some youngsters this was more a test of courage than anything else; in some instances, however, it could turn into deadly earnestness. Peter took photographs of German planes at the airport with his friends Roy Mourant and Victor Huelin before running out of film; these he would develop himself and then circulate around school. He also contrived to assemble a map of the German island fortifications.

On November 6, 1943, NCO Soltan and three other members of the *Feldgendarmerie* called on the Painter home at Hinemoa, New Zealand Avenue in St Saviour. The door was answered by Mrs Painter who was told that the *Feldgendarmerie* had information according to which her son Peter was in possession of a wireless, cameras and photographs of military importance, requiring them to carry out a routine house search. There is evidence to suggest that they were following up on a denunciation.[111] The Painters had retained a wireless set and unlike many other families made no secret of their reception of the news. After the war Mrs Painter stated that they had carried *'the news to many people'* as well as *'allowed some to come to listen when there was something of importance'*.[112]

The Germans who had come to search the Painter home and who probably never expected to unearth anything more damning than a radio set, were in for a major surprise. When Soltan searched the boys' bedroom he made a fatal discovery: a few days before the house-search Peter had taken a World War I souvenir pistol from its hiding-place under the bedroom floorboards and placed it in his wardrobe. This automatic pistol, a German Mauser in good condition, belonged to Mrs Painter's brother, from whose house - which had been requisitioned by the Germans - it had been salvaged. Mrs Painter's frantic explanations were aborted by Soltan, who cut her short with: *'This is most serious. I fear that I will go hard with you over this. It is much too serious for me to overlook it.'* In addition, the house-search produced the Painters' wireless, cameras and three photographs of military

---

[110] From a letter of Edward Mossop to Mrs Painter, 3 June 1945, s. Painter Papers.
[111] PRO. KV4/78/65169. 'Collaborators in the Channel Islands' by J.R. Stopford, 8 Aug. 1945.
[112] PRO. WO 311/11. Post-war statement of Dorothy Mary Painter to the British Military Authority in Jersey, n.d.

objects.[113] A keen DIY man, Peter was an avid experimenter with little valve radios and the spare parts the search squad found were earmarked as evidence pointing to the existence of '*a secret radio manufacturing atelier*'.[114]

Suicidal as it may seem, the frequent German calls and promises of amnesty for the voluntary surrender of firearms – one of the last in August 1943 - prove, above all, that these orders were ineffective and that the Germans were still making discoveries. Undoubtedly, many Jersey people still regarded this as a pecadillo and few imagined that the banality of a souvenir pistol could secure them a slot in a concentration camp. It also appears that the deterrent effect of the concentration camp concept, which was quite important as a tool of domination in Germany, did not produce the desired effect. Though some knowledge of concentration camps had filtered through to the Channel Islands, it is very unlikely that any member of the islands' community had a precise idea about what these institutions exactly stood for. The Channel Islands, whose benign political history offered little precedent for brutality, were little prepared for the Nazi onslaught. While most people probably sensed that little good was in store for those sent away, nobody could predict that their fate would be as sinister as it eventually turned out to be. Worrying as the disappearance of several Jersey people on the Continent was, the connections and conclusions were probably too convoluted to be drawn at the time. What therefore appears suicidal with the benefit of hindsight was not automatically comprehensible to those trapped in the woes of the Occupation.

Peter and his father were to present themselves at the Feldgendarmerie in Bagatelle Road the following morning at 9 o'clock. Although the youngster assumed full responsibility, the interrogating officer rejected his account because of his age. As a former Infantry and RFC officer who had served during the First World War, the English-born Clarence had some trouble explaining how a pistol could have merely sentimental value. Besides, Clarence Painter suited the German profile of an underground movement activist and therefore was held to be fully responsible. When the interrogation ended at 1 p.m. the Painters were allowed to return home; Clarence Painter, however, was required to report back three hours later. At 5:30 p.m. Peter and his brother John returned with the news that their father

---

[113] Luckily, the Germans never discovered a pile of other photographs of military objects and a map of the island which Peter had marked with the fortifications and which were hidden in an ornamental top in the boys' bedroom. Information provided by John Painter.
[114] Information given by Roy Mourant.

had been taken into custody and that clothing, blankets and food could be taken to the prison every Saturday and Wednesday. The next day the Painter home was raided again, apparently with the expectation of recovering a transmitter. However, the Germans found little else of significance - a few unspectacular scrapbooks of airforce pictures and some airforce literature belonging to John. These trophies, surely seized in compensation for the frustration of not having achieved a more dramatic breakthrough, proved worthless to the subsequent inquiry.

The next day Mrs Painter went to the Feldgendarmerie to plead for her husband. Once again she stressed the souvenir character of the pistol, declaring that the family had never owned any ammunition and that it had not been fired. Though Soltan's real opinion is a matter of conjecture, he was apparently prompted to say *'We believe all that you and your husband have told us and will send your statement to the court.'*[115] In any case, at this point in the inquiry, his opinion was of little importance, as the bureaucracy had already started working on the case. Meanwhile, the whole family, including John and his older sister Joan, a teacher at Victoria College Prep, were interrogated individually. Sometime later John, who was in particular danger, was called up to the court at Westbourne Terrace, Wellington Hill and severely reprimanded for the photographs which had been found in his collection. Eventually, however, unlike his brother Peter, he got off the hook, probably because he was still attending college and had not reached military age. Had the German raid taken place sometime after his 18th birthday in February 1944, he might well have suffered the same fate as his father and brother.

The nature of the Painter case and the special attention it received from the German administration is confirmed by a tiny, yet rather telling deviation from a normal administrative practice. Before putting any islander on trial in their court, FK 515 made it a routine matter to enquire of the Attorney General whether any previous convictions existed. In the Painter case the relevant request of November 13, 1943 bore a stamp reading 'very urgent' in red ink. More importantly, and in addition to this standard procedure, the German court official handling the file - a man called Böhm - requested a second report *'detailing the previous conduct, manner of life, general reputation and political convictions of Clarence Painter and Peter Painter.'*

---

[115] PRO. WO 311/11. Post-war statement of Dorothy Mary Painter to the British Military Authority in Jersey, n.d.

[116] This leads the author to the conclusion that there was no agreement on how the Painters were to be dealt with, a thesis confirmed by Roy Mourant. He clearly remembers having been able to approach his friend Peter - while a court martial was deliberating in the States Building - and spending a few hours chatting to him. If the German law officials had been unanimous in their opinion that the Painters were dangerous terrorists, this would have been impossible.

The events in this case link it closely with the application of the NN decree. Each case was examined by the German court in charge who conferred with military intelligence whether the conditions for a trial before a military court in the occupied territories existed. If the military refused the liability, the prisoners were instantly handed over to the Secret Field Police, or the SS. As we have seen, 'possession of a fire arm' was one of the many offences which the NN decree had been designated to cover. Anyone found in the possession of *military* arms was in particularly severe trouble, as a mere suspicion of their use against the occupying forces was deemed sufficient for a death sentence.[117] This would have invariably been the fate of the Painters and it must be assumed that FK 515, eager not to pass any death sentences on islanders, were keen to wash their hands of the Painter case and decided in favour of deporting them under the NN decree. The instructions for the enforcement of the NN order are very specific: in cases where there were *political* reservations against the immediate execution of a death sentence, the culprits were to be transported to Germany.[118] It must be assumed that there were, indeed, political reservations against pronouncing a death sentence in the Painter case, thus the long deliberations. An example of the 'velvet glove' in practice.

Four days before Christmas 1943, when Joan Painter called at the prison gate with food for her father and brother, she was informed that future visits were unnecessary. A few days later the same German warder revealed to the

---

[116] Letter dated 13 Nov. 1943 from court of FK 515 to Attorney General, re. previous sentences of Painter senior and junior; asked to supply information, Mr Mourant, the chef de police at St Saviour Parish Hall replied: '...*nothing detrimental is known to me concerning their previous conduct, manner of life or general reputation (...) I am not aware of their political convictions.*', s. Mourant to Duret Aubin, 15 Nov. 1943, in: JAS. D/Z. Law Officer's Department, 1943/18. Sentences and prosecutions by Field Command and Troop Courts.

[117] Kosthorst, Erich/Walter, Bernd, *Konzentrations- und Strafgefangenenlager im Dritten Reich. Beispiel Emsland. Dokumentation und Analyse zum Verhältnis von NS-Regime und Justiz*, Düsseldorf, 1983, 2862.

[118] Directives for the prosecution of criminal acts against the Reich and the occupying power (enforcement instructions), 7 Dec. and 12 Dec. 1941, in: Kosthorst/ Walter, op. cit., 2862.

Painter family that Clarence and Peter had been sent to France and that their whereabouts were to remain secret.[119] They were not to learn until June 1945, through Roger Hardy, a French concentration camp survivor, what fate had befallen their loved ones.[120]

The first stage of their ordeal took them to the Cherche-Midi prison in central Paris where they arrived on December 23, 1943, two days after their departure from Jersey. Incarcerated there two weeks earlier, Hardy encountered both Painters the next morning. They celebrated Christmas and New Year's Eve together, but on January 6, 1944, as was practice for many NN prisoners, the Painters were sent to Natzweiler-Strutthof concentration camp, 31 miles south of Strasbourg in the Vosges mountains of Alsace. A place frightfully exposed to the north winds and fog, Strutthof was the name of a skiing hotel that had existed there before the war.[121] It was one of the smallest concentration camps in Nazi Germany and had been set up after Albert Speer, Hitler's architect, had noted the granite deposits in the area on an inspection tour. The DEST (German Earth and Stone Works Ltd.), an SS enterprise, acted on Speer's suggestions and by autumn 1940 a project was launched to quarry the granite. The first batch of prisoners to arrive was of 300 Germans in May 1941. The growth of this camp was slow and only on August 15, 1942 did Natzweiler become available for the Gestapo's routine posting of prisoners. By the end of 1943 it numbered 2,000 inmates. Most worked in arms production, the overhauling of Junkers aircraft engines for example, and around 500 were employed in the quarries. 1944 witnessed a spurt in activity, as Natzweiler became part of a programme to relocate armament plants in subterranean facilities. Correspondingly, numbers rose to between 7,000 and 8,000 in the main camp and 19,000 in the satellite camps. The year 1944 also saw Natzweiler become one of the prime destinations for members of the French Resistance, among them many NN prisoners who were assigned the worst type of work on road construction projects and in the quarries. Natzweiler had an exceptionally high mortality rate and claimed a total of 25,000 lives, the majority of them French and Jewish. In August 1943 the construction of a gas chamber inside the former

[119] PRO. WO 311/11. Post-war statement of Dorothy Mary Painter to the British Military Authority in Jersey, n.d.

[120] Roger Hardy died in August 1945, as a result of the deprivations he suffered. Information provided by John Painter.

[121] The Painters appear in a register of NN prisoners which was established by the French priest and former NN at Hinzert, Joseph de la Martinière. Clarence received the camp number 6868 in Natzweiler and then, together with his son, the number 81560 in Gross-Rosen, s. Musée de la résistance et de la déportation, Besançon, de la Martinière Files concerning NN prisoners.

hotel commenced. It is here that 130 prisoners transferred from Auschwitz, mostly Jewish, were killed, for inclusion in the skeleton collections of Dr Hirt, a Nazi anatomist at Strasbourg's Reich University. The gas chambers were also used for medical experiments with antidotes for phosgene, a poisonous gas and antityphus injections tested on human guinea pigs - gypsy prisoners from Auschwitz. As the Allies approached, the main camp was disbanded in August 1944; the survivors were sent on a death march to Dachau. Altogether, Natzweiler is believed to have hosted 45,000 prisoners.[122]

The Painters spent three months in this extremely hostile environment which they survived - despite the severity of the regimen. Paradoxically, they were exempted from work, possibly due to their nationality, but had to appear for the excruciating roll-calls. On April 19, 1944 they left together with Hardy and numerous other captives for Wohlau in Silesia, where they arrived three days later. They were detained there for two weeks and then sent to work at a camp in Dietzdorf, a Krupp factory 25 miles from Wohlau producing armoured turrets for aircraft. Around August 20, after four months in this factory, they were sent to work on a canal where they remained until October 1944. Due to the marginally better conditions in both camps they were able to pull through; however, when they were transferred to Gross-Rosen, by this time a notoriously bad camp, their condition worsened rapidly. Characteristically, they had passed through Breslau prison on their way, but by this time in 1944 NNs were no longer put on trial and instead were sent directly to concentration camps.[123]

Gross-Rosen in Lower Silesia was established on August 2, 1940 as a satellite of Sachsenhausen concentration camp and was located in the vicinity of a granite quarry which was, as in many other camps, exploited by the DEST. From May 1941 to February 1945 it operated as an independent camp with over 50 satellite camps erected on the sites of a variety of infrastructure projects and armaments, the worst of which were to be found in the Sudetic mountains. The number of prisoners grew from 1,487 (1941) to 90,314 (1944) and on the eve of its liquidation, Gross-Rosen recorded 97,414 detainees. It is estimated that a total of 125,000

[122] *Encyclopedia of the Holocaust*, op. cit., entry 'Natzweiler'.
[123] Musée de la résistance et de la déportation, Besançon, de la Martinière Files concerning NN prisoners. NN trials were suspended in September 1944.

prisoners passed through this camp where Jews comprised the largest group of inmates, as well as casualties.[124]

Peter, suffering from pneumonia, died in the arms of his father on November 27, 1944 and his body was cremated in Gross-Rosen. Battling with grief, Clarence Painter managed to overcome the shock and his own condition improved slightly over the following weeks. However, when the Russian advance forces came to within 13 miles of the camp, 40,000 prisoners were moved out, five days before its liberation on February 13, 1945.[125] Clarence, at this stage suffering from a severe case of erysipelas was loaded onto a train and sent to Dora-Mittelbau concentration camp. Léon Halkin, a Belgian survivor, described the evacuation:

> At the Gross Rosen station, we climbed into the metal wagon; about 100 per car. We had no coats, no pullovers, no blankets. It was cold and the wind whistled into the car from underneath. Two SS [in the car] guarded us at the time. 'Criminal prisoners', who were in the majority, organized themselves to steal our bread and clothing. What to do? We were only a handful of Belgians and French in the middle of such a hostile group. Among the Poles, two former kapos were seen. They were well built, warmly dressed, hardy and fearsome. [...] The train was made up of about thirty wagons. It stopped often for long periods. In order to prevent us from escaping, we had been squeezed to the back of the wagon by the SS. There was no room to stretch, however, by being crushed, we kept warm. Daybreak brought new miseries: cold, fatigue, hunger and thirst. Standing up, we were forced to hold on to each other, like animals in a circus. Several of us did not wake up any more and there were those who tore the clothes from their bodies. The SS let them do it, and ordered that we pile the dead in one corner. They were totally nude, an occasional shot created more cadavers. [...] The last morning, Sunday, 11 February 1945, the SS again ordered us to throw the dead on top of the railway tracks; no doubt to remove the terrible stench of decaying cadavers. This totally revolted us and our spirits collapsed. The rain chilled us to the bone.

---

[124] *Encyclopedia of the Holocaust*, op. cit., entry 'Gross-Rosen', 623.
[125] Ibid., 352.

Our convoy stopped once more, but this time we had arrived. It was Dora! Dora in the Harz Mountains! [...] The doors to our cattle car opened. We were given brief orders to get out. There were no duck-boards, no pavements, only the stones, which constituted the road. We fell out of the wagon, one after the other onto the stones. The SS immediately put paid to those who could not get up. I heard shots! I saw it happen! Hanging on to my comrades, I dragged myself to the roll-call place.[126]

Clarence Painter's succumbed to this ordeal on the third day of the journey. The exact circumstances are unknown, however, according to Roger Hardy's testimony his body was incinerated on arrival, at the Dora crematorium.[127]

On June 2, 1945, news of the Painters' tragic fate appeared on the front page of the Evening Post. This aroused a wave of emotion in the island and letters of sympathy started pouring into the bereaved home. It was the words of P A Tatam, the acting vice-principal of Victoria College, in a letter to Mrs Painter, which perhaps struck the chord most profoundly and expressed the paralysing helplessness and indignation felt by many islanders:

With the deepest sorrow I have heard the terrible news today. I cannot bring myself to believe that such a foul deed has been committed - it seems inconceivable. On behalf of Victoria College I offer you our heartfelt sympathy on the shadow which has fallen so heavily on you and your family.

I am completely unable to express, adequately, my feelings of horror. The clouds have indeed been very thick over your path, and none of us has been able to give you any help during these long anxious months of waiting and hoping. We admire you and we are proud of you for the wonderful courage you have shown during the terrible ordeal through which you have passed. I most earnestly

---

[126] Halkin, Léon, *A l'ombre de la mort,* Gembloux, 19652, 145-150, passage translated by Peter Hassall.

[127] For the paragraph on the Painters' deportation and the circumstances of their deaths, s. letters of Roger Hardy to Dorothy Painter, in: Painter Papers; PRO. FO 950 741. Note of G C Littler (FO) to Dr Burckhardt, International Tracing Service, re. Painter jr., 21 Sept. 1964.

hope that the time will come when you will be able to enjoy brighter and happier days. Believe me,

Yours very sincerely,

P A Tatam[128]

James Houillebecq[129]

James Edward Houillebecq was born on February 24, 1927 to a family who farmed in the parish of St Saviour. He was a pupil at De La Salle College and had not long left school when, in May 1944, a German search party discovered gun parts and ammunition buried on the premises of the Houillebecq home, Alpington Villa in St Saviour. James had associated with a group of other youngsters and when they stole a gun from the Germans, James undertook to conceal the disassembled parts without the knowledge of his parents or his sister Nancy. The entire family was arrested, separated, put into solitary confinement and interrogated by the Secret Field Police. Although his parents and Nancy were released after a few weeks, James remained in jail. Henceforth, as in the case of the Painters, the family was able to bring food and clean clothes to the prison gate, while their sole means of communication with James were notes smuggled in and out of prison.

Judging by his offence, the circumstances of his disappearance, the absence of trial proceedings and the complete lack of documentary evidence, it is probable that James, as well, was a Jersey NN prisoner. He was deported in August 1944, on what must have been one of the last boats transporting prisoners from the island, and taken to Fresnes prison, ready to be transferred to Germany. At Fresnes James befriended a young Englishman whose family resided in France and who had been arrested together with his father, a resistance worker forced underground and betrayed by a Gestapo informer. Subsequently, James Houillebecq and the young man were sent to Neuengamme concentration camp, outside Hamburg, and each vowed to contact the other's family if one of them died and the other survived. The young survivor kept his promise and told the Houillebecqs after the war that he had last seen James alive when entering the camp hospital. For many

---

[128] s. Painter Papers.
[129] JAS. B/A/W/85/5. Bailiff's War Files. War graves, grave registration report form of J E Houillebecq; PRO. FO 950/741; L'Amy, op.cit., 7/8; Information provided by Nancy Aylward.

thousands of prisoners this was the last stage of their ordeal in Hitler's concentration camps and James Houillebecq, prisoner no 37354, died around January 29 1945. The family never found out more, for the young survivor, severely traumatised as he was, decided to cease all further contact with them; his name remains unknown.

The tragedy continued, for having received the definite news of her son's untimely death, Mrs Houillebecq's health degraded rapidly and she died a short time later, *'of a broken heart'*, as her daughter Nancy says.

5. Compassion with a Capital C - Louisa Gould's 'Family Affair'

Louisa Gould (née Le Druillenec) from St Ouen was one of seven Jersey residents arrested on the grounds of action motivated by genuine compassion, in late spring 1944.[130] Their story highlights the moral obligations felt by a number of Channel Islanders who would not stand by, but who engaged in action on behalf of the slave labourers who had been herded together in cattle trucks and transported to the Channel Islands. Carted there from the four corners of Europe, thousands of them were to end their days toiling for the Axis war effort.[131] Louisa Gould's 'crime' lay in having sheltered one of these slave workers, a Russian, for twenty long months following his escape in October 1942.[132] She epitomises a charitable attitude based on the belief that one's own hardship does not justify turning a blind eye to the sufferings of others.

Louisa Gould, Harold Le Druillenec and Ivy Forster were three of the nine children of Vincent Le Druillenec, a seaman, who moved to Jersey from Brittany some time in the second half of the nineteenth century. Such was the age gap between the children, people often mistook the eldest brother to be Harold's father. In fact, Vincent Le Druillenec died when Louisa was in her twenties and Harold and Ivy were young children. Born in Jersey on October 7, 1891, Louisa was already widowed at the time of the Occupation and ran a general store ('Millais Stores') at La Fontaine, Millais in the parish of St Ouen. Both her sons had received scholarships to Victoria College and her elder son Edward later continued his studies at Exeter College, Oxford. Afterwards he was Languages and Games Master at Colchester House School, Bristol and at the outbreak of the war he volunteered and took a commission in the Royal Navy Volunteer Reserve. He was trained and appointed to HMS Bonaventure as an anti-aircraft control officer. Louisa's life was turned upside down one fateful day in July

---

[130] The seven people were Alice Gavey, Louisa Gould, Ivy Forster, Dora Hacquoil, Harold Le Druillenec, Berthe Pitolet and Elena Le Feuvre.

[131] According to estimates, at least twenty hidden slave workers survived the Occupation in Jersey, some of them having relied on the help of islanders 'for nearly two years', s. Bunting, Madeleine, *The Model Occupation – The Channel Islands under German Rule 1940-1945,* London, 1995, 217.

[132] Information provided by Rex Forster.

1941, when a Red Cross Message notified her that Edward had been killed in action in the Mediterranean four months earlier.[133]

About seventeen months later she was approached by Feodor ('Bill') Buryi, a fugitive Russian seeking a safe shelter. When 'Bill' told her that he had nowhere to go, Louisa Gould felt it was her obligation to prevent another mother from losing her son: *'Then you are coming with me. I have lost one of my boys in this war and the other is away and I'll try and make up by looking after you.'*[134] In a newspaper article published after the Liberation, 'Bill' said that she was the most kind-hearted lady he had ever met. 'Bill' soon became an integral part of her life, assuaging her pain at the loss of her own son. His presence at Louisa's store became ever more apparent, for after a first critical period had elapsed she began to nurture a false feeling of security. Louisa, who was a very outspoken and courageous person, also had a hidden radio and passed on the news to customers. Her frankness was to seal her fate and served as a passport to Ravensbrück.

Feodor Buryi was born in 1919 to a Smolensk peasant family that moved to Tomsk in Siberia when he was a small child. 'Bill' did well at school and in 1939 he was selected to study photography in Moscow for 12 months. Like millions of his countrymen, 'Bill' was called up when the Germans launched Operation Barbarossa, the invasion of the Soviet Union. He served in the air force until October 1941, when his plane was shot down and he escaped death as the only survivor of the 3-man crew. 'Bill' parachuted into an area that was encircled by German troops and joined Red Army ground units in the fighting. However, after five days he was taken prisoner.[135] Convinced that the Wehrmacht held nothing good in store for Soviet prisoners and acutely aware of the German contempt for the international standards governing their treatment, 'Bill' escaped one day later, in the hope of joining a partisan unit.

The type of war the Germans fought in Eastern Europe differed greatly from military campaigns in the West. From its inception, it assumed the character of a war of extermination aimed at destroying the jewel in the crown of an imagined Judeo-Bolshevik conspiracy. This entailed exterminating the Jews

---

[133] 'Well-known Jerseyman's Death in Action - Brilliant Scholar and Sportsman', in: *Evening Post*, Jersey, 15 July 1941.

[134] 'A Russian Officer's Story - His Escape from Jersey PoW camp - How He Was Hidden and Fed for Two and A-Half Years', in: *Evening Post*, Jersey, 10 May 1945.

[135] Hillsdon, Sonia, *Jersey-Occupation Remembered*, Norwich, 1986, 118; 'A Russian Officer's Story - His Escape from Jersey PoW camp - How He Was Hidden and Fed for Two and A-Half Years', in: *Evening Post*, Jersey, 10 May 1945.

and enslaving the Slavic peoples who were considered only a rung above the Jews in the Nazi racial hierarchy. With such paranoid precepts determining German action, the perpetrators assumed that Slavs did not merit the protection accorded to prisoners of war by the Geneva Convention. For this reason, Red Army prisoners could expect little from their German captors: Jews and political commissars were immediately singled out and shot on the spot while hundreds of thousands of other Soviet prisoners starved to death in open-air camps, particularly during the first months of operation 'Barbarossa'. In 1942, however, racked by serious labour shortages all over Europe, the Germans discovered the potential of Soviet prisoners as a source of labour. Instead of letting them perish from starvation and disease after a few weeks, their potential as a labour force could be harnessed to the Reich's benefit. In consequence they were put to work, often under gruesome conditions.

During the winter of 1941/42 'Bill' went underground and managed to remain undetected until the beginning of the spring offensive, when the Germans rounded up all soldiers on the run behind their lines and put them into PoW camps. 'Bill' stayed in such a camp until June 28, 1942 and was then transported with 200 other prisoners in a nightmare journey across Europe, finally arriving at St Malo from where they were shipped to Jersey. Eventually, they ended up in labour camp *Immelmann*, at the foot of Jubilee Hill in St Peter.[136] A few weeks after his arrival 'Bill' made his second attempt to escape, only to be recaptured yet again. As a lesson to others, his captors stripped 'Bill' of his clothes, made him load a wheelbarrow with stones and cart it around the camp compound until he dropped. All his movements were accompanied by the thrashes of the guards who forced the rest of the camp population to participate as onlookers. Afterwards, 'Bill' was left standing naked in the open all night until his strength was totally consumed. The realisation that it was preferable to risk his neck than to be at the mercy of brutes may have prompted 'Bill''s third attempt at flight. Later, he would explain his action by quoting a Spanish proverb: 'It is better to die on your feet as a man, than on your knees as a dog.' Within days he devised a plan to escape from a work party outside the camp. The timing was good, as the guards had received their pay and would engage in heavy drinking and all 'Bill' had to ask from his fellow prisoners was to divert

---

[136] Hillsdon, Sonia, op. cit., 118; Ginns, Michael, *The Organisation Todt and the Fortress Engineers in the Channel Islands* (Channel Islands Occupation Society, Archive Book No. 8), Jersey, 1994, 12.

their attention for a moment. This escape, on September 23, 1942, proved successful.

Subsequently 'Bill' was quartered by René Le Mottée, a sympathetic farmer who, in addition to his family duties as the father of five children, kept one escapee in his house, another in a store and a third one in his shed. 'Bill' joined the Russian in the shed and spent much of the daytime in the house. He stayed with René Le Mottée for three months, but had to leave when the Germans started searching all the houses in the vicinity for railway sleepers that had been removed as firewood. 'Bill' then approached Mrs Gould, whom he knew already and told her that he had nowhere to go.

All interviewees describe Louisa Gould as a remarkable person, but concede that she mistakenly believed in the trustworthiness of some ill-disposed neighbours. Sheltering was an act of conscience based on individual or family decisions and there was little or no liaison between the people hiding Russians who were usually painstakingly security-conscious. This was the attitude adopted by Ivy Forster and her family.[137] In December 1942 they had taken in Grigori ('George') Koslov, another Russian on the run. Like 'Bill', Koslov was a young man in his early twenties who had been taken prisoner in 1941. He arrived at labour camp *Immelmann* after 'Bill''s escape, in October 1942 and was forced, until his own escape, to work on the Five Mile Road fortifications. Rex Forster, Ivy's son, remembers that although there were occasions when he would take 'George' to the swimming-pool at Havre des Pas, he would stop short of telling school friends who came to visit him about the 'secret' in the attic. Groping for an explanation of Louisa's behaviour he reaffirms that most Jersey people were not fully aware of the consequences of acts of defiance and that they never imagined being sent to a concentration camp. Such beliefs were reinforced by the actual return to the island of some people sent by the Germans to prisons on the Continent. Well beyond 1942, this was quite a frequent occurrence, especially with 'essential workers'.

Her false sense of security was to prove Louisa's downfall: holding on, perhaps too blindly, to the continuing validity of her moral universe, she saw little reason to take more than the basic precautions and was finally denounced by her neighbours. These, it appears, were mainly interested in the £100 reward.[138] However, their letter of denunciation, intended for the

---

[137] Rex Forster says that during the Occupation he knew one other Jersey family, the Metcalfes, hiding a Russian called Michail.

[138] PRO. KV4/78/65169. 'Collaborators in the Channel Islands' by J.R. Stopford, 8 Aug. 1945.

German Feldkommandantur, but incorrectly addressed to 'Victoria College' (instead of 'Victoria College House', the annexe taken over by the German administration), first landed on the desk of vice-principal Pat Tatam, in charge of the College's affairs since 1940. He steamed the letter open, read the content and then readdressed it, thereby creating a 24-hour delay. Meanwhile a bicycle messenger was despatched to warn Louisa about the impending danger. Louisa immediately removed all evidence of 'Bill''s presence in the house and Alice Gavey, her maid, undertook to hide the radio set under a large box that acted as a step down into the hen-house, one hundred yards away in an adjoining building. At 6 o'clock the next morning 'Bill' left for the Forster house where he stayed for the following five days.[139]

However, in the hurry Louisa had not been thorough enough, for she overlooked some items which the Germans found during one of their several ensuing searches: a camera that had belonged to her late husband and, more importantly, Christmas gift labels that had been attached to presents given to 'Bill' and which clearly identified Louisa and Ivy as the givers. Eventually, they also discovered the radio. Louisa was arrested with Alice Gavey and entered prison on May 25, 1944.[140] One week after Louisa's incarceration, the German 'search party' raided the Forster house and arrested Ivy; but the Forsters had calculated this possibility and taken precautions. When the Germans arrived both Arthur Forster and his son were out - and so was 'George' Koslov. He and 'Bill' had meanwhile been entrusted to Bob Le Sueur who moved them into his office. Bob, a young clerk, who almost single-handedly ran the Jersey branch of the General Accident Life Corporation during the Occupation, had met 'Bill' because Louisa Gould had taken out an insurance policy with his company. A week later two of Louisa's closest friends were arrested: Berthe Pitolet, a French housekeeper who had lived in Jersey for 25 years and worked in town, and Dora Hacquoil, a schoolteacher. Pitolet was a regular visitor at Louisa's house and would spend three or four weeks at a time with her. Hacquoil joined Louisa and 'Bill' in the daily nine o'clock wireless listening ceremony in Louisa's bedroom.[141]

Then it was Harold Le Druillenec's turn: although not directly involved in sheltering 'Bill', he was implicated in the case. The fact that Ivy and Harold

---

[139] 'A Russian Officer's Story - His Escape from Jersey PoW camp - How He Was Hidden and Fed for Two and A-Half Years', in: *Evening Post*, Jersey, 10 May 1945.
[140] Information provided by Rex Forster.
[141] 'My Story...Dora Hacquoil - Harbouring Russians', *Jersey Evening Post*, 2 Feb. 1995.

were registered at their sister's shop where they collected their weekly rations provided a clue. Harold took advantage of his sorties to St Ouen in order to listen to the radio and it is probable that the informer(s) gave Le Druillenec's name along with the others, but not that of his wife Phyllis or Ivy's husband Arthur. The latter worked long hours during the Occupation and therefore is unlikely to have accompanied his wife to St Ouen, save on very rare occasions such as Christmas 1943. Neither Arthur Forster, nor Rex, nor Phyllis Le Druillenec were questioned by the German police. When the author interviewed Phyllis in 1997 he was at first sceptical about one of her initial remarks, namely that the case had been something of a 'family affair'. In the end, however, she proved to be well on the right track. Naturally, their imprisoned relatives would have done their utmost to keep as many people as possible out of the affair and in this respect the tactics of the 'Le Druillenecs' were so successful that charges against Elena Le Feuvre, Louisa Gould's neighbour and the owner of the property at La Fontaine Millais, were dropped.[142] Dora Hacquoil also stated later that she owed her relatively lenient sentence to Louisa Gould's intervention:

> I was charged with listening in, but Lou vowed and declared that I always arrived too late [...] They accepted her word [...] a week later [...] she, Harold and Bertie were transported to the Continent [...] But for her statement I should have suffered the same fate.[143]

That the court found it difficult to verify the role of each of the accused is evident from their failure to prove Harold Le Druillenec's implication on the basis of available evidence; not that this presented an obstacle to a jurisprudence which, in the words of Advocate Valpy, operated on the dubious premise that 'being arrested equalled being guilty'.[144] In their attempts to base the trial on firmer ground, the discovery of Louisa's radio came in handy. The trial ended on June 22, 1944 and while the sentences were being read out the detonations of the battle that was raging on the Normandy coast were clearly audible in the courtroom. Le Druillenec was sentenced to five months on the sole grounds of his *'prohibited reception of wireless transmissions in company with other persons'*. Louisa Gould received a tough two-year sentence for her failure *'to surrender a wireless receiving apparatus',* her *'prohibited reception of wireless transmissions'* and *'aiding and abetting breach of the working peace and unauthorised*

---

[142] JAS. D/Z Law Officer's Department. Convictions and prosecutions by troop courts.

[143] 'My Story...Dora Hacquoil - Harbouring Russians', Jersey Evening Post, 02/02/1995.

[144] Information provided by Advocate Valpy.

removal' (as the offence of giving assistance to escapees was defined in the German judicial jargon).[145] In an example of shrewdness, Ivy Forster escaped deportation through the concerted efforts of the Prison Governor and Raymond Osmont, a trainee doctor, who was able to interchange medical samples and certify tuberculosis after she had been moved to the General Hospital. This manoeuvre got her off the list.[146]

Up to 1944 it had been common practice to retain Jersey prisoners earmarked for deportation in Gloucester Street prison for some time, before sending them on. However, during the first half of 1944 the period between verdict and deportation shortened considerably. The Germans' restlessness was attributable to the threat of imminent Allied landings. Things began to move even more quickly by June 1944. With people on a waiting-list to serve their prison sentences, the Germans now disregarded all procedures and started removing as many people as possible, anticipating the severing of the French link. These steps coincided with the evacuation *en masse* of forced labourers and those German soldiers serving prison sentences in Jersey. On June 29, 1944, twenty Jersey people sentenced for 'political crimes', among them Gould, Le Druillenec and Pitolet, boarded a vessel that formed part of a convoy of six ships and various escort vessels leaving Jersey the same night. Its passengers presented a curious mix of individuals: 634 prisoners of the SS Construction Brigade I in Alderney, spirited away in order to prevent them falling into Allied hands alive, 58 accompanying SS men, 458 OT workers, 28 civilian and military prisoners, 43 foreigners, 46 women and one British PoW.[147] However, due to fear of Allied interception, they returned to Jersey where all passengers disembarked in the early morning hours of June 30. The following night the procedure was repeated and this time the convoy succeeded in slipping through to St Malo via an alternative route.[148] It was to be one of the last trips taking Jersey prisoners to the Continent before the link was cut off several weeks later. The preliminary destination for the three prisoners was Rennes in Brittany,

---

[145] JAS. D/Z Law Officer's Department. Convictions and prosecutions by troop courts.

[146] This is one example of how German fear - in this case of infectious diseases - could be exploited successfully by clever and observant people. After the war Ivy Forster went on to become the first woman States member. She died in June 1997 at the age of 90, s. 'Obituary', *JEP*, 7 July 1997.

[147] 'War Diary of the Sea Transport Officer, St Malo', cited in Ginns, Michael, *The Organisation Todt and the Fortress Engineers in the Channel Islands* (Channel Islands Occupation Society, Archive Book No. 8), Jersey, 1994, 136.

[148] Sinel, op. cit., entry of 29 and 30 June 1944; Interview with Rex Forster.

from where Harold was soon moved to Belfort, in Eastern France,[149] while the two women remained behind. Rennes prison was badly hit when the nearby railway station was bombed during the Allied advance, offering Berthe Pitolet an opportunity to escape into the street from where she was picked up and hidden until the liberation of the city by American troops, less than a week later. Louisa, however, stayed put, probably because she was wary of lessening her friend's chances who, being French, had few problems in passing entirely undetected. Therefore, when the chaos subsided Louisa Gould was put on a train that eventually took her to Ravensbrück, the women's concentration camp 56 miles north of Berlin. This camp had been established on May 15, 1939, with a first contingent of 867 women arriving from Lichtenburg concentration camp three days later. Prisoner numbers rose from 2,000 by the end of 1939 to 10,800 by the end of 1942. In 1944, 70,000 women arrived at the main camp and its 34 satellites which were attached to military industrial plants. The main camp had 26,700 prisoners in 1944 and by early February 1945 a total of 106,000 women had passed through Ravensbrück.[150]

Le Druillenec was to see his sister one more time before they were absorbed into the concentration camp system: by some stroke of divine coincidence his carriage stopped next to hers at Belfort station and they were able to exchange a few words. It was Harold's birthday and Louisa managed to hand her brother a tin of tobacco. Harold later described Belfort as 'a slave-market' where the fit were separated from the unfit by the thousands, for further distribution into the concentration camp system. During their stay, prisoners whiled their time away giving lectures and Harold chipped in with a talk on the Constitution of the Channel Islands. At the time he was totally oblivious of his final destination - a concentration camp. As he later testified, *'it never occurred to me that I was to endure anything more severe than a few months' simple imprisonment'.*[151] On September 1, 1944 Harold arrived at Neuengamme, just outside Hamburg, with a party of French and Belgian political prisoners. Neuengamme, in Harold's estimation, was *'a typical concentration camp, clean, well-organised, run with German efficiency'* and with its fair share of sadism. It *'was a central camp, a pool*

---

[149] Le Druillenec's deposition at the Belsen Trial, in: Phillips, Raymond, ed., *Trial of Josef Kramer and forty-four others (The Belsen Trial),* London, n.d.
[150] *Encyclopedia of the Holocast,* op. cit., 'Ravensbrück.'
[151] For whole section, s. BBC Archives. BBC feature programme 'The Man from Belsen', based on the experiences of Harold Le Druillenec, 12 Apr. 1946; s. also Cottrell, Leonard, 'The Man from Belsen', in: British Broadcasting Corporation, *BBC features,* London, 1950.

from which labour was drawn for its subsidiary camps'.[152] Neuengamme had been established on 13 December 1938 as an external unit of Sachsenhausen concentration camp. The SS camp was established because the Nazis sought to reactivate brick production there for the huge public structures planned in Hamburg and the first prisoners were housed in a disused brick factory. The DEST signed a contract with the city in April 1940, after which a canal was dug to connect the camp with a tributary of the Elbe river and a siding laid to link it to the railway network. By June 1940 it became an independent camp with a prisoner population of about 1,000 and numbers were boosted in the autumn of 1941 by an influx of thousands of Russians. In 1942 private firms such as the Walther weapons factory asked for prisoner labour and numerous annexes were set up in the shipbuilding and armaments industry. By 1944 the main camp had reached a population size of 12,000 with around twice that number in satellite set-ups. Jewish transports from Poland and Hungary during summer 1944 brought in another 13,000 prisoners. Most of the new prisoners were sent to satellite camps. In 1945 Neuengamme had 70 such annexes, among them Sylt camp in Alderney which housed the *SS Baubrigade I* (SS-Construction Brigade I) after its arrival in March 1943. The total number of prisoners sent to Neuengamme ranged around 106,000 and it is estimated that 55,000 prisoners perished there.[153]

Le Druillenec was sent to a satellite camp in Wilhelmshaven, one of the principal naval bases in Germany, where he was made to work as an oxy-acetylene welder. In his BBC radio play written in 1946, a fellow prisoner, an American with Belgian nationality, briefs the new arrivals on the basic principles of life and death in the concentration camp:

> Well, there are one or two things worth knowing. The first is to recognise that your Block Alteste [sic, Block Elder, n.b.] is God. And, barring escape, which is pretty hopeless, the only chance you've got of staying alive for long is to get on the right side of the Block Alteste [...] They're all prisoners, you see, but privileged prisoners, and they're responsible to the SS for camp discipline. They've got powers of life and death. The second thing to remember is that they're all mad, and when I say mad, I mean mad. You'll see things going on here that'll drive you nuts if you try to figure them out - guys

---

[152] BBC Archives. BBC feature programme 'The Man from Belsen', based on the experiences of Harold Le Druillenec, 12 Apr. 1946; BBC Talk, 25 Sept. 1945.
[153] *Encyclopedia of the Holocaust*, op. cit., 1057; Bunting, op. cit., 186-189.

beaten to death for stealing a swede, guys tortured for weeks and then killed because a Camp Chief didn't like their faces. Don't worry about it. Don't argue with yourself about it. Don't judge it by the standards of a sane world.[154]

Soon many of the fellow prisoners Harold befriended, fell ill and died, owing to conditions created by 'extermination by work' and a more than inadequate diet. On Good Friday 1945 the camp was evacuated, followed by what Harold called *'the most terrible part'* of his story: having injured his foot he was loaded into a cattle truck with other prisoners - 450 prisoners into four wagons. They remained trapped inside *'for five days and five nights, without food, without water, without sanitation'*. Outside Lüneburg the train was caught up in a raid and a bomb scored a direct hit on one of the wagons loaded with over 100 prisoners. And when the 250 survivors of the journey where divided into two parties, Harold was in a group loaded onto lorries and driven to Bergen-Belsen. In 1946, when he returned to Lüneburg for the Belsen trial, he was to find out that on this occasion again he had narrowly escaped death, as the 100 prisoners who had remained behind in the field outside Lüneburg were summarily executed.

The notorious Bergen-Belsen started off rather late in the war, on April 30, 1943, as a clearing house for a select number of Jews designated for exchange with German nationals in Allied countries. Included were Jews from neutral countries, some with South American papers and others with connections abroad. Only a few of these detainees were actually exchanged and they became bargaining material for the SS during the last months of the war. In March 1944 the situation changed and Belsen became a regular concentration camp, with a take-in of prisoners who were classified 'ill' or 'unfit to work'. The first such transport arrived in late March 1944 from Dora and was put in a section of the camp without any facilities. The majority of these arrivals were Hungarian Jews, and similar transports - among them Anne Frank and her sister in a convoy from Auschwitz - continued to arrive at Belsen until the end of 1944. On December 2, 1944, the camp count stood at 15,257 prisoners, over half of them women. When the camps in the East were evacuated, numbers at Belsen continued to rise, from 18,465 to 44,060 between January and April 1945. By then conditions had become utterly chaotic and the number of deaths during those months

---

[154] BBC Archives. BBC feature programme 'The Man from Belsen', based on the experiences of Harold Le Druillenec, 12 Apr. 1946.

has been estimated at 50,000, with an outbreak of typhoid killing 35,000 from January to mid-April 1945 alone.[155] With no facilities to dispose of the carcasses, these were heaped like rubbish onto burgeoning mountains of flesh and bones. And the Nazi extermination logic continued until the end: although the Red Cross had delivered 500 blankets and enough food to fill a room 12x15x10 feet from floor to ceiling, neither these supplies nor the large quantities of medicaments were ever distributed.[156] The last days at Belsen were a horror of apocalyptic proportions, as 'soup' distribution ceased almost entirely and the water supply was cut. Harold witnessed cases of cannibalism, and skeletal prisoners simply dropping dead from terminal exhaustion and disease as they were made to drag the corpses of the deceased to burial pits. The stench over the camp was abominable and after the SS abandoned the camp, the Hungarian guards went on a rampage, taking aim indiscriminately at prisoners and shooting them like rabbits. When the British army liberated Belsen on April 15, 1945, thousands of unburied, decomposing bodies were strewn across the camp compound, whilst, according to one account, more were piled into a huge mass grave. About 40,000 men and women, over half of them needing urgent medical treatment if they were to live, were crammed into eighty-two wooden huts, each 100 feet by 200 feet and about 8 feet at the highest, some of them rotten, with no water, no food, no functioning lavatories.[157] Harold survived these last nine nightmarish days as one of the walking dead, in an inferno impossible to visualize. Belsen was, as he later described, *'the foulest and vilest spot that ever soiled the surface of this earth.'*[158]

After the war he often wondered why he had ended up there, and his surviving manuscripts give an idea of his complete incredulity and shock at the sight of SS guards and emaciated prisoners when his train ground to a halt inside the compound of Neuengamme. It is indeed puzzling why this group of Jersey prisoners went straight to concentration camps, without the customary detour via a prison. After all, they had received prison sentences. There have been several hypotheses as to this occurrence. Michael Ginns, chairman of the Channel Islands Occupation Society, believes that Gould, Pitolet and Le Druillenec came to be associated with the SS because they

---

[155] *Encyclopedia of the Holocaust,* op. cit., entry 'Belsen'; Schwarz, Gudrun, *Die nationalsozialistischen Lager,* Frankfurt 1991, 149.
[156] Lasker-Wallfisch, Anita, *Inherit the Truth 1939-1945. The documented Experiences of a Survivor of Auschwitz and Belsen.* London 1996, 93.
[157] MacAuslan, Alan, *Darling, Darling Meg. Belsen? Where's that?,* Edinburgh-Cambridge-Durham 1996, 171.
[158] BBC Archives. Harold Le Druillenec, BBC Talk, 25 Sept. 1945.

were put in the military wing of Jersey Prison at the time the prisoners of SS-Construction Brigade 1 were in transit from Alderney to St Malo. According to Ginns, conditions were chaotic and in the confusion their fate had simply converged with that of the SS prisoners.[159] This goes some way towards explaining what happened to this group, but one must not minimise the fact that in Nazi Germany things were done by the book, even if bombs were falling on the home front and chaos was rife. Somewhere in the line of command a decision had been reached that the military had more urgent tasks to attend to than shifting civilian prisoners from one prison to another, and that these should now be dealt with directly by the SS. In order to arrest and send people to concentration camps the Gestapo still operated along the lines that had been set in the combat against political opponents of Nazism in Germany after the 1933 take-over. Administrative and police detention procedures had been greatly facilitated by the passing of emergency decrees following the Reichstag blaze in Berlin, in February of that same year. Since then, the police could issue detention orders to hold suspects in 'protective custody', affording the Gestapo virtually unlimited powers of arrest and confinement. Most basic democratic rights were nullified through the 1933 emergency decrees. 'Protective custody', which was invariably followed by concentration camp detention, became the Gestapo's most widely used tool of repression and persecution, first in Germany and later in occupied Europe. Although some islanders returned to Jersey after having served their terms in French prisons, this practice became increasingly uncommon after 1942. Channel Islander Robert H B Bell was sentenced on January 22, 1942 to nine months' imprisonment for receiving stolen property. On December 3, 1942 the Bailiff of Jersey was officially informed that Bell had been placed in 'security detention'[160] in Dijon from where he would be taken to an internment camp.[161] This policy was officialised with the French authorities in March 1943, when the military governor prohibited the release of all British prisoners who had served their terms in French penitentiaries and ordered them to be handed over to the Gestapo, *'for transfer to internment camps'.*[162] Consequently, prisoners from the Channel Islands were sent to internment or concentration camps after their

---

[159] Ginns, Michael, op. cit., 113/14.

[160] A form of administrative detention practised in the occupied territories.

[161] Government House Jersey. Lieutenant Governor's Files. 50/4. Certification by H F C Ereant, Attorney General of Jersey, 22 Nov. 1966.

[162] Archives de Paris. The Chief of the Military Administration in France to the French Ministry of 163 Justice, 11 Mar. 1943, attachment to list of Channel Islands prisoners in French penitentiaries.

release from French prisons. The coordination of both measures posed no problem whatsoever for the Gestapo, as the military government in France had abandoned all police prerogatives - amongst them the supervision of internment measures - to them in the second half of 1942.[163] The orderly practice continued and despite a notable hastening of procedures in spring 1944, at that time Jersey prisoners such as Paisnel and Marsh continued to be sent to penal institutions in occupied France under the authority of the military governor and in Germany under the Reich Ministry of Justice (RMJ). A few months later, however, the entire German penal system established in France collapsed and all prisoners automatically came under immediate Gestapo control. When Gould, Le Druillenec and Pitolet were deported this had been enacted already, but only on September 24, 1944 did Wehrmacht High Command rubber-stamp the new reality, conceding that all prisoners from the occupied Western territories could be sent directly to concentration camps without serving their prison sentence first.[164] The hand-over of power to Himmler's ideological warriors, the SS, came at a time when the military situation on the Western front was going from bad to worse, but it also followed the political emasculation of the army and the conservative elites after the failed attempt on Hitler's life on July 20, 1944. At this point the Nazi Party and its formations were to reach the pinnacle of their power, ruling entirely on their own terms (with the only exception of the German business leaders clustering around Speer).[165] The historical irony is that by the time the Nazi dictatorship stood in its fullest bloom, it was also doomed. In their own little way this group of Jersey prisoners was enveloped in a maelstrom of much wider political and military proportions. And none of their actions had had any causal link with the forces they were being exposed to.

The relatives of Harold Le Druillenec and Louisa Gould had little reason to rejoice when Liberation Day finally came. Instead an overwhelming sense of numbness accompanied their wait for news about the relatives from whom they had not heard since their departure in June 1944. Some of their worries dissipated when information finally trickled in that Harold had survived and was in a hospital in England. But not in their wildest dreams could they imagine the state he was in when he was brought back from Belsen. Even worse was the total blank concerning Louisa. Answers eluded

---

[163] Thomas, Jürgen, op. cit., 106.

[164] Ibid., 109.

[165] This last remaining independent power block came to the foreground in April 1945 when Speer disobeyed Hitler's suicidal order to have Germany's future economic viability destroyed.

them for one long, agonising year, although Harold's story must have alerted them that something genuinely sinister might be in store. The truth finally emerged in the form of a small woman dressed in black who presented herself to the Forsters, one day in 1946. Mrs Tanguy was a hotel proprietor from Rennes in France, and she was survivor of the concentration camp of Ravensbrück. Her account of Louisa's fate categorically dispelled all hope that she might still be alive. The horrified family was to learn the story of how Tanguy had befriended Louisa in the camp and how, in order to survive, they had shared the burden and worked in tandem; until that fateful day of February 13, 1945, when Louisa, invalided by then, was selected and sent to a hastily improvised, but operational gas chamber.[166] Before Louisa Gould was sent in, Tanguy had solemnly pledged that if she survived she would go to Jersey as an emissary on her behalf and break the news to her family.

It was in Ravensbrück that the nightmare of last minute gassings – something that had been averted or sabotaged in other camps - became a reality. In January 1945, when the camp still had 25,000 female prisoners - among them twelve British and fourteen Americans - Schwarzhuber, one of the SS underlings, was called before the Camp Commandant and told that Himmler had ordered the dirty work for Führer and Fatherland to continue unabatedly. Soon, however, the execution method which was *de rigueur,* namely to shoot prisoners in the back of the neck (a fate suffered by British SOE agents Viollette Szabo, Lillian Rolfe and Denise Bloch), revealed itself as too slow. Therefore, in order to accelerate the speed of killing, all women who were ill or unable to march were targeted for asphyxiation in a gas chamber set up by SS personnel evacuated from Auschwitz. Located next to the crematorium, its dimensions were about 29 x 15 foot, enough to have the SS squeeze in approximately 150 women. During the following six weeks Schwarzhuber was to supervise a daily roll-call at 2:00 p.m., during which he selected for the gas chamber.[167] During that period alone about 2,400 women were exterminated and nothing came in the way of this

---

[166] PRO. FO 950 766. 'Index to names of British subjects in enemy concentration camps and statistical survey of camps', May 1946, document established by the War Office.
[167] PRO. WO 235 317. Ravensbrück Trial, depositions of Johann Schwarzhuber, the Commandant of the Protective Custody Camp, and Ruth Closius Neudeck, a female guard, Hamburg, 1946.

murderous routine until the Swedish Red Cross was granted permission to evacuate prisoners in late April 1945.[168]

The news of Louisa's death spread quickly and as the family were making preparations for a memorial service a letter arrived on April 2, 1946 from Madame Ballard, a second French survivor who had known Louisa prior to and during their time at Ravensbrück. Madame Ballard was the niece of a Jerseywoman, Marie Gruchy of Beaulieu, St Clement, and she had come to know Mrs Gould during the transfer from Rennes to Belfort. Her account offered further details, describing to the family how the prisoners were loaded onto cattle trucks, and how for the entire duration of their 15-day journey across France they received food or water only when the train stopped in one of the stations. Another 15 days were then spent at Belfort, before Madame Ballard joined Louisa in a convoy of women destined for Ravensbrück. Both women soon became friendly and on arrival they were quartered with German and Polish common law prisoners from whom they suffered abuse. They slept next to each other, indulging in memories of Jersey and sharing stories about their relatives and friends. Louisa spoke with natural pride of her two sons, passing around photographs of her deceased son Edward and her grand-daughter. She left a deep impression on many prisoners for whom she set an example of courage and sangfroid in the *'heroic way in which she withstood the suffering'* in the camp. Similar to her brother at Belfort she gave English lessons to her fellow prisoners, a task she accomplished *'in good spirits which was one form of her courage'*. Finally, one month after their arrival at Ravensbrück, Madame Ballard and Mrs Gould were separated when the former was taken to an aircraft factory 10 miles east of Berlin, never to meet again.[169]

Harold survived his war…by a narrow margin. Despatched to Epsom Hospital for treatment after liberation, his weight at that time was barely five stone. He was suffering from septicaemia and a mental disorder and was on heavy medication. However, he could count on the full support of his wife who moved to England and was able to visit him daily. Although he recognised her, he spent most of the first weeks in a state of hallucination, with at times comical effects. Imagining himself a millionaire, he prompted his wife on one occasion with the question: *'So how do you like the mink coat I bought you?'* As other survivors who had been starved for months on end and who went almost completely without

---

[168] Kogon, Eugen/Langbein, Hermann/Rückerl, Adalbert et al., *Nationalsozialistische Massentötungen durch Giftgas,* Frankfurt 1983, 261-263.
[169] Letter of Mme Ballard to Ralph Gould, 2 April 1946, in possession of Ralph Gould.

food during the last weeks of the ordeal, Harold was ravenous and hoarded additional food in his locker. Finally, after four months, he pulled through, only to return to Germany, in order to get back to where he saw his duty and give evidence at the Belsen trial held by a British military court in Lüneburg, in September 1945. Seven months later, on April 12, 1946, he scripted and narrated a radio play about his concentration camp experiences which was aired on the BBC. All this demanded prodigious inner resources; his lucid prose which, sixty years on, has lost none of its gripping power, ranks amongst the best *Lagerliteratur* ever written. As one may surmise, the post-war years were not untroubled, as he struggled to disentangle himself from a clinical condition, Holocaust survivor syndrome. Soon after the war, probably in 1947, when he was walking in town with his nephew Rex during the Christmas period, a Salvation Army band started to play *Silent Night, Holy Night.* Rex recounts that Harold paused abruptly and stood still, transfixed and with a dramatically altered expression on his face. As soon as he had steadied himself, he told him that the carol brought back agonising memories of Christmas Eve 1944 at Wilhelmshaven when the prisoners were made to stand out in the chill to take the daily roll-call for hours on end, under a clear wintry sky, speckled with stars. That night the star of Bethlehem also shone over the Nazi concentration camps. The mockery continued on Christmas Day when prisoners attended a grotesque Christmas celebration staged by their very tormentors, during which *Silent Night, Holy Night* was rendered by a concentration camp choir. This was just one example of how Harold's memory was frequently provoked and although he readjusted comparatively well, relatives say that in private moments 'it' was never far away. Harold Le Druillenec returned to his profession and continued in his duties as the headmaster of St. John's school in Jersey, where he died in 1985.

As to the two Russians fugitives, Feodor ('Bill') Buryi and Grigori ('George') Koslov, both were entrusted to the care of other hosts, after their move to the office of Bob Le Sueur's General Accident Life Corporation. Both men survived and *'were living independent lives by the end of the Occupation, having been able to find jobs and get food on their false papers',* due to Dr McKinstry, the medical officer of the Jersey Public Health Department.[170] Bob provided linkage with the outside world, for his profession brought him in contact with a wide range of people. He soon helped 'Bill' on to Mrs Dorothy Huelin of Trinity Hill where he stayed for a fortnight and then moved him to the home of two conscientious objectors,

---

[170] Bunting, op. cit., 220; Information provided by Bob Le Sueur.

Mike Frowd and René Franoux, who had arrived in Jersey in 1940 and occupied a flat at 7 Grosvenor Terrace. 'Bill' would resurface periodically from the sheltering anonymity of their large Victorian house,[171] only to return from his outings with boasts about the copious meals he had received from another source. It was only after the war that Bob discovered this benefactor as having been the Woodhalls. They were a couple hiding two Russians in the flat they were allowed to keep after the German military had requisitioned their hotel, the Mayfair, as a recreation center (*Soldatenheim*). Despite her Austrian origin, Mrs Woodhall had nothing good to say about the Nazis - two of her closest relatives had been imprisoned – but her leanings were unknown to the Germans flocking to the ground floor. This was probably also the last place where the German police would consider looking for Russian fugitives. One of the better examples of how simple psychology could be used to one's advantage, if only one knew how to work it.

When the war ended 'Bill' returned to the Soviet Union. It appears that he was approached by British Intelligence, with the idea of installing him as a 'sleeper', before his departure. Although he declined the offer, his welcome back home was none the better. As all repatriated Soviet citizens he was greeted with suspicion and remained under surveillance for the next twenty years.

Koslov, on the other hand, seems to have had no illusions about how Stalin would treat returning Soviet PoWs and civilian forced labourers. The authorities' suspicion and apprehension about their return had two main causes: for one thing they were intent on rooting out and eliminating those Soviet citizens who had collaborated with the Germans, and there were thousands. Secondly, they feared the effect of an extended stay in foreign lands on the ideological purity of their citizens. They suspected that their repatriates had been 'spoilt', having been exposed to new ideas, or worse, that they were perhaps working for foreign intelligence. In any event, Koslov's reasoning for hanging on in the West was sound. Due to be turned over, he escaped from Guildford transit camp, but was recaptured. Subject to military discipline, this latest feat of bravado equalled desertion and he was acutely aware that he owed the NKVD (the precursor of the KGB) an explanation. In a way this left him no other choice than to elude all repatriation efforts by continuing to apply the escape and risk-taking skills acquired as an occupation fugitive. The last the Soviets were to hear of him

---

[171] Hillsdon, Sonia, op. cit., 118. Another shelterer was Mr Williams of Roseville Street.

was when he jumped off an army jeep bound for their Brussels Embassy. Koslov went undercover, resurfacing when things had calmed down and later settling in West Germany.

Post-war recognition for what Gould, Forster and Le Druillenec had accomplished was slow and there were times when the family felt as though they had 'done something wrong'. For a long time all public debate was stalled by the myth that those engaged in activities which had irked the Germans had risked 'rocking the boat'; an argument often upheld without any regard as to whether these activities of defiance were illegal under the law or not. As goes for all groups of offenders, the relationship between those who had assisted fugitives and the island authorities was not an easy one. It was finally Britain's cold war enemy, the Soviet Union, who opened up the issue. In March 1966 they honoured twenty Jersey people, among them Louisa Gould (posthumously), Ivy Forster and Harold Le Druillenec, by awarding them gold watches.[172] By that time the Jersey authorities had already loosened up on the issue, otherwise they would have not associated themselves as closely with this gesture as they did: when he arrived in the island the chargé d'affaires at the Soviet Embassy, Mr Vassev, was officially greeted by Bailiff Le Masurier who gave him a tour of the States Building. On the photograph taken during the ceremony and printed in the Jersey Evening Post of March 29, 1966, Mr Vassev is pictured in conversation with Senator Ralph Vibert and Harold Le Druillenec took the occasion to give a short, eloquent speech. However, Guernsey was still nowhere to be seen in this commemorative effort. This was already recognized at the time and in his speech Mr Vassev emphasised that the honours bestowed on Jersey people *were in recognition of all in the Channel Islands who helped, including Guernsey.*[173]

Later in his life Harold Le Druillenec was also awarded a high French decoration, the Ordre de la Libération, instituted by General De Gaulle, and an MBE on his retirement from teaching. An appropriate commemoration of their deeds in the island, however, was still riddled with controversy, and all the island could bring themselves to do was to erect a generic memorial to all deportees. The first island memorial specifically referring to Louisa Gould only came after Harold's death, in 1995, when a permanent plaque was affixed to the wall of La Fontaine, her St Ouen home.

---

[172] The other seventeen people were Albert Bedane, Claudia Dimitrieva, François Flamon, René Franoux, Royston Garrett, Leslie Huelin, John Le Breton, Norman Le Brocq, Mike Le Cornu, René Le Mottée, Francis Le Sueur, Robert Le Sueur, Dr R McKinstry, Augusta Metcalfe, Oswald Pallot, Leonard Perkins and William Sarre, s. Bunting, op. cit., 325.
[173] 'Russian presentations', *JEP*, 29 Mar. 1966.

Frank Le Villio

At some point in his journey, Le Druillenec was afforded the company of another deportee, Frank Le Villio. This Jersey youth had been sentenced by decree of the troop court on 19 June 1944 for 'serious military larceny'.

Two previous convictions show that this was not the first time Le Villio had been in trouble with the authorities: in March 1942 he was sentenced, together with two other young Jerseymen, to three months' hard labour for breaking into the store of a Mr Dupré and stealing groceries worth £8.4.2; this was the second burglary at the store within one week, but the Royal Court could only prove his involvement in the last one and placed him on two years' probation. Within ten months Le Villio was apprehended again, for bicycle theft. He received a three-month sentence which, this time, was duly executed. So when Le Villio appeared before a German court for an offence against the German military in 1944, their harsh judgement was largely influenced by the fact that he had been previously convicted. No mitigating circumstances were acknowledged and Frank was deported to France.

His life had not been a happy one. François René Julien Le Villio was born on 13 September 1925 in St Saviour as one of the five children of a seaman. Frank spent his childhood at Sacré Coeur orphanage in Rouge Bouillon, as his mother died when he was two years old and his father signed on a liner for seven years when Frank was aged five. At Sacré Coeur the children were subject to a very strict régime. Girls and boys were cordoned off and unable to communicate. Thus separated from his sisters, Frank suffered terrible isolation. When their father returned after seven years, he bought the Rising Sun, a pub in Charles Street. Although they were now able to leave the orphanage and live with their grandmother, the children's overall situation showed little sign of improvement as Mr Le Villio showed no interest in his son's future and remained a virtual stranger to the other children. In this situation the girls pragmatically chose the security of early marriages.

Those who knew Frank testify that he was an independent-minded, kind and generous youth who deviated from the straight path owing to a lack of parental love and guidance. Therefore, though his actions give little cause for commendation, we ought not to draw hasty conclusions. The perceptive Harold Le Druillenec paints a sympathetic picture of Frank Le Villio in his 1946 radio screenplay and there must have been adequate reason for a man with such profound knowledge of human nature to do so. Harold, in fact, felt deeply protective of Frank - the latter was only eighteen years old.

When he met Frank's two sisters in Jersey after the war he confided to them, in a voice choked by tears, that Frank had been '*through a lot of pain*'. Le Druillenec's intuition is further compounded by earlier observations made by Oscar Williams, the Jersey probation officer, in March 1942. He remarked that, when interviewed, Frank '*did not appear to realize the gravity of the offence but promised to amend, if given an opportunity.*' He did not forget to stress that '*(t)his lad was placed at the Orphelinat du Sacré Coeur at the age of 2 years and left at the age of 12, during which time his conduct was most satisfactory.*' His work record was equally good. Athough not an achiever at school, he was described as a '*good, steady worker*' by one pre-war employer, Huelin Ltd., and as '*honest and willing*' by another, the Commercial Art Co. Ltd. The officer therefore concluded: '*I am of the humble opinion that he has no inherent vice and that the commission of the offence was to a great extent due to the present day condition*'.[174]

In theory his sentence of three months should have been executed in Jersey. And on June 21, 1944, as was standard procedure, the troop court sent a request for Le Villio's sentence to be executed in Jersey to C W Duret Aubin, the Attorney General. Le Villio duly entered prison to commence his sentence on June 27, but during the interlude the Germans had obviously changed their minds, deciding to disregard their own principles and to include Le Villio in the next shipment of 'undesirables' to France. A second communication of the troop court, dated July 1, 1944, therefore revised the prior decision, asking for the request for execution to be returned to the court and informing Aubin that Le Villio was on his way to Fresnes.[175] The Germans, as we know, were emptying the prison of as many inmates as possible and they were certainly not inclined to hesitate over their treatment of repeat petty offenders. Le Villio's profile fitted their definition of an 'undesirable' to the letter and he stood no chance of being exempted from deportation. Therefore, when his sister Raymonde arrived at the prison in order to intervene on his behalf, all she could do was watch in dismay as her brother was bundled into a vehicle bound for the harbour. Deported on the same boat as Le Druillenec, Gould and Pitolet, Frank's three-month-sentence was earmarked for execution in France. However, in the chaos of the German evacuation of France he was transferred straight to Fresnes and then, some time before the liberation of Paris, to Belfort. It was on this

---

[174] JAS. D/Z/H5/97. Law Officer's Department. Case no. 43. Probation officer's report on home surroundings of Le Villio, 28 Feb. 1942 (hearing), 13 Mar. 1942.
[175] JAS. D/Z Law Officer's Department.

journey that he met Le Druillenec, with whom he was sent to Neuengamme. They were separated several weeks later when Harold was sent to Wilhelmshaven and although they spent the final days of the war in Bergen-Belsen, they were both unaware of the presence of the other Jerseyman in the same camp. And this is hardly surprising, considering the abject conditions. Following his repatriation to England in spring 1945, Le Villio was treated for TB with steroids in Nottingham and on weekends he paid regular visits to a nearby aunt. But, despite his efforts to build a new life by taking up employment as a railway porter, he soon had to quit as his health deteriorated beyond recovery. Frank sensed that his days were numbered and although he was the beneficiary of a generous allowance his last months were, hardly surprisingly, restless and erratic. On 26 September 1946 he eventually succumbed to the lasting effects of his incarceration, at the age of 21.[176] Le Villio's fate confirms a sad truth, namely that survival was not just a matter of physical strength. Counterintuitive as it may seem, adolescents stood less of a chance to survive the camps, and their aftermath, than middle-aged men.

---

[176] JAS. L/C/24/D2. Joe Mière Collection: death and birth certificates of Frank Le Villio.

6. An Icon Turned Martyr - the Ogier Case

Unlike his fellow islanders portrayed in this book, Advocate Ogier died neither in a concentration camp nor in a penal prison, but in an internment camp. This may seem outside the remit of the memorial book project. The inclusion of his name on the memorial is, however, eminently justified when one considers the circumstances of his death. Firstly, his untimely death was precipitated by an initial two-month period of interrogation and imprisonment at Fresnes in spring 1943. Then his second deportation, from Jersey to Biberach internment camp, was motivated by political reasons, as he had been branded an 'undesirable'.

Born on June 15, 1881 at St Saviour to Lydia Jane (née *de Gruchy*) and William John Ogier, a partner in the reputed local law firm *Larbalestier & Ogier*, Léonce L'Hermitte was one of four brothers who attended Victoria College, Jersey. A keen sportsman, he excelled as the captain of the school cricket and rugby teams. Later attending Jesus College, Oxford, he graduated with an honours degree in law and was called to the Bar at Lincoln's Inn. Eventually returning to practise the law in Jersey, Leonce teamed up with Jack Le Cornu, with whom he successfully carried on his father's practice after the First World War.[177] In 1910 Ogier had married a Welshwoman, Emma Lilian Carter, and they subsequently had three children: Kenneth, Barbara and Richard. The latter had chronic health problems, a mysterious malady initially diagnosed as encephalitis. This saw him being led from one specialist to another, with no cure in sight.

The Occupation separated the family: Barbara and Kenneth lived in England; Emma, Leonce, Emma and Richard stayed on in Jersey. Worse than separation was to befall them two-and-a-half years into the Occupation: on February 12, 1943, the Ogier family home was raided by the German police. During their search they found a map on which Richard had been marking fortifications. The German initiative, one may surmise, was prompted by an informant, whose suspicion was probably aroused by Richard's frequent solitary wanderings around the island, during which the map had been pieced together. The house-search also produced a baby box camera belonging to Kenneth.[178] Upon this discovery Ogier was

---

[177] Ogier Papers; Victoria College Newsletter, 1943, 8/9.

[178] According to uncorroborated information Kenneth Ogier boarded the last train out of Prague where he had been working as an English language tutor for 12 months, on 31 Aug. 1939. He is said to have worked for a British intelligence agency during the war, on the basis of his

immediately arrested together with Richard and interrogated. The German authorities in Paris clearly suspected a major plot, for in early March 1943[179] the two Jerseymen were shipped to Paris for interrogation at Gestapo HQ and later to Fresnes prison where they were questioned by one Major Formanek, attached to the military court. It was Formanek who suspected that Richard was suffering from a brain tumour and recommended that he be admitted to St Anne's Hospital in Paris. Meanwhile, his father stood trial and was condemned to six months' imprisonment in May. However, the entire charge of espionage against Ogier and his son was so flawed that the court had not hidden its great difficulty in upholding the verdict and recommended its immediate suspension. Therefore, once the sentence had been read, Ogier was pardoned by the military commander of Paris and sent back to Jersey.

German courts in France did not have a reputation for parsimoniousness. Indeed, for an unprecedented situation of this nature ever to arise, communications between the German court in Paris and the service instigating Ogier's transfer to France must have been quite abysmal. What is all the more astounding is that, under normal circumstances, all Ogier could have hoped for was to be sent straight to an internment camp for Allied nationals, despite the pardon. That he was granted permission to return home was extraordinary. Richard stayed on in Paris at the neurosurgical unit at St Anne's Hospital where his condition was diagnosed as Parkinson's disease. No treatment was possible at the time, but Richard remained there until his repatriation to London in November 1944.[180]

When his father arrived back in Jersey on May 24, 1943 a crowd turned out to offer him a warm welcome. In a letter recounting the story to his sister Barbara after the war, Kenneth Ogier wrote:

> Everybody from the dustmen up would stop him to welcome him home and he was showered with gifts of food. This welcome seems to have been the chief reason for his second deportation, he became too much of a hero. One German officer admitted as much. When he arrived he was tired and a little weak after his experiences but with all this

---

knowledge of Czech. After the war he went on to become a senior official for UNESCO in Paris where he died in September 1996.

[179] Sinel, op. cit., entry of March 4, 1943.

[180] s. Ogier Papers. Richard died in Paris when his heart failed after an operation, on March 4, 1966.

kindness soon picked up again [...]. Many people have told me how Dad told them how well he was and how happy and how these weeks were the happiest of his life. He loved being home again.[181]

Ogier had become an icon for the island population and the popular enthusiasm which greeted his return was a bitter pill for the German rulers of the island. Compromised by their flawed decision to deport Ogier and his son, some high-ranking Germans in Jersey were irritated by this popular reaction. That displays of public discontent which surpassed a narrowly-defined level invited harsh counter-measures is well attested, however, in this case they cannot have been too sure about how to react, hesitating for six long weeks before initiating further action. Finally, around July 10, 1943, the Secret Field Police was at Ogier's door-step again, telling him that he had a few hours to get ready for deportation to Biberach internment camp. *'The devils are adept at this cat and mouse game'*[182] was Mary Deslandes' reaction in her Occupation diary on this blow that caught Ogier completely unaware. What nobody knew at the time was that Ogier was seriously ill with cancer of the intestines.[183] The main symptoms of the illness are anaemia and weight-loss and it is not surprising that his condition went unnoticed, as most people in occupied Jersey were suffering from the emaciation caused by an insufficient diet. The severe physical and psychological strain and the shock of unexpected deportation triggered his rapid degradation, and upon his arrival at Biberach from Compiègne, on July 15, 1943 he was immediately admitted to the camp hospital. Ogier was known for his good nature and he tried to give everyone in the camp an impression of cheerfulness. In his letters he reassured his wife, referring to his condition as *'a very bad cold'* and promising: *'I shall keep on smiling in spite of my bad luck'*. [184]On 21 July he wrote a last letter to his partner Le Cornu in Jersey, telling him that he was much better and how he enjoyed the *'wonderful scenery'* and the *'two terrific thunderstorms'* that had occurred in the vicinity of the camp. The self-deprecating Ogier was still unaware of how serious his condition was, for he asked Le Cornu to send him *'a small pack of snuff as I need some to wash off my colds.'*[185] It must

[181] Letter of K N Ogier to B Sandover, 17 July 1945, in: Ogier Papers.

[182] 'The Diary of Mary Winifred Deslandes June 1940 to May 1945', entry of July 18, 1943, in: *An Island Trilogy. Memories of Jersey and the Occupation by Mary Robin, Basil de Carteret and Mary Deslandes,* Jersey, n.d.

[183] s. Ogier Papers.

[184] Ogier Papers. Letter of Ogier to his wife, Biberach, 18 July 1943.

[185] Ogier Papers. Letter of Ogier to Le Cornu, Biberach, 21 July 1943.

have been around this time that he was fatally moved from the hospital back to the barracks where he was assigned top bunk. Shortly afterwards he collapsed and was taken to Ulm municipal hospital where he was given a blood transfusion. However, this did not save Ogier's life and he died on August 1, 1943, barely two weeks after his arrival in Biberach.[186] Two relatives interned at nearby Würzach, Percy and Evelyn Aste, (née Ogier), were present at his deathbed and recounted the last moments of 'Ogre' (as he was called) in a letter to his sister Maud in England. On July 28 they had received a telephone message telling them that Ogier was in hospital:

> It was such a shock for we thought he was home. Nurse took me over the next morning; as soon as I saw him I knew he was dying, for he was in a coma, but three times he came around, saw me and said, 'Evelyn, the girls and Percy'. It was heartbreaking, if only you had been with me. He had haemorrhage of the intestines, lost two litres of blood and his heart was very weak; He had the best medical attention and all kindness. Friends of his, Captain Woodrow and his wife, were in the same hospital and she was always in his room. The authorities asked me if I would like his body cremated because, by so doing, we can take his remains back to Jersey to be buried when we leave [...]. Ogre loved his island so much and, as all say, he was so loved by all, that I feel we have done the right thing, tho (sic) I felt awful signing the paper that this should be done [...]. We just cannot believe this is true, we are stunned it is so cruel (sic). I can write no more.[187]

Ogier's ashes were returned to his beloved Jersey by the Astes and laid to rest at St Saviour's cemetery. Both were repatriated to England in the months preceding the end of the war, as part of an exchange of 125 Channel Islands internees.[188]

---

[186] Ogier Papers. British Red Cross Message to Ogier's sister in Berkhamsted, Herts., 6 Mar. 1943; message of Arthur Harvey to J F Le Cornu, Ogier's partner, Biberach, 2 Aug. 1943.

[187] Ogier Papers. Percy and Evelyn Aste to Aunt Maud, 3 Aug. 1943.

[188] King, Peter, *The Channel Islands War 1940-45*, London, 1991, 150.

7. The Kreuzburg Internment Trap

-The Rossi Case

On 25 February 1943 Marcel Rossi and his father Jean Marie were sent to Kreuzburg/Silesia as part of the internment measures intended against residents of the Channel Islands.[189] Marcel did not survive the war.

Kreuzburg internment camp, though a former lunatic asylum, was not the most unpleasant place to spend the war in Germany. The solid building lodged 350 people, among them 200 Jews with British passports. Bullying the camp population was never a practice of the camp administration and Douglas Tanguy, a former Jersey internee at Kreuzburg, only recalls one suicide occurring in the camp during his time there. He still recalls how he was startled one day in February 1943, learning from his hairdresser that he had been selected for deportation to Germany. Stunned, Douglas summoned his courage and proceeded to College House, where he was informed, rather laconically, that the occupying authority thought it a 'better idea' to send him to Germany than to let him loiter about in Jersey. Contrary to the September 1942 deportations, which affected the non-indigenous British population of mainland origin, this later measure also included many people born in the Channel Islands, mostly men. Douglas also recalls a few 'mainlanders', among them a former Mosley bodyguard by the name of Pleasants ('a not very pleasant character') and three conscientious objectors. In his opinion what weighed most heavily on internees was the fact that the duration of their detention was undetermined. However, life at Kreuzberg was quite tolerable and Douglas reckons that overall Kreuzberg internees were *'luckier than those in other camps',* as there were many opportunities *'to kill time'.* The camp population was an amazing mix of personalities who ensured that distraction was plentiful: foreign legionaries, a university professor, actors, artists, musicians and several professional sportsmen who had all been surprised by the German advance. Douglas, a professional musician, soon found his niche in camp life. He formed the Kreuzberg Trio with Charles Haboreiter and Victor Hammett, two British musicians trapped in Europe by the German advance. Musicians were obviously in short supply and Douglas still recalls with a chuckle how he was approached by a German officer charged with entertainment for the Allied PoWs at nearby Lamsdorf camp and who had slipped into the role of a music agent. This

---

[189] JAS. B/A/W/80 Bailiff's War Files. List of persons evacuated from Jersey, n.d.

way the Kreuzberg Trio were afforded a most welcome three-week break from their camp and came into contact with other detainees.

Whiling away their time was easier for artists or craftsmen than for people with skills rendered superfluous by the sealed camp environment, and it is not hard to imagine that the Rossis - motor mechanics - would have found this challenge more difficult to negotiate than others. Still, as Douglas reminisces, the Rossis seemed to have come to grips with their camp existence, Jean leading a very quiet life and his son Marcel, a tall and attractive young man, spending most of his time keeping fit with physical exercise.[190] Jean was born in Jersey in 1898, of a family originating in Italy. After the First World War he married an Englishwoman, Lilian Maud Baker, and the couple's son Marcel Fortuné was born in Long Sutton, Lincolnshire on December 14, 1921. Like his father, Marcel was a dual Italian-British national and the family returned to Jersey where Jean worked at St Helier Garages until the German arrival in 1940. At the time the two Rossis were deported in 1943 they were living at Ypriana, in Chestnut Avenue, St Saviour.

The Rossis' fate in Hitler's concentration camps is difficult to elucidate, for having arrived in Kreuzburg on March 1, 1943 they were removed between nine and twelve months later, first to Oppeln prison, and subsequently to a concentration camp, Blechhammer, situated 18 miles to the West of the town of Gleiwitz. Initially, Blechhammer was established in April 1942 as a forced labour camp for Jews from Silesia employed on the construction of the Upper Silesia Hydrogenation Works. The number of prisoners increased to 5,500 and on April 1, 1944 Blechhammer became satellite number four of Auschwitz. On January 21, 1945, 4,000 Blechhammer prisoners where taken on a death march which reached Gross-Rosen on February 2.[191]

At this camp Jean Rossi was separated from his son and sent to Dachau, the first Nazi concentration camp established in March 1933. Jean Rossi was liberated by the American army in Bavaria in April 1945, but Marcel, who was sent to Flossenbürg concentration camp, died there, shortly after his arrival in February 1945.[192] After his liberation Jean Rossi spent a few months in England for medical treatment and then joined his wife who had stayed behind with Jersey relatives. For years he tried to ascertain what had

---

[190] Interview with Douglas Tanguy, summer 1997.
[191] *Encyclopedia of the Holocaust*, op. cit., 218, 352.
[192] PRO. FO 950 766. Index to names of British subjects in enemy concentration camps and statistical survey of camps.

befallen his son, but no survivors came forward with news of Marcel. Jean died in 1967, having never discovered the full story.

The fate of the Rossis is a conundrum as it defies the pattern of routine in Kreuzburg. They were the only known case of permanent removal of internees from this camp. Even escapees and those involved in the misappropriation of food or other misdemeanours were always returned to the camp. Word spread very easily and it is therefore inconceivable that the reasons for their removal could have been related to occurrences in the camp. The only way the Rossis differed from the rest of the camp population was through their dual citizenship and the only real clue offered to unravelling the mystery is one secret note the author found in what remains of the *Wehrmacht* High Command files. This document of April 15, 1943, explicitly alludes to the Rossis and claims that they were Italians, wryly stating that Italian nationals were not affected by the order to deport Channel Islanders to internment camps in Germany.[193] For one thing this document proves that the Rossis' case had been passed onto the highest echelon of the German military hierarchy for clarification. It also reinforces camp rumours circulating at the time that they were removed because they were considered Italians. If they were considered Italians, rather than British, the Rossis would have been affected by German counter-measures taken after Italy's disintegration and subsequent capitulation in September 1943. How their fate had been brought to the attention of the Wehrmacht High Command can only be surmised, but there is one hypothesis which is more plausible than others: while keeping a low profile in the camp, they may have initiated steps, on arrival, to have their case reviewed - with a view to being released - by arguing that their Italian nationality should have precluded them from internment measures intended at 'enemies of the Reich' and other undesirables. It is not unknown for internees to have been released, if they could argue a convincing case. One has to remember that the process of categorization of 'objective enemies' or 'undesirables' singled out for internment was extremely discretionary and volatile. Much depended on how willing German officials were to consider any objections - on the grounds of health or age for example - and what interpretation they gave to other, often rather self-referential evidence based on their flimsy assumptions. The most spectacular case of a release from internment was perhaps Jerseywoman Esther Pauline Lloyd who - despite being a registered Jew - successfully petitioned her way out of Biberach and was sent back to

---

[193] BA-MA. RW/4/624. OKW Wehrmacht HQ to Quartermaster (IV), FührerHQ, Secret Note Nr. 01675/43, re. Italian nationals Rossi, 15 Apr. 1943.

Jersey in 1944. What the Rossis could not have calculated was how fast the winds of war, at this later stage, could change and how rapidly yesterday's allies could become today's enemies. Therefore they may have well been carted off to prison in September 1943, to be integrated into the masses of Italian civilian and military internees[194] taken prisoner and deported to Germany. Branded traitors, these were singled out and made to live and work in appalling conditions. Thence it was only a short step into a concentration camp. It would have been enough for the Rossis to refuse signing a declaration committing them to work for Germany. At some stage they could have also been subject to an order of Himmler, the SS leader, issued on September 9, 1943. This stipulated that 'work related offences' - another rather elastic legal construction – on the part of Italian workers could be countered through an immediate concentration camp transfer.[195]

---

[194] Italian military personnel taken prisoner in 1943 were refused the status and the protection enjoyed by PoWs. Already considered traitors, they were forced to opt for continued cooperation with Germany. Many were punished for their refusal to sign up for the new Fascist army Mussolini was setting up with the assistance of the SS. The mortality rate of Italian forced labourers in Germany was on par with that of Russians, s. Herbert, Ulrich, *Fremdarbeiter-Politik und Praxis des Ausländer-Einsatzes in der Kriegswirtschaft des Dritten Reiches*, Berlin/ Bonn 1985, 259; Cajani, Luigi, 'Die italienischen Militärinternierten im nationalsozialistischen Deutschland', in: Herbert, Ulrich, ed., *Europa und der Reichseinsatz. Ausländische Zivilarbeiter, Kriegsgefangene und KZ-Häftlinge in Deutschland 1938-45*, Klartext Verlag, 1991, 295-316.

[195] Grossmann, Anton J., 'Fremd-und Zwangsarbeiter in Bayern 1939-45', in: *Vierteljahreshefte fur Zeitgeschichte*, 34 (1986), 481-521.

8. The Fatal Escapades of a Small-Time Juvenile Delinquent

If it was not for one solitary file at the Bundesarchiv, nothing could tell us about the fate of Walter Dauny.[196] As in the Le Villio case, Dauny's troubled youth was devoid of guidance and parental love, making his formative years very unsettled. His case reflects the partial fragmentation of public order during the Occupation years and the vacuum of meaningful authority that it created. This was nothing extraordinary and a fair number of Channel Islanders - especially those who were adolescents - admit that their behaviour was not always in tune with what would have been socially acceptable under normal circumstances. In particular stealing from the occupier acquired an aura of glamour and was considered entirely legitimate.

Walter Allen Stanley Dauny was born in St Peter, Jersey on April 4, 1926, but was soon left without a mother, who died when he was only one year old. Subsequently, he was raised by his aunt and uncle who lived at 8 Bath Street, St Helier. Although his father remarried later and took Walter back in, the relationship with his step-mother was full of friction. Walter's family ties had little effect in taming his unruly tendencies and Walter Dauny was an unloved child. This is nowhere clearer that in his uncle's essentially negative statements to the German *Feldgendarms* investigating his nephew's case in 1943. On this occasion he declared that his nephew deserved being deported from the island. Even with little or no knowledge of what was going on in German prisons and camps, it is inconceivable that he did not sense that this could only have the gravest of consequences for Walter.

Leslie Le Sueur, a classmate at La Motte school, is one of the few people who remember Walter Dauny from the time he was living in Bath Street, as they played football together in the same team. Leslie left school in March 1940 and it was not before sometime in 1942/43 that he saw Dauny again, who by then was working on a construction project at Blanchet House, St Peter. [197]

In January 1943, Dauny ran into his first trouble when he was apprehended for stealing an unknown amount of Cognac together with another man

---

[196] For whole section, s. BA-ZNS. Z 726. Court of the 319th I.D., Jersey branch: Investigations into the case against Walter Dauny.

[197] Information provided by Les Le Sueur.

whose name he obstinately refused to reveal. Sentenced by the court of FK 515, he served a five-month term which ended in June 1943. When he left prison he took up employment with Elsche & Co., the largest German contractor in the island, who was building a new electricity plant at St Peter. Walter now moved to town and rented a bed-sit in Roseville Street, from where he carried out yet more pointless thefts. Clearly, Dauny was not somebody who knew how to thrive on crime; there is nothing to indicate that he sold or bartered parts of his loot, most of which was found by the Feldgendarmerie when they searched his lodgings in January 1944. The articles he assembled represented no real value and did not improve his level of subsistence. If his behaviour was supposed to be the *début* of an apprentice crook, he showed little talent as he limited himself to uselessly hoarding a variety of items, in ludicrous quantities. No doubt Dauny was compensating for loneliness, lack of love and attention. A compulsion to please appears in the case of a theft he carried out for one of his neighbours, a woman employed as a hairdresser at the German harbour office who, when questioned later, denied all association.

Dauny sleep-walked his way into petty crime which became his favourite pastime: in October 1943 he entered through an open window into the clubroom of the Safety Coach Ltd. in Green Street, St Helier and removed a total of 248 (!) books, mostly detective novels, murder mysteries and other light fiction. Dauny took considerable risks, because with such a large number of books to be carried, he had to come back several times. This example alone demonstrates conclusively his state of blissful oblivousness to danger. Later that month not one, but three pairs of roller-skates disappeared from Cleveland Garages, all of which were later found unused in Dauny's bed-sit. Indeed, Dauny had some nerve because, as he later stated, when he did not like the soup served every lunch-time to Elsche workers, he walked down to a German unit stationed not far from his worksite at St Peter who served him some of their own German soup. This, no doubt, was tastier, for he made it a habit to come back daily. Finally, during one of these lunch-time visits in November 1943, Dauny could no longer resist the temptation of four pairs of military boots in an unlocked box, all of which disappeared into his bag. As with the rest of his collection, Dauny arranged his loot in a neat little row in his bed-sit, not realising that the Germans did not suffer fools gladly. However, fate was soon to catch up with him: on the evening of January 5, 1944, Dauny's landlord arrived at the Feldgendarmerie claiming that his tenant Walter Dauny was unruly, had threatened his maid with a knife and that he didn't want him any longer in his house. With him he had brought one pair of military boots which, as he said, might be of interest to Germans.

Whether or not Dauny had behaved badly towards his landlord, the latter's action was profoundly reprehensible. Again this episode demonstrates that denunciations in dictatorial regimes can serve entirely personal purposes, among them the possibility of ridding oneself of an unwanted person.

Dauny's trial took place on February 8, 1944 and the court of the 319th I.D. gave him a nine-month term for serious larceny. As one German lawyer willingly conceded, Dauny's acts were not those of a criminal mind, but of an immature youngster. However, this is where all empathy stopped. After all one could hardly expect the Germans to have given thought to the issue of tackling juvenile delinquency. What irked them most, of course, was the fact that Dauny had helped himself to German property. Therefore, in the view of the court, the general interest of the authorities by far exceeded the simple theft of four pairs of boots, a point stressed in the verdict: *'It must be clear to the local population that German property must not be touched. Those who offend against this principle must be severely punished.'* [198] German irritation acquired a farcical tone in the prosecutor's indignation over the fact that Dauny had responded to the 'hospitality' of the Wehrmacht with theft.

Walter Dauny was to pay dearly for his *faux pas*. Sometime before February 25, 1944, he was sent to St Lô, where he stayed for two weeks. On March 7, 1944 he was transferred to Villeneuve St Georges, the prison where he was to serve his entire term until October 4, 1944. After the German withdrawal from France he disappeared; his file gives no further clues as to his subsequent fate and he is presumed to have died in a concentration camp.[199]

---

[198] Verdict of the Court of the 319th I.D., Jersey branch, in: BA-ZNS. Z 726. Investigations into the case against Walter Dauny.
[199] JAS. L/C/24/A/5. Joe Mière Collection. List of political prisoners in the Channel Islands 1940-1945; information provided by Geoff Delauney.

9. Without a Trace - June Sinclair and Peter Johnson

Two Jersey offenders, June Sinclair and Peter Bruce Johnson, disappeared into the abyss of the Third Reich's camps and prisons without a trace. The little we know about them is based entirely on oral testimony. Both had moved to the island before the Occupation and they had few attachments and no family ties there. In the grey days of the Occupation social isolation increased vulnerability, explaining why their disappearance went unnoticed.

June was a half-Jewish orphan from London who came to Jersey before the war. Joe Mière remembers her because she was his next door neighbour at 27 Midvale Road, St Helier and her picture was taken on a beach outing with Joe and his mother, one sunny Sunday afternoon. Little is known of her apart from the fact that she worked at one of the hotels requisitioned by the German forces, probably the Continental or the Mayfair, and that sometime in 1940/41 she confided to Mrs Mière that her closest relatives had been killed in the Blitz.

A genuine city girl, June was quick-tempered and did not suffer fools easily. Therefore, when she was molested by a German soldier at the hotel where she was employed, she retaliated rapidly by slapping his face, and it seems that the ensuing *mêlée* degenerated dangerously. Like many other women in occupied Europe, she was swept into the concentration camp system and ended her days in Ravensbrück, where she is presumed to have died in 1943, aged 23.[200]

Peter Bruce Johnson was an Australian deaf-mute, an impediment which must have greatly magnified his isolation. Nothing is known of his fate, but there is a high probability that he was subject to measures targeting people with a physical or mental impairment, including deportation as an undesirable. It is a well-established historical fact that the disabled were the Nazis' first genocidal victims and that tens of thousands were gassed in Germany, and other countries, as early as 1940. Johnson was sent to France in 1943 and thence to Dora-Mittelbau concentration camp, in the Harz mountains.[201]

---

[200] Information provided by Joe Mière; 'In Memory of Those Who Never Came Back', *JEP*, 8 Nov. 1996.

[201] JAS. L/C/24/A/5. Joe Mière Collection. List of political prisoners in the Channel Islands 1940-1945; Dora-Mittelbau was also the final destination of Clarence Painter.

This camp, situated three miles from the town of Nordhausen, was first mentioned on August 27, 1943 as an external unit of Buchenwald and it became a concentration camp in its own right, with 23 branches, on October 28, 1944. Thousands of prisoners were transferred there in the second half of 1943 in order to excavate underground tunnels for the site of a huge plant for the manufacture of V2 missiles, which became operational in late spring 1944. Dora can only be described as a 'meat grinder', to the point that its mortality rate was higher than that of any other concentration camp in Germany. The first group of prisoners sent from Buchenwald included several hardy individuals who organised sabotage and managed to slow down production. When they were detected, these underground leaders, together with many others - altogether 200 - were hanged in public. On March 25, 1945, there were 34,500 prisoners at Dora-Mittelbau, most of whom were sent on a death march to Bergen-Belsen on April 1.[202] The chances that Johnson survived any of these hecatombs are minute.

---

[202] *Encyclopedia of the Holocaust*, op. cit., 399.

Conclusion

The twenty lives encountered in the preceding pages give a sufficiently broad idea of the diverse forms of defiance that developed in occupied Jersey. Although each case is unique, there is good reason to determine and generalise patterns of dissidence which can be categorized along five main lines. Some cases, however, do not fall squarely into one of these categories. This is certainly the case of Gould, and of Hassall and Audrain whose escape attempt bears features of resistance (escape being an act of resistance), but also of a particular brand of dare-devilishness characteristic of youths.

The first type encompasses genuinely subversive action or open defiance, of which the dissemination of uncensored radio news was the most common manifestation. This was an offence that came very close to making an explicit political statement. The majority of the people portrayed in this book died because of this offence, which amounted to a deliberate refusal to comply with the demands of the occupying authorities. The most openly defiant of these intrepid people was undoubtedly Canon Clifford Cohu who prioritised his determination to boost morale in the island over his own safety.

The protagonists of the second category of defiance were those who reacted against the severe shortage of supply and the breakdown of a fair system of distribution. They considered this as an imposition upon them, by the drain on the island resources through the fortification program and German garrison, and they took a liberal view on ownership rights, and in particular German ownership rights. Most of them were neither resistance heroes nor petty criminals but in most cases ordinary people struggling for survival. Although such activities lack the element of selflessness, a summary condemnation would be unfair without bearing in mind the harsh realities of occupation, which tended to push people to - let's say - 'unconventional' forms of survival.

That the food situation was dramatic throughout almost the entire occupation is welldocumented.[203] In 1941, R. N. McKinstry, the Jersey

---

[203] For a society of affluence such as ours where - according to the latest figures - about half the population is above their recommended weight levels, it may be difficult to imagine the impact of food restrictions. It is all the more unfortunate that many journalistic accounts of the Channel Islands Occupation have an annoying tendency to ignore the structural roots of the

medical officer, already warned that the rations fell short of the requirements of healthy life: while for example the recommended ration for a manual worker was a minimal 3,000 calories, the distribution only yielded a meagre 1,500. For other categories, children excepted, the discrepancy between need and availability was similarly dramatic. While additional carbohydrates could be supplied through potatoes, the most critical food bottle-neck was the deficiency in fats and proteins, supplied through milk, butter, oil, meat, fish, nuts, beans, peas and lentils. This rendered the population more susceptible to diseases of the respiratory tract, especially tuberculosis. [204] Despite McKinstry's pleas on how to improve the local diet, and despite the genuine attempts of the authorities to ameliorate this situation, there was never enough food to go round for everyone. The effects of malnutrition, as predicted, soon kicked in: increasing lassitude, fall in stamina, lowered resistance to disease, rising mortality from tuberculosis and other infections, increased maternal and infant mortality.[205] In Guernsey the situation was no different: Charles Russell Jekyl Randall, a retired RAF group captain living in Guernsey, stated that already prior to his deportation to Germany, in February 1943, the inhabitants suffered from malnutrition, detailing that *'death certificates lodged in the Greffe definitely state, in certain cases, that death was partly due to this cause.'* That malnutrition was a killer was not Randall's private opinion, but established fact, as demonstrated by a statement signed by Guernsey doctors, which Randall personally handed to Dr Brosch, the FK representative.[206] There is nothing to indicate that the situation improved after his departure. If anything, it got worse: in May 1943, following Allied air raids on supply ships, rations were lowered by the Germans. By spring 1944 the flow of supplies from mainland Europe slowed down to a trickle, which dried up completely in the wake of the Normandy landings. When the Red Cross ship Vega docked in the Channel Islands, they were starving.

By no means can this category of offenders be lumped together with criminals or black-marketers profiteering on the backs of their fellow

---

surge in crime, quoting the phenomenon entirely out of context. The objective of this manipulatory device is to create moral outrage, thereby priming readers for the catalogue of other alleged moral depravities to follow. A classic example of sensationalist exploitation.

[204] JAS. D/Z/H5/174. Law Officer's Department. R N McKinstry to the President of the Department of Public Health, May 1941.

[205] s. Garnier, Val, *Medical History of the Jersey Hospitals and Nursing Homes during the Occupation 1940-1945*, London, 2002.

[206] PRO. TS 26/197. Charles Russell Jekyl Randall, handwritten notes to British war crimes investigators, 1945.

islanders. This point is also stressed by the Jersey prison chaplain who wrote after the war:

> My touch with the prisoners is close and personal and I can vouch for the fact that many of them are not criminally minded and would not have stumbled in ordinary times. The plain fact is that the period of the occupation was abnormal and very trying; that it pressed on some much more than others; that moral standards had degenerated throughout the community generally; and that the prisoners in question were by no means the only or the worst offenders.[207]

Finally, even law-and-order proponents whom such arguments cannot convince must admit that – without exception - the punishment of offenders was hugely disproportionate to the severity of the offences. The harsh treatment of any type of non-compliant or unconventional behaviour had much in common with practice in Nazi Germany where 'misdemeanours' such as turning up late for work repeatedly or alcohol addiction were included in the Nazi catalogue of antisocial behaviour; which could secure the offender a slot in a work reeducation camp.

The third category comprises acts perpetrated by adolescents. The young were particularly adversely affected by the effects of hunger and demoralization. The combination of these two factors is what post-war officials, both in Jersey and in Whitehall, came to call the 'exceptional circumstances of the occupation.' While the action of youngsters was often motivated by patriotism, and contained elements of defiance, they could not always invoke the same degree of either noble intention or reflection that may have characterised other acts of opposition.[208] Some cases were simply mindless and immature provocations, others bore characteristic daredevil elements of 'flirting with danger' and taboo-shattering, both so typical of teenagers. The older generation had less influence over the young whose preferred target was pre-war peace-time propriety. The absence of many fathers made the job of reining in unruliness that bit more difficult for Jersey mothers. In addition, most youngsters found an excellent hate figure in the Germans and it does not require much imagination to see why the occupier presented a particularly gratifying target for teenage ridicule. The young were also scathing about the

---

[207] JAS. D/Z/H5/456. Citation from correspondence Duret Aubin to J B Howard, Home Office, 21 June 1945.
[208] Although they were young, the author does not include the long list of Jersey escapees in this category.

authority of the island officials and their parents' painful accommodation with the enemy. Naturally, the only authority they respected – and this is more than exemplified by the numerous escapes - lay across the water. The fact that these mostly harmless activities - a normal feature of all societies - entailed consequences as dire as death in a concentration camp puts the tragedy of the young Jersey offenders into perspective.

Not only youngsters lost orientation in an environment of confusion and moral ambiguity, which no longer provided clear standards of behaviour. In a correspondence of July 1945 concerning the possibility of an amnesty, the Home Office endorsed the island authorities' view that it was '*necessary to discrimate very carefully*' between crimes which had been '*detrimental to the common welfare*' and those '*cases in which the offender may have had real doubt as to where his duty lay or may have committed the offence in the belief that he was injuring the interests of the enemy and not of the Islands*'. The point was aptly illustrated with the not-so-uncommon example of '*a farmer (who) may have thought that by holding back food from the civil or military authorities and selling it surreptitiously to civilians he might be helping the Islands.*' [209]

A last category of offenders, probably the most tragic, does not fit into any category at all. These were circumstantial victims who committed no punishable act as such, but who were sucked into the system of destruction, on the basis of prejudice, suspicion or affiliation to a group of people that had received the label 'enemies of the Reich'. Marcel Rossi was such a victim. His sole 'crime' was that he held dual Italian-British nationality and was in the wrong place - an interment camp in Germany - at the wrong time - after the capitulation of Italy in September 1943, when Italians became subject to fierce counter-measures on the part of their former German ally.

Despite the evident focus of this book on those who died in deportation, it must be noted that many Jersey people who survived their imprisonment continued to suffer from their wartime deprivations, both mentally and physically. And, as demonstrated in the cases of Sinclair and Johnson, there may also have been a small number of islanders whose disappearance into Hitler's camps and prisons went entirely unrecorded, most likely people who had moved to the island before the Occupation. Finding a satisfactory answer to how many people this may have involved and who they were, has proven beyond the scope of this project. Some doubt lingers as to whether a final word on this issue will be possible at all.

---

[209] JAS. D/Z/H5/456. Home Office (Markbreiter) to Duret Aubin, 16 July 1945.

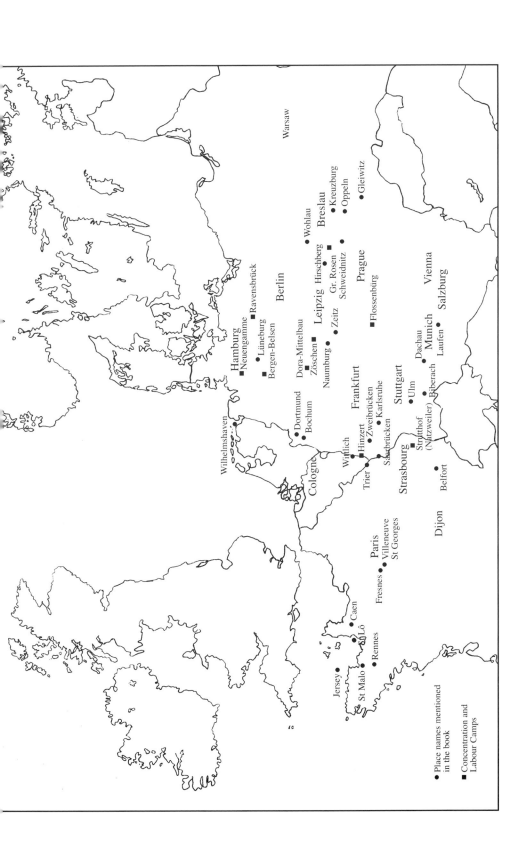

Warsaw

Breslau
Kreuzburg
Oppeln
● Gleiwitz
● Wohlau

Hirschberg
Gr. Rosen
Schweidnitz
Leipzig
Zeitz
Prague

Berlin

Ravensbrück
Hamburg
Neuengamme
Lüneburg
Bergen-Belsen

Dora-Mittelbau
Zöschen
Naumburg

Flossenbürg

Vienna
Salzburg
Dachau
Munich
Laufen

Wilhelmshaven

Dortmund
Bochum

Frankfurt

Stuttgart

Ulm
Biberach

Cologne

Wittlich
Hinzert
Zweibrücken
Karlsruhe
Saarbrücken

Trier

Struthof
(Natzweiler)

Strasbourg

Belfort

Dijon

Paris
Villeneuve
St Georges

Fresnes

Caen
St Lô
Rennes

Jersey
St Malo

● Place names mentioned
  in the book

■ Concentration and
  Labour Camps

Joe Tierney

Arthur Dimmery

George Fox

Canon Clifford Cohu

John Whitley Nicolle

William Marsh

Emile Paisnel

Frederick Page

Clifford Queree

After their failed attempt Gould and Hassall were taken to the Pomme d'Or Hotel, the seat of the German Harbour Police in Jersey

Dennis Audrain

Maurice Gould's grave in Howard Davis Park, St Helier

Peter Hassall in 1942

Maurice Gould

SS-Special
Camp
Hinzert 194

Wittlich pris

Above: 'Work' in the Concentation
Camp. Hundreds of prisoners perished
hauling blocks of granite up the
'staircase' leading from the quarry at
Mauthausen

Right: Biberach Internment Camp

Above: Peter Painter

Right: Gross-Rosen concentration camp. The sign above the entrance reads 'Arbeit Macht Frei'

Below: John Painter

Clarence Painter

Above: Peter Painter in happier days

Left: June Sinclair

Right: Frank Le Villo 1940/1

Below: Frank Le Villo, whilst receiving medical treatment in 1945/46. The effect of the steroids treatment is clearly visible in his bloated physical appearance.

Advocate Leonce Ogier

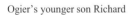

Fresnes Prison, near Paris

Ogier's younger son Richard

James Houillebecq

Feodor Buryi

Ivy Foster

Edward
Muels

Louisa
Gould

Walter Dauny

John Soyer

Harold Le Druillenec MBE

Marcel Rossi

Major General Müller [left] Commander of 319th Infantry Division and head of overall command in the Channel Islands from May 1941 to September 1943. He was the driving force behind the June 1942 wireless ban

Colonel Knackfuss

The scene of a memorable 'wireless case' in occupied Jersey: St Saviour's Church and Parish Hall

Major General Graf von Schmettow in 1944. An internal power struggle engaged von Schmettow and Müller and the wireless issue was one of the areas where they diverged. Von Schmettow was Müller's predecessor as Befehlshaber of the Channel Islands and resumed this post after Müller's departure in 1943

Gloucester Street prison, St. Helier

Escapees were met by the Duchess of Kent after the occupation

The Memorial to the 'Jersey Twenty Two' St Helier Harbour

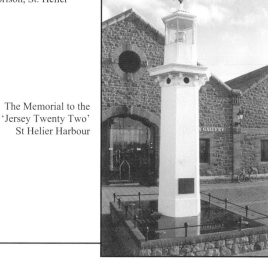

Above: Secret Field Police headquarters at Silverside, Havre des Pas

Right: Feldgendarmerie headquarters in Bagatelle Road

PART TWO

IMPRESSIONS OF AN OCCUPATION

1. *Inselwahn,* Security Obsessions and Radio War

Little has been said about the broader historical context against which 'offences against the occupying authorities' have to be measured. The following chapter will deal with the changes arising out of the German fortification scheme for the Channel Islands and the impact it had on life in the islands. The fortification of the islands undertaken on Hitler's personal directive was one of the most important factors in dictating relations between the German occupier and the island population, and most areas where islanders and Germans clashed were associated, however remotely, with the fortification work. These contentious areas were the obstruction of work, the hiding of escaped forced labourers, the lack of supply which put many people in a desperate position and the retention of wireless sets. Through the prism of the fortification programme the true nature of Nazism was evident. It entailed a dramatic increase in the number of soldiers, civilian workers and members of the Organisation Todt (OT), the German labour organisation, in the Channel Islands. Increasingly, forced labourers were shipped to the islands and obsessive security demands became commonplace. As a result of the changes brought about by the fortification programme, the occupying authority needed to deal more swiftly and ruthlessly with popular dissent, thus leading to ever-greater expeditiousness in their treatment of the local population. Step by step, a constant and progressive radicalisation of German attitudes took place, leading to mounting repression. It is quite reasonable to believe that, had Hitler's *Inselwahn*[210] not prevailed, the Occupation would have evolved very differently.

A meeting at his HQ, on October 18, 1941, provided Hitler with an ideal opportunity to display (as he had done on previous occasions) his obsession with the Channel Islands, his only British possessions. Prone to think in terms of prestige rather than utility, this was the perfect occasion for the former corporal to prove what a bogus strategist he was. Although the overall military situation in the Channel had shown no sign of change and Britain's prospects were still bleak, he was to commission a gigantic fortification programme that could hardly be justified in strategic terms. Hitler conjectured that Britain was under severe political pressure from her Soviet ally, allegedly demanding that she engage with the enemy. With all British footholds in Europe apart from Malta and Gibraltar lost, Hitler was

---

[210] Literally: Island madness.

firmly convinced that North Africa and the Channel were the two theatres of war where the British would try to regain the initiative. He therefore argued that if they succeeded in retaking the islands this would cause severe disruption to German convoys in the area.[211] Characteristically, none of the professional soldiers present dared to contradict him, although he cited no 'hard' evidence to support his argument and although the Germans had little intelligence of British long-term planning. In fact, Churchill had been in favour of ventures to retake the islands as a much-needed morale booster in 1940 and Lord Mountbatten argued the case of retaking Alderney on several occasions in 1942, but in the end such plans were rejected by other members of Britain's Chiefs-of-Staff Committee as too risky and too costly.[212] This illustrates conspicuously the leadership structure in the two camps and points to one of the major differences in the way they were waging war. Decision-making on the British side involved a common and concerted effort and was based on mutual consent; similar tendencies in the German camp were badly hampered by the all-imposing will of one individual. Decidedly, this was the Achilles heel of the Axis war effort, for this individual, Adolf Hitler, based many of his moves on little more than intuition and preconceived ideas.

With the Führer's pet project naturally overruling all other considerations, immense pressure built up to tighten security measures and deal harshly with all offenders. There were two major areas of concern to the Germans. First, there was the possibility that civilian workers engaged on the fortifications would obstruct the progress of work or even engage in acts of sabotage. It was therefore important to maintain discipline at all times and repress severely all manifestations of disobedience among the workforce. The second concern was that members of the civilian population, taken here in its widest sense, would acquire details of the building programme and transmit this information to the enemy. This was a possibility which, increasingly, began to obsess the German military ranks.

The obsessions were reinforced by some powerful paradoxes. First in the labour issue. The contradiction here was that while the Germans were desperately short of labour, they were equally desperate not to let civilian workers recruited among the local population get an insight into their building work, especially not the sensitive military projects. Another

---

[211] BA-MA. OKW RW/4-625. General of Engineers and Fortresses at Army High Command (ObH), Protocol of meeting at FührerHQ on 18 Oct. 1941 re. fortification work in British Channel Islands.
[212] Bunting, op. cit., 224-5.

disadvantage of local civilians was that many made it an issue of 'going slow' on the work, with the highest rates of absenteeism and the lowest rate of efficiency among all groups of workers.[213] The lack of discipline among Channel Islands workers is for example attested by a list which Goetzky, a German contractor in Guernsey, sent to his client, OT-Normandy (Section 'Gustav'), on June 26, 1942. This detailed the names and attendance of 38 Guernsey workers in his employment. '*Some of the workers*', it was stated, '*completely failed to turn up for work and others stopped working after a very short time*', absenting themselves for days without an excuse. Almost all Guernsey employees also made it a point to obstruct the work in progress. According to the report, '*the majority* [of the Channel Islands civilian workforce, n.b.] *are extremely reluctant to engage in regular work [...] Other foreign workers* [in this case French and Belgians, n.b.] *have adapted themselves to the German work ethic though their food is no better and though they are separated from their families.*'[214] By this time the FK's Guernsey branch, the *Nebenstelle,* also endorsed the view that British absenteeism was becoming alarming: Inspector Zachau of the *Nebenstelle* therefore reported the case to the court of the FK 515 in Jersey. He supported his move with the claim that a continual rise in such unruly behaviour was endangering the work discipline and preventing the conclusion of important military installations on schedule. While requesting that the court take over the Goetzky case, he suggested that a more extensive interpretation be given to the military governor's 'Protection of the Working Peace Order' of November 6, 1941 and that the punishment of all culprits be conducted in a '*perceptible manner*'.[215]

---

[213] BA. ZNS. Court martials. General correspondance. W11/104-107, November 1940 - March 1944, collection of Files (319th I.D.): Correspondance between the court of the 319th I.D. and the Nebenstelle Guernsey of the Feldkommandantur, re. unauthorised absenteeism of English civilian workers, June/July 1942. The remaining court documents at the Guernsey Archives give precious indications that German troop courts were mainly dealing with the slackening discipline among their own troops, but many cases also dealt with British and Western European civilian workers. Another case is perhaps noteworthy: On 4 Aug. 1943 a German contractor, the Gewerkschaft Windsheim, Spezialbau-Einsatz West (based in Cologne) wrote to Fortress-Engineers HQ (Festungs Pi Stab 19, Abt. 2/II) that William John Upson of 4 Rue Flére, Vale, Guernsey worked a total of ten hours during the period 22 July – 4 Aug. 1943 (4 hrs on 22 July and 6 hrs on 29 July) and then left work without being excused, in: Guernsey Archives. FK23-3.

[214] BA. ZNS. Court martials. General correspondance. W11/104-107, November 1940 - March 1944, collection of Files (319th I.D.): Letter of William Goetzky, Contractors to the OT-Normandie, Abschnittsleitung Gustav, 26 June 1942, re. unauthorised absenteeism of English civilian workers, re. Order for the Protection of the Working Peace.

[215] Ibid., Note of Inspector Zachau, Nebenstelle Guernsey, to Court of FK 515, 13 July 1942.

Surely, it would be unwise to profess that patriotism alone accounted for this situation; there was rather a mixture of different motives at work here. Some civilians were attracted by German work because it was supposed to yield certain advantages, such as better wages or a better supply of sparse commodities, which was greatly facilitated through the possibilities of theft from the places of work.[216] Some of those recruited also cherished illusions about better rations when they started work, but these were soon to be dispelled by the harsh reality. Over time this became a major source of dissatisfaction, and many absentees at Goetzky's attributed their poor performance to sickness and weakness caused by an inadequate diet. What remains, however, regardless of the motivations, is the plain fact that Channel Islanders were not good employees and did not volunteer in droves to work for the Germans, at least not the way some authors would like to make us believe.

Channel Islanders would not endure bad work conditions, as they were marginally better protected than foreign labourers. First of all because the Germans did not want to alienate the island population and, secondly, because the island authorities could act as a buffer between civilian employees and the Germans and protect them from the worst types of abuse. Their nuisance factor was increased in as far as they had to be treated and paid comparatively well and could not be hoarded into mass lodgings where their movements were easy to control. Islanders went home after work and had plenty of outside contact. Plans were therefore devised to prevent the employment of local civilians on the most sensitive sites or in locations where they could get a good picture on progress made on the fortification of the islands. In order to counter the dependence on the local workforce, foreign labour, and in particular forced labour, was brought into the islands. However, the different nationalities of these workers barely concealed their one common denominator. They all had little good to say about their new masters and as a consequence the Germans soon became apprehensive that Channel Islanders might plot sabotage and espionage by joining forces with the foreign labour.[217] Thus one putative security threat followed another, thereby increasing the German potential for highly disproportionate misrepresentations. The situation was quite surreal: the world had seen few occupying powers carrying out prestigious military projects commissioned expressly and supervised attentively by their

---

[216] Ginns, Michael, op. cit., 66/67.

[217] For a comprehensive breakdown of the different types and nationalities of foreign labour shipped to the Channel Islands by the German occupier, s. Ginns, Michael, op. cit.

venerated supreme chief, and with no choice other than to employ thousands of mistrusted enemy civilians and PoWs. Naturally, paranoia thrived.

The protection of their fortress began to dominate the German mind, most of all because their security procedures were lax. Improvement in this area was urgently called for, as demonstrated by one incident reported to the head of the Secret Field Police, (the 'Gestapo of the Wehrmacht') at Abwehr [218]HQ in France on March 16, 1942. In this case, the entire extension plans of the Jersey Luftwaffe[219] base had simply disappeared[220]. Similar deficiencies were spotted by Abwehr officers surveying security procedures on the French coast: surveillance of the workers was minimal and the Abwehr drew the conclusion that '*members of enemy intelligence were active amongst the workforce and had detailed information on the fortifications*'.[221] Finally the Abwehr decided that maximum security could only be achieved by effectively blocking all channels of transmission between the islands and Continental Europe. However, it was soon realised that virtually no secret would remain intact if security procedures were to be concentrated in the extensive harbour area of St Malo, which the Abwehr acknowledged was impossible to control. Tactical considerations dictated the concentration of measures of control on the islands, where the element of natural geographical separation from mainland Europe could be exploited. On April 7, 1942 Abwehr France indicated in a report the measures it deemed necessary to achieve this task. They were to include a reduction of all movements between the islands and the Continent, tight control of the Channel Islands harbours and the coastline, strict censorship of postal services, a ban on pigeons, the billeting of workers and measures of deterrence against the civilian population. Also included in the catalogue of suggestions was a ban on all wireless sets owned by the civilian

---

[218] Military Counter-Intelligence

[219] BA. MA. RW/49 97: Abwehr Command France (F/IIIc), Channel Islands - Commitment of labour resources, protective security measures 1942-1944. Communication of Army Group Command D, Chief-of-staff to Abwehr Command France, Head of GFP West, 16 Mar. 1942.

[220] The term in German is Geheime Feldpolizei (GFP). There was no Gestapo as such in the islands, however GFP included many Gestapo members in their ranks who had been drafted into the forces, s. Gessner, Klaus, 'Geheime Feldpolizei - Die Gestapo der Wehrmacht', in: Mallmann, Klaus-Michael/Paul, Gerhard (Ed.), *Die Gestapo – Mythos und Realität*, Darmstadt 1995, 492-507.

[221] BA-MA. RW/49 97. Abwehr Command France (F/IIIc), Channel Islands - Commitment of labour resources, protective security measures 1942-1944. Communication of Army Group Command D, Chief-of-staff to Abwehr Command France, Head of GFP West, 16 Mar. 1942. Report on fact-finding mission to coastal area Dieppe 24-26 Mar. 1942.

population.[222] As an immediate counter-measure the reinforcement of the German forces was taken up and on April 10, 1942 thirteen additional Secret Field Police were despatched to the Channel Islands.[223] Some days later, Abwehr France adopted the report's recommendations concerning the seizure of wirelesses in a communication to their Berlin HQ, on the grounds of the possibility of converting radio receivers into transmitters or the camouflaging of existing transmitters as receivers.[224] Radio receivers and transmitters are very different in that one performs the opposite function of the other, namely converting voice to radio waves and vice versa. However, in doing so they use the same functional blocks essentially in reverse order. In the vacuum tube era the components required to make a transmitter were very similar, if not identical, to those in a radio receiver. The conversion was not a task for the layman, but a radio amateur could easily manage.[225] A confiscation could, theoretically, be based upon international law. The Hague Convention provides for this eventuality, stipulating that the occupier may seize *'all appliances [...] adapted for the transmission of news [...] even if they belong to private individuals'*.[226] Whether such a heavy-handed approach was justified is another question; especially as nobody had asked the Germans to turn the islands into a fortress and stir up a security scare of their own making. Nevertheless, after the war, no war crimes investigations were launched with regard to the wireless confiscation, as was done for the Alderney atrocities, the deportations of Channel Islanders and other measures of collective punishment.

The Abwehr's vision of Channel Island realities was inspired by measures carried out in occupied France which, despite its geographical proximity,

---

[222] BA-MA. RW/49 97: Abwehr Command France (F/IIIc), Channel Islands - Commitment of labour resources, protective security measures 1942-1944. III H, summary report on secret measures of prevention taken in the Channel Islands, 7 Apr. 1942.

[223] BA-MA. RW/49 97. Abwehr Command France (F/IIIc), Channel Islands - Commitment of labour resources, protective security measures 1942-1944. Communications of Army Group Command D, Chief-of-staff to Abwehr Command France, Head of GFP West, 16 Mar. and 30 Mar. 1942.

[224] BA-MA. RW/49 97. Abwehr Command France (F/IIIc), Channel Islands - Commitment of labour resources, protective security measures 1942-1944. Communication of Army Group Command D, Chief-of-staff to Abwehr Command France, Head of GFP West, 16 Mar. 1942; Abwehr Command France to Abwehr HQ at OKW, re. intelligence reports on OT workers, 16 Apr. 1942.

[225] Correspondence with Jane Horrell, Department of Electrical and Electronic Engineering, Imperial College London, December 2003 (in possession of author).

[226] Laws and Customs of War on Land (Hague IV), Annex to the Convention: Regulations respecting the law and customs of war on land, Section III: Military authority over the territory of the hostile state, article 53, 18 Oct. 1907.

was a very different place. In France and in the Low Countries transmitters had been discovered that were used by resistance cells in order to maintain radio contact with London. Equally, the resistance received instructions through the BBC programmes. The Abwehr was not well acquainted with the special situation in the Channel Islands where no serious cases of sabotage occurred and where German troops had little to fear and they clearly thought that, as in other countries, the development of resistance and sabotage in the islands was merely a matter of time. The enthusiasm with which some islanders responded to the V-sign campaign in spring 1941 only served to confirm such strong beliefs about the effectiveness and direction of the British Radio War. The distortion of German vision is indicated by the reasons assigned for the reinforcement of the Secret Field Police: a preventive step designed to keep track of *'intentions to build resistance movements, acts of sabotage and terrorist groups and to build a reliable network of informers among the workers and the island population.'* [227] The venture yielded a plentiful harvest, evident in the rising tide of denunciations. With prejudice and erroneous interpretations of the Channel Islands being all the rage, distortions were only to be reinforced by a panoply of flawed reports: Lieutenant-Colonel Bleibtreu, the officer in charge of the Abwehr advance party at St Malo, spent a week in the Channel Islands on a fact-finding mission, from April 29 to May 6, 1942. In his final report he claimed that the security risk presented by the civilian Channel Islands workers living with their families was by far greater than that presented by foreign OT workers. He asserted that:

> In the event of an English attack, sabotage and open revolt have to be reckoned with. Advance troops recruited among the population will face little difficulty in disrupting communications throughout the limited island territory and carrying out extensive sabotage. In fact, the English have already attempted to organise themselves under the command of an English Major,[228] pretending that they were

---

[227] BA-MA. RW/49 97. Abwehr Command France (F/IIIc), Channel Islands - Commitment of labour resources, protective security measures 1942-1944. Communication of Army Group Command D, Chief-of-staff to Abwehr Command France, Head of GFP West, 16 Mar. 1942; Abwehr Command France to Abwehr HQ at OKW, re. intelligence reports on OT workers, 16 Apr. 1942.

[228] Bleibtreu was referring to Major Crawford Morrison, the Jersey Air Raid Protection (ARP) warden who had set up a secret information-gathering network. Like most other endeavours of this type, its activity was based on the initiative of individuals and no directives were received from the UK. By planting agents in German employment they were able to conduct an

taking air raid precautions. In the opinion of the Feldkommandantur's (Intelligence officer) this air raid organisation has a military character and has an excellent structure. Although the Feldkommandantur has taken all the necessary steps, it should be borne in mind that the actual wire-pullers sent from England have not been apprehended.[229]

Bleibtreu suspected three channels through which information could be smuggled out of the islands: first of all deficient control of the ships going to France, and in particular the OT workers on leave who were able to take information out. Secondly, a direct sail-link to Britain via the smaller islands. His allusion to the escape attempt of Gould, Hassall and Audrain, which took place during his stay, brought out this perspective.[230] Had he been in the islands for longer he would have discovered that such escape attempts were not common and that they only started occurring on a massive scale after the liberation of the Cotentin peninsula in summer 1944.[231] And as much as the three boys had been encouraged by Vibert's example, others harbouring similar ideas would have been deterred by their failure and subsequent disappearance into the Night and Fog. Thirdly, Bleibtreu's phantasmagoria prompted the claim that the island population was in possession of better radio sets than the troops, and that these could easily be converted into transmitters. Naturally, with fact and fiction as indistinguishable as they were, 'could' equaled 'would', bestowing an aura of conspiracy on individual acts mostly motivated by 'news hunger'.[232]

---

extensive survey of the fortifications in the Island. The work carried out by these agents was sophisticated and information was also collected on the morale of the troops, what they talked about and how they reacted to British broadcasts. Major Morrison was deported in September 1942 and the ARP was disbanded on 15 May 1943, s. L'Amy, op. cit., vol. 2 (3-6); Bunting, op. cit., 203.

[229] BA-MA. RW/49 97. Abwehr Command France (F/IIIc), Channel Islands - Committment of labour resources, Protective security measures 1942-1944. Report by Lt.-Col. Bleibtreu (Officer-in-command at Abwehr advance post St Malo) on experiences of his fact-finding mission to the Channel Islands, 29 Apr. to 6 May 1942, 8 May 1942.

[230] Bleibtreu's 'findings' had an impact on the interrogation of Hassall and Gould at Gestapo HQ in Paris. According to Peter Hassall the Germans suspected the involvement of ex-military officers in the planning of their escape, s. Hassall, Peter, synopsis of his memoirs, 8.

[231] Richard Mayne: 'People who escaped from Jersey during the occupation', in: *Channel Islands Occupation Review 1975*, 22-24.

[232] In his book on radio crimes in Germany Michael Hensle demonstrates that the majority of radio offences were not politically motivated, but the result of 'news hunger', s. Michael Hensle, *Rundfunkverbrechen – Das Abhören von 'Feindsendern' im Nationalsozialismus*, Berlin, 2003.

Bleibtreu called for swift action in order to tackle the 'security threats' and gleefully recommended the deployment of undercover agents. As a follow-up to Bleibtreu's mission two agents, 'researcher Willy' in Jersey and 'researcher *Renard* (Fox)' in Guernsey, were camouflaged as OT welfare assistants and issued with IDs allowing them to enter the harbour areas. Their principal task was to recruit German agents among the workers and the civilian population. Another nine 'researchers' were posted to St Malo, Granville and Cherbourg, maintaining contact via Bleibtreu's office in St Malo.[233]

However, doubt must linger over the question as to whether security was the sole, or even main, rationale for the wireless ban. It was most likely the brainchild of the military commanders in the islands who were deeply irritated by the ways in which the local population turned wireless reception into a psychological weapon and who enlisted the Abwehr security establishment on their own side, to oppose the opinion of the Feldkommandantur. Especially in the beginning of the Occupation, people routinely turned up the volume of their wireless sets such that they were clearly audible outside their houses. Already in 1940 we can see Jersey police following up 'noisy wirelesses' and giving the owners a shot of warning. In November of that first occupation year the Attorney General himself was forced to write to the Constable of St Helier that it was '*very important indeed for the public to stick to the rules*' and that it had to understand that wireless reception was '*for private enjoyment*' only. Law enforcers were instructed to watch carefully for breaches of this provision and give offenders a shot of warning. Accompanying this note was a mention reading '*I am told that the radio can be heard at about 2 p.m. in Windsor Road blaring out of a house in that thoroughfare.*'[234] The following day the offender, George Le Put, received a visit by Jersey police and was cautioned about his conduct.[235] Although an offence under German orders, this seems to have had absolutely no effect: eight months later Duret Aubin had to instruct the Constable of St Helier again that the practice was

[233] BA-MA. RW/49 97. Abwehr Command France (F/IIIc), Channel Islands - Commitment of labour resources, protective security measures 1942-1944. Report of Lt-Col. Bleibtreu (Officer in-command at Abwehr advance post St Malo) on experiences of fact-finding mission to the Channel Islands, 29 Apr. to 6 May 1942, 8 May 1942.
[234] D/Z/H5/97. Law Officer's files. Duret Aubin to Cuming, 28 Nov. 1940.
[235] D/Z/H5/97. Law Officer's files. Police report, 29 Nov. 1940.

to stop at once and that everyone should keep volumes down and windows shut.[236]

But regardless of the nuisance value created by 'noisy wirelesses', the military were also looking for easy solutions to their security problems. It is possible that a large part of their irritation owed much to the 'scandalous' fact that the troops in the Channel Islands could, through the civilian population, avail themselves of sources of information; a practice which, in Germany, was punishable with the death penalty. According to Bleibtreu's Abwehr report mentioned above, the BBC news beamed to the islands *'was especially geared to influencing the German soldiers.'*[237]

Parallels for tight control of the airwaves exist for other countries, but the Channel Islands were the only place in Europe where wirelesses were banned altogether.[238] Similar plans had also been drawn up for occupied France, but faced with a territory bearing no comparison with the size of the Channel Islands, and a serious manpower shortage, this scheme soon had to be abandoned; only in a territory as limited and cut off as the Islands could such a measure be contemplated. In a post-war statement, Lieutenant-Colonel von Helldorf said that the divisional commander, General Müller,[239] was in favour of the wireless confiscation, whereas Colonel von Schmettow, at that time the island commander of Jersey, and Colonel Knackfuss, the Feldkommandant, opposed it. In this (and in many other questions) Müller was strongly influenced by his divisional intelligence officer, Captain Selig, who was also an advocate of total evacuation of the civilian population.[240] Von Helldorf had become von Schmettow's ADC in

---

[236] D/Z/H5/97. Duret Aubin to Constable of St Helier, 7 July 1941.

[237] BA-MA. RW/49 97. Abwehr Command France (F/IIIc), Channel Islands - Commitment of labour resources, protective security measures 1942-1944. Report of Lieutenant-Colonel Bleibtreu (Officer in-command of Abwehr advance party St Malo) on experiences of fact-finding mission to the Channel Islands, 29 Apr. to 6 May 1942, 8 May 1942.

[238] The only other case of a comprehensive confiscation effort was in the Netherlands where 800,000 wireless sets were seized after the strikes of April-May 1943. There is no indication, however, that continued listening was reprimanded , s. Hensle, op. cit., 62-3.

[239] PRO. WO 309/192. The British War Crimes Investigators characterised Müller as a *'typical Prussian officer'* who *'easily went into a temper'*. Knackfuss is more favourably described as a *'very jovial type. Used to wear a monocle and was clean shaven. Speaks Italian fluently and looks a bit like an Italian'*. According to a report available to the investigators Knackfuss was *'relieved of his post in 1944, court-martialed as a result of his opposition to Müller and his anti-Nazi behaviour generally'*.

[240] PRO. WO 309/192. Statement by Freiherr von Aufsess, 9 Sept. 1946. He outlined Müller's ideas: *'This evacuation was to be carried out for military reasons, because, if the islands were to be built up as a fortress, there could be no question of having civilians there apart from*

November 1940, at a time when the garrison comprised a few battalions and anti-aircraft detachments. Müller became the key actor in the histrionics of German power-play when he arrived in spring 1941 with an additional division and replaced von Schmettow as the head of overall military command in the Channel Islands. Until Müller's posting home in 1943, von Schmettow's position was reduced to keeping an eye on the island fortifications and the troops in Jersey.[241] Von Helldorf's job during that time was confined to procuring supplies for the troops in Jersey. The internal power struggle for authority in the Channel Islands reached its climax in April 1943 when divisional command demanded the complete dissolution of the Feldkommandantur 515, the German civil affairs unit, and transfer of its duties to the 319th I.D.. However, these steps were thwarted in unison by the competent superior authorities in France, the Oberbefehlshaber (OB) West,[242] and the Military Governor in France,[243] who insisted on the usefulness of the FK 515.[244]

Wireless bans were nothing new: such was the symbolic importance of the apparatuses that taking them away from the population became one of the staple items of occupation rule. One of the first of these bans occurred in Guernsey in 1940, as a way of punishing the population for the support given to British military personnel. Again in 1941 wirelesses were confiscated in retaliation to the V-sign campaign. On the night of 28 to 29 June 1941 V-signs were painted on the houses, roads and walls in the Rouge Bouillon district. The Feldkommandantur decreed that had the culprits not been found by 3 July, the district would have to furnish civilian night guards. In addition, a fine was to be paid and all radios in the district were to be confiscated. Although this ruling was contrary to the Hague Convention - which outlaws collective punishment - the Jersey authorities encouraged people to deliver information on the culprits.[245] This call for collaboration seems to have had little effect, as police searches had to be initiated which dragged out the affair over another week. When these

---

those who could supply themselves with food and promote the supply of food.' According to his statement, officers were discussing the possibility of a lengthy period of siege and emphasising the advantages of a small population. Aufsess concluded: *'The Feldkommandantur was opposed to all of these plans.'*

[241] PRO. WO 309/192. Statement of Oberstleutnant Hans W von Helldorf re. Channel Islands, 27 Dec. 1945.

[242] German Military High Command in Western Europe.

[243] The term in German is *Militärbefehlshaber in Frankreich.*

[244] s. relevant files, in: BA-MA. RH 26 319/10.

[245] JAS. D/Z/H5/186. Notice, 1 July 1941. The notice was signed by Duret Aubin, Cuming and Mourant, the chef de police.

yielded no results, the measure was implemented, on 9 July, although the Germans decided to drop the imposition of a fine. A repeat situation occurred in October 1941, when 100 wirelesses were confiscated in response to V-signs appearing at West Park Pavillion, the Royal Square and the Ritz Hotel. The Feldkommandantur was not enthusiastic about this measure, as it created additional workloads and strained their relationship with the island authorities. It was also unpopular, as the Feldkommandantur did not have the resources to avoid lapses in the implementation. As experienced administrators, they realized that anything but a strict application of disciplinary measures could have the opposite effect of rekindling opposition. As they were left with the task of implementing the measure, they opted for a lenient application, granting many exceptions. Elderly or sick people received their radios back; one Susan Wimble, aged 80, on the grounds that she had only moved into the area after the appearance of the V-signs.[246] This type of collective punishment had some elements in common with the draconian measures imposed in Eastern Europe from where some military personnel may have learnt a dehumanizing lesson or two.

The Feldkommandantur fought an uphill battle against the gross simplifications to which troop commanders were subject in their reasoning and their tendency to use disciplinarian measures whenever challenged. They realized that this would lead to an inevitable deterioration in the relationship between Germans and Channel Islanders, perhaps even an escalation of violence. The radio confiscation was the one issue where they attempted to take a principled stand - and more or less failed. The prevalence of troop commanders over the running of the Occupation meant that this could never be a 'model occupation'. Many troop commanders viewed the Channel Islands as just another conquered territory, and counteraction to any perceived threats – while less brutal than in other places - was swift and expedient. It certainly bore none of the political niceties characterizing the approach of the Feldkommandantur.

That combat troop commanders had for a long time eyed a comprehensive wireless confiscation as the magic catch-all solution to their problems is attested through a letter of September 12, 1941 sent by Dr Casper, the chief FK administrator in the Channel Islands, to his immediate superior authority at St Germain,[247] outside Paris. In this communication he stated that the

---

[246] JAS. D/Z/H5/186. Law Officer's Department. Dr Reffler to Duret Aubin, 22 Dec. 1941.

[247] Casper's immediate superior was the head of administrative zone A at St Germain. For administrative purposes occupied France was divided into four zones. The head of each

319th I.D. had asked that measures leading to the confiscation of radio sets be taken in order to avenge an anonymous, obviously defamatory English poem that had been sent to the Division. Casper, in unison with von Schmettow, asked his superior not to take the divisional command's arguments seriously, as the reception of a simple poem in his eyes provided no sufficient basis to retaliate in such a manner.[248] Casper had obviously understood the specific set of circumstances at work in the islands, where radio confiscation risked rocking the steady course of occupation government, and that ultimately it would do more harm than good and overstretch the Feldkommandantur.

Other perceptive people proffered their views and a report written in February 1942 by Major Kretschmann of *Abwehrstelle* Paris was also more objective about the situation. Kretschmann wasted no time dwelling upon whether receivers could be converted into transmitters as he regarded the entire radio issue as one of marginal importance. In his opinion the transmission of precise details of the fortifications was difficult via the wireless and he noted that other convenient modes of information transfer were available. More likely channels - infinitely trickier to deal with - were personal, freight and postal traffic.[249] However, in the heated atmosphere of 1942, voices urging rational consideration of the facts were out of tune with the prevailing paranoia which demanded ever more rapid and drastic measures, the more ruthless the better. As must be sufficiently clear, the Nazi dictatorship had little place for people with reservations.

The FK realised that preserving the population's autonomy in listening to their radios bore no potential harm and would not constitute a seedbed of revolt as long as Britain's chances of retaking the islands were minimal. Fearing a deterioration of relations with the population who, as they did not forget to stress *'had up to then acted in the most correct manner'*,[250] the FK objected to the wireless confiscation, not least because it was the authority

---

administrative zone was accountable to a chief administrator who was based at the Majestic Hotel in Paris where the German military governor in France (*Militärbefehlshaber in Frankreich*) was headquartered.

[248] BA-MA. RW 35/537 35/537. Reception of enemy broadcasts. FK 515, Casper to Chief of Administrative Zone A (Northwestern France) of Military Government in France, re. confiscation of wirelesses in the Channel Islands, 12 Sept. 1941.

[249] BA-MA. RW/5 243, 5/243. Foreign Section/Abwehr, III H, report on a journey to the Channel Islands, 10 Feb. 1942.

[250] BA-MA. RW/49 97. Abwehr Command France (F/IIIc), Channel Islands - Commitment of labour resources, Protective security measures 1942-1944. Communication of OKW/Foreign Section/Abwehr to OB West Army Group Command D, May 1942.

responsible for implementing such an order. They knew that instead of neutralising potential trouble-spots, this measure may have the opposite effect. Further excuses were sought by the FK in order to counter the impending measure and they went as far as claiming that the remaining broadcast link with Britain had so far protected the Channel Islands from air attack.[251] Their action was not motivated by philanthropy, but pure political intelligence. They anticipated, quite accurately, that a measure of such fundamental importance would deliver the fatal blow to an already tarnished image of legitimacy they were trying to fabricate and shatter any remaining illusions of an orderly and 'correct' occupation. Clearly, it was reasonable to assume that islanders would consider this move to have overstepped the line and the measure therefore bore all the ingredients to become a 'shot in the foot'. However, against a united and determined alliance of combat troop commanders, counter-intelligence and Wehrmacht High Command, all of whom insisted on the harmful effects of BBC-transmissions on the population, more reasonable voices stood no chance of prevailing. With military intelligence appearing on the scene, things began to hot up in spring 1942 and several high-rank meetings were called on the wireless issue. By this time the unsubstantiated perception that wireless retention was a major peril had been endorsed by Berlin, thereby becoming conventional wisdom. A ban was now a foregone conclusion and the ensuing discussions centered around the 'how' rather than the 'when'.

On May 6, 1942, Colonel Martini of the Wehrmacht High Command told the participants of a two-day meeting at Abwehr HQ France in St Germain-en-Laye that Hitler had given maximum priority to the work in the Channel Islands and that the Wehrmacht had raised no objections to the confiscation of radios and photographic equipment. The representative of the military governor in France beat a retreat on the issue, trying to fend off their involvement with a set of legal arguments seeking to establish that the FK 515 was not the competent authority to carry out and enforce such measures. Many different services were involved in the preliminaries to this measure, creating, in the process, a great deal of paperwork which touched upon diverse areas of occupation government. One of the most common topics in these internal discussions was the allusion to a presumed difference between British-born and native Channel Islanders. That this issue was raised at all shows the Germans' limited understanding of the

---

[251] BA-MA. RW/49 97. Abwehr Command France (F/IIIc), Channel Islands - Commitment of labour resources, Protective security measures 1942-1944. III H, summary report on secret measures of protection in the Channel Islands, 7 Apr. 1942.

Channel Islands culture. It was a German *idée fixe,* nurtured by Nazi researchers, that a substantial difference existed in the character of native and non-native Channel Islanders, and that the latter posed a greater potential danger to German interests. The May 6 meeting reconfirmed the existence, in the minds of the Germans, of a distinct line between indigenous Channel Islanders and the remainder of the population. Branded 'dangerous', it was suggested that the evacuation of at least all males belonging to the second group should be given serious consideration.[252] Significantly, differential treatment went beyond measures such as the deportation of those originating from the mainland, as finalised in September 1942. Four days after the meeting at St Germain, Abwehr HQ in Berlin detailed measures destined to restrict the movements of the civilian population between the islands and from the islands to the Continent. Again it stressed that particularly strict standards should be applied to all those of mainland origin.[253] Cruickshank's official history of the Channel Islands Occupation further supports the thesis that differential treatment also influenced the practice of the German courts and that mainland-born people received heavier sentences than islanders and were likely to be sent to France.[254] The principle appears to have influenced some of the cases portrayed in this book: Arthur Dimmery, Frederick Page, Clarence Claude Painter and June Sinclair.

On May 30, 1942 the commander of the 319th I.D. informed Knackfuss, the Feldkommandant, about the decision of 7th Army Command to confiscate the civilian population's wireless sets - on the basis of the Hague Convention, which authorized the confiscation of wireless transmitters. FK

---

[252] BA-MA. RW/49 97. Abwehr Command France (F/IIIc), Channel Islands - Commitment of labour resources, Protective security measures 1942-1944. Note on meeting of 6-7 May 1942. Colonel Martini reiterated that *'originally, the total evacuation of the islands had been envisaged, but that this had been abandoned because of concerns about possible reprisals.'* The other participants at this meeting included representatives of the Abwehrleitstelle Frankreich (Abwehr Command France), Armeeoberkommando 15 (High Command of the 15th Army), Heeresgruppe D (Army Group D) and the Militärbefehlshaber (military government in France).

[253] BA-MA. RW/49 97. Abwehr Command France (F/IIIc), Channel Islands - Commitment of labour resources, protective security measures 1942-1944. Suggestions of Foreign Section/Abwehr, III, 11 May 1942. It was also detailed that foreign workers were now to be replaced by PoWs, that all the British civilian workforce would be concentrated on building sites with a low security priority, that they should be replaced by foreigners as drivers and that the general ban on photography in the islands was to be extended to members of the Wehrmacht and the OT.

[254] Cruickshank, Charles, *The German Occupation of the Channel Islands,* London, 1975, 339-40.

515 was instructed to proceed with the implementation of the measure.[255] One week later, on June 6, the Bailiff of Jersey was informed of the decision and requested to prepare the execution of the Order. The population was notified about the details of the collection procedure in the *Jersey Evening Post* of June 8, and two weeks later a total of 10,050 wireless sets had been handed in.[256] In the end, the FK's prognosis proved right, as the measure provoked non-compliance and put further strain on the already over-stretched tasks of the German police force and courts in the islands. There were definite signs that islanders' willingness to accommodate was waning; the 'velvet glove' approach was being unmasked. The Bailiff of Guernsey, Victor Carey, made his frustration clear in a letter of June 8, 1942, addressed to the Field Commandant, in which he expressed his *'great disappointment',* particularly as *'the local authorities have always endeavoured to act strictly in accordance with the rules laid down by the Hague Convention'.*[257] These words were symptomatic of islanders' increasing weariness with broken German promises. During the following months it became clear that a large number of people in the Channel Islands were not prepared to surrender their last link with the civilised world and that prison sentences of up to six weeks and heavy fines of up to 30,000 marks (£3,000) were not a sufficient deterrent. In November 1942 Knackfuss found himself in the unenviable position of having to report this unsatisfactory state of affairs to his superior authority in St Germain. Under pressure from General Müller, Knackfuss asked them to pass an order threatening the death penalty for continued non-surrender of wireless sets or, alternatively, give the FK 515 *carte blanche* to hand out longer prison sentences. As a consequence a provision penalising wireless retention and the dissemination of news was included in the 'Order for the Protection of the Occupying Authority' issued on December 18, 1942 by the German military governor in France. If the maximum sentence was not passed on an islander, this was due to the policy of the FK whose court had authority over the wireless cases. On the other side, from now on the FK could vary the prison sentences in any manner they deemed appropriate.[258] Far from taking steam out of the Germanic bulldozer, this incident

---

[255] BA-MA RW 35/537. Reception of enemy broadcasts, 319th I.D. to FK 515, 30 May 1942.

[256] JAS. B/A/W/30/94. Bailiff's War Files. Papers relating to the order to surrender wireless sets 1942-43.

[257] Ibid.

[258] BA-MA. RW 35/537. Reception of enemy broadcasts, Chief of administrative zone A of the military government in France, concerning the confiscation of radio sets in the Channel Islands, 7 Nov. 1942.

illustrates that inter-German rivalry and leadership contests added to the burden of the population.

The wireless episode lays bare an important determinant of the Occupation: the differences of perception and rivalry between German services. Both the FK and the combat troop commanders had their own ideas about how occupation should be conducted. The significance of these divergences and their overall impact on civilians warrants a digression on occupation government. In notable contrast to the situation in other occupied countries, the combat troops exerted more than the usual influence over the running of this occupation. This - together with the absence of racial prejudice against the civilian population[259] and the prestige attributed to the possession of the Channel Islands - was the most decisive element in forging German policy toward islanders. As a general rule, manpower shortages made the Germans adopt a formula of 'indirect administration' in occupied Europe, and the Channel Islands were no exception. This 'control administration' (*Aufsichtsverwaltung*) was loosely modelled on the example of British colonial administration and could be compared to 'hands off' management. The stress lay on the surveillance of all domains of state and society, but direct interference in key strategic areas only. In addition, the FK 515 also had a responsibility to provide the troops with supplies. Cut off from their pre-war sources of food imports, extreme scarcity was rampant in the Channel Islands during long periods of the five-year occupation. Therefore, not surprisingly, food production and agriculture were at the top of the FK's overall agenda. Other duties included masterminding finance and economy in the islands and passing directives to the island authorities for execution. On a more unpleasant note, the FK also supervised the German police force, had jurisdiction over islanders who flouted German regulations and implemented anti-Semitic measures, wireless confiscations and deportations. This mandate brought FK officials such as Dr Casper and Baron von Aufsess in close working contact with island officials. Although technically members of the armed forces, the German administrators were recruited directly from civil service positions. Before coming to the Channel Islands, Casper, for example, had been a *Landrat* (county councillor). His first wartime posting was to the French city of Evreux where Jean Moulin, later to become leader of the French Resistance, served as prefect. Although they received military ranks, the administrators were not professional soldiers, and this discrepancy led to a

---

[259] Needless to say, this did not include the Jews in the island. The stress is on racial prejudice and this book demonstrates to a sufficient extent that other forms of prejudice against civilians existed.

great deal of resentment from the latter. Skilled in the craft of reconciling conflicting interests and with an eye for the public good, they also outdid their military counterparts intellectually. Politically, they belonged to the conservative right, which meant that they probably approved those elements of Nazi ideology which coincided with their own world view: revision of the Versailles treaty, establishing Germany as the European hegemon, anti-liberalism, exclusion of Jews and other minorities and a hefty dose of anti-communism. However, they were not blind and fanatical Nazis and could be open to reason. Many conservatives grew increasingly disillusioned with the regime, especially when they realised that it was leading Germany into an abyss. Naturally, such men could be expected to develop a more nuanced understanding of the challenges their power was facing in the Channel Islands. Therefore they were prone to claim that army officers were overreacting and they did not seek to impose themselves on sensitive issues such as the Freemasons dossier. They also never made it a secret that they considered the presence of civilians beneficial, reiterating that without them the occupiers would be faced with a desert to which everything would have to be imported from France. This is why they opposed the radio confiscation and probably also the deportation of islanders to internment camps. Indeed, it would be interesting to know what they made of Hitler's *Inselwahn* in their private moments. In all this they were at odds with the military commanders who had the support of the Wehrmacht hierarchy. At one time these were quite favourable to the evacuation of the entire island population. Although this never materialized – the Feldkommandantur's argument of the 'desert to which everything would have to be shipped' having prevailed - they did not hesitate to use the threat of evacuation. [260]

---

[260] Cruickshank writes that the argument was adopted by Jodl, and thus became the dominant paradigm within the Wehrmacht High Command, Cruickshank, op.cit., 89.

2. Resistance, *à la Jerriaise*

Asked why no particular honours were conferred on Jersey offenders immediately after the war, relatives and friends make little attempt at concealing their past disappointment. Misconceived ideas of this story of tragedy and suffering, which did not fit squarely into official history, made a thorough appreciation difficult and led to the subject meandering under a veil of silence in the decades following the end of the war. Only the establishment of the memorial to the 'Twenty' marked the beginning of a new chapter in the relationship of the island with those who 'offended against the occupying authorities'.

The reasons for the long silence on the topic of the 'missing people' were manifold. The first culprit on this count would, undoubtedly, be the fact that Jersey resistance was not considered 'spectacular' enough to be taken seriously. Critics of the island record compounded the erroneous belief that Jersey acts of defiance compared unfavourably to other exploits of resistance that took shape in continental Europe. Another handicap was the post-war adoption of the all-imposing British perception of the war in the island culture of memory. This led to a marked uneasiness in the islands to place their own occupation experience in the context of the general European experience. Islanders subsumed their experience under the UK war paradigm of the 'bulldog spirit', of victory against all odds, thus avoiding confrontation with the 'murky waters' of European wartime collaboration. The clash of two diametrically opposed visions within island memory created a lasting conflict which has shaped the ideology of memorialisation ever since. On the whole, Jersey resistance was not considered as something special or worth investigating, especially when viewed through the spectacles of the motherland's six-year war effort. Beliefs about the 'inadequacy' of Jersey resistance were compounded by many of the people who resisted (such as Louisa Gould) who often saw nothing extraordinary in what they had done. They saw their deeds dictated by simple decency and they were definitely loath to self-styling themselves as heroes. One may also consider psychological factors such as shame and frustration, meaning that many islanders felt the things they had done to oppose the Germans were simply not enough.

It is hard to imagine today how heavily politicised the question of resistance was in the immediate post-war years. As we have already noted, the only resistance which counted was resistance which could lay claim to removing the Nazi regime by force. Simple acts of defiance or opposition did not qualify for attention and were seen as side-shows or diversions. Every former occupied country was actively engaged in making its wartime record appear as heroic as possible. Armed resistance became a matter of honour as it could be manipulated into national myths of self-liberation from the Nazi yoke. This was particularly in evidence in France: in August 1944 de Gaulle prevailed in his insistence that the first Allied troops to enter Paris were to be the Second Free French division of General Leclerc. Such symbolic gestures were instrumental in rebuilding shattered pride and in driving forward national reconciliation. Focusing on armed resistance also kept many countries from dealing with the more controversial aspects of occupation and made them get on with reconstruction. The celebration of resistance assured continuity and avoided political, institutional and economic turmoil which would have inevitably followed had thorough purges been initiated. These attempts to politicise resistance were not always truthful to historical facts and they tended to emphasise armed action to the discredit of other more subterranean or subtle forms of civilian resistance. As we have already mentioned in a preceding chapter, nobody attempted a cost-benefit analysis or dared to question the effectiveness of armed combat over civilian subversion. While there were economic benefits in adopting a forward- looking and optimistic attitude and in avoiding an investigation into the past, there was also a moral cost to this post-war choice: it is the unresolved issues of the day which have come back to haunt the children and grandchildren of the wartime generation.

The shortcomings were already revealed at the time, as the political context was to colour the historiography of subsequent decades. Despite the large output in publications, European resistance has been subject to little analytical history, not least because of a trying lack of reliable sources and instruments of measurement. It has gone largely unnoticed that historical research still owes us an authoritative evaluation of European resistance during the Second World War. The absence of comprehensive and reliable models has allowed an often monolithic picture of resistance to prevail. Masses of public and academic resources were lavished on the spectacular aspects of armed resistance. This one-sided focus often swept alternative approaches of inquiry as well as interest in other forms of resistance under the carpet. Professor Alan Milward of the London School of Economics was one of the earliest critics of this view, still widespread in the 1970s, which presupposed a strategic value of armed resistance. At that time many historians were dedicating disproportionate amounts of attention to armed manifestations of resistance, without setting out a pertinent basis to their inquiry first. As a result of these intellectual defaults, these accounts often painted a rather hagiographic picture. Milward's principal criticism was that this approach failed to measure the real impact of armed resistance on influencing the outcome of the war in terms of military and economic gains. In an article on the economic and strategic effectiveness of resistance he therefore repeated his claim that European resistance had achieved very little in strategic terms and that its real importance lay in a very different area:

> It is in the moral and psychological dimension that resistance assumes its greatest value. Most resistance was personal, isolated and unique, and in affecting the ultimate outcome of the war was entirely unimportant compared to the co-ordinated and carefully controlled actions of real armed forces. But for each individual the act of resistance did have a psychological value of immense importance. On this level resistance is neither strategy nor tactic but response. It was the ultimate affirmation of every human being's right to his own individuality. The myriad acts of petty defiance do testify to the unquenchable fire of humanity.[261]

Perception has changed in the last two decades. Previously, in Germany the debate on resistance had been monopolised by the leading heads behind the failed July 1944 plot on Hitler's life. This focus led to an automatic belittlement of other acts and forms of resistance. In the early 1980s Martin Broszat, of the Munich Institute of Contemporary History, was one of the first historians to break the ice with an ambitious project on Bavarian civil society under National Socialism.[262] One of the innovations his team came up with was the concept of *Resistenz* (medico-biological resistance; synonymous with 'immunity'), as opposed to *Widerstand* (political or armed resistance). Broszat used *Resistenz* in order to measure the immunity of civilian society against the Nazi ideological onslaught. Broszat's criticism was similar to Milward's and he saw a need for a redefinition of

---

[261] Milward, Alan S., 'The Economic and Strategic Effectiveness of Resistance', in: Hawes, Stephen/White, Ralph, eds., *Resistance in Europe 1939-1945* (based on the proceedings of a symposium held at the University of Salford, March 1973), London, 1975, 201-2. In retrospect, resistance was also of great importance as it set the scene for the painful post-war rebuilding process. In the immediate aftermath of the war it was those who could put forward claims that they had participated in the Resistance who enjoyed an almost automatic legitimacy in the eyes of the nation. The legacy of resistance was of vital importance and determined the course of post-war political life in many European countries.

[262] Broszat, Martin/Fröhlich, Elke/Wiesemann, Falk, eds., *Alltag und Widerstand. Bayern im Nationalsozialismus*, Munich, 1987, 6 vols.

the resistance paradigm. According to him the premises of resistance history in Germany were too centered on attempts to remove Hitler from power and neglected projects with other, more civilian objectives. Similar orientations were behind a recent project on the salvage of Jews in Nazi Germany, conducted at the Berlin Centre of Antisemitism Research. This studied the profiles and motivations of people who had hidden Jews during the Nazi period.[263] Again no question of removing the Nazi regime, which would automatically have discredited such research only a few decades ago. But although saving Jews during the Holocaust did not shorten the war, it would be impossible to regard such deeds as 'resistance of a lesser kind'. This example demonstrates where excessive use of the paradigm of armed resistance leads to. Studies of civilian reactions to the Nazi regime have led to a reappraisal of the varied forms of European resistance. These newly emergent schools of the social and economic history of the Occupation also no longer talk of 'occupation' as a generic term, but acknowledge how much the circumstances prevailing in each country influenced the various 'occupations'. Resistance was heterogeneous, assuming many different facets and was discernible in a variety of armed, spiritual and moral forms. The most important concept to have emerged from this debate in recent years is the notion of 'civilian resistance'. The concept brings an interesting new dimension to resistance research and presents an effective challenge to the enduring controversy about the value of civilian action as opposed to armed resistance. The most influential and meticulous study on the subject of Second World War civilian resistance is Jacques Semelin's *Unarmed against Hitler. Civilian Resistance in Europe 1939-1943*.[264] Broadly, civilian resistance is defined by the action a society devoid of arms and faced with an aggressive occupier can devise in order to preserve its integrity. It also expresses the potential of civil societies to defend themselves when the armed option has failed. Civilian resistance exists in two forms: as a natural complement to, and in support of, armed resistance; or as a type of resistance pursuing genuinely civilian targets, such as preserving the independence of a country's institutions. It operates on two levels - institutional and popular. An overwhelming amount of evidence now suggests that, especially in occupied Western and Northern Europe, civilian resistance achieved more in real terms than guerrilla warfare, a fact

---

[263] Beate Kosmala, Claudia Schoppmann, eds., *Überleben im Untergrund. Hilfe und Rettung für Juden in Deutschland 1941-1945*, Berlin, 2002.
[264] Semelin, Jacques, *Sans armes face à Hitler. La résistance civile en Europe 1939-1943*, Paris, 1989. (English transl. *Unarmed against Hitler. Civilian Resistance in Europe 1939-1943.* Westport/London 1993.)

also recognized, in retrospect, by many military historians.[265] And, indeed, numerous cases exist where German rule in Europe met the limits of its power when faced with dedicated collective action. One example of this was the massive go-slow movement of the French railway-men, which caused severe disruption to German movements during the crucial first weeks of the Normandy landings. This was one of France's most important contributions to Allied victory. Equally impressive were the rescue of the Danish Jews with the help of their Gentile countrymen, and their escape to Sweden and, on a smaller scale, the Rosenstrasse protests of German women for the release of their Jewish spouses in Berlin, both in 1943.[266] Such action is determined by factors which Semelin outlines as follows: the predominant factor defining a society's capacity to resist is group solidarity, as this determines the extent of social cohesion. The second factor determining the capability of civilian resistance is the attitude of the wartime leaders in the occupied countries, and whether they have lent legitimacy to German measures. Next follows the strategy of the occupier towards each occupied country, a shifting variable in occupied Second World War Europe. German intervention in the affairs of the occupied countries differed greatly and was most commonly - but not exclusively - determined by racial ideology. Poland was in the way of German dreams of *Lebensraum*, therefore it was to vanish from the map of Europe. Its culture was liquidated and the population was left with a choice of serfdom or extinction. The people of Western Europe never had to endure such extremes of brutality and France's authoritarian Vichy regime retained a sizeable degree of autonomy until 1942. Denmark was also able to preserve her democratically elected government and her institutions until 1943; in neighbouring Norway, on the other hand, German intervention was more direct, channelled through a downright collaborationist leadership. To resume Semelin's theoretical framework: the societies best resisting the Nazis had a high degree of social cohesion, leaders that had steered clear of

---

[265] s. Lidell Hart, Basil, 'Lessons from Resistance Movements', in: Roberts, Adam, ed., *The Strategy of Civilian Defence*, London, 1969.
[266] For details s. Semelin, Jacques, *Unarmed against Hitler. Civilian Resistance in Europe 1939-1943*, Westport/London 1993. The rescue of the Danish Jews is one of the best-documented episodes of the Holocaust. For a survey of publications s. Goldberger, Leo, ed., *The Rescue of the Danish Jews - Moral Courage under Stress*, New York, 1987. A monograph of the Rosenstrasse episode is also available, s. Stoltzfus, Nathan, *Resistance of the Heart - Intermarriage and the Rosenstrasse Protest in Nazi Germany*, New York/London, 1996.

the Germans and a relatively benign place in the Nazi racial hierarchy. This was important, as it precluded genocidal ravages.[267]

In the occupied Channel Islands, resistance never assumed the proportions of a collective effort. For all situations where individual action is the only detectable form of resistance, Semelin suggests the terms 'dissidence' and 'disobedience'. Naturally, the most intriguing question in this context must be why the numerous acts of defiance in the Channel Islands did not consolidate into the collective act of resistance. What is amply clear is that in comparison to other occupied countries, resistance in the islands was indeed in an embryonic stage. It has been frequently insinuated that this was linked to an equal or even greater disposition to fraternisation and collaboration in the islands than in the rest of Europe. Typically, such views are professed without any plausible explanation. A closer look, however, shows that no evidence exists to underpin the claim that Channel Islanders were greater or lesser collaborators than other Europeans. If some aspects of the Channel Islands Occupation were strikingly different, this would have been related, above all, to a marked difference in physical conditions, rather than to mental attitudes or genetic make-up.

France's foremost authority on the Second World War, Professor Jean-Pierre Azéma, estimates that one million French people, a figure representing roughly three percent of the population, had become militants or active supporters of the Resistance by spring 1944. No comparison is intended with the diligent and heroic action of some French Resistance movements but, if figures have anything to say about a general willingness to confront the occupying force, the Channel Islands have little reason to shy away from comparisons with the rest of Europe. As mentioned in the introduction, 4,000 sentences were pronounced during the Occupation for breaking German law in the Channel Islands. This figure represents a sizeable part of the population. To this should be added the number of Channel Islands escapees that ran at 225. The civilian population's boats had been confiscated in 1941 and all escapees and would-be escapees took great risks, demonstrated in the cases of those who were shot, drowned or arrested in their attempts to leave the islands.[268] One may conclude that

---

[267] Preface by Jean-Pierre Azéma, in: Semelin, op. cit., 9.

[268] JAS. L/C/24/A/5. Joe Mière Collection. For offences against the occupying authorities, 2,600 sentences were passed in Jersey and 1,400 in Guernsey (these figures bear no relation to the Channel Islanders deported to internment camps in Germany). Of the escapees 150 came from Jersey, 75 from Guernsey. Escaping from Guernsey to France was riskier because of the longer distance involved and the danger of being spotted by German vessels. For a lists of

these figures point to a latent predisposition for more active forms of resistance in the Channel Islands, on at least the same order of relative scale as in France. Account should be taken of the fact that human behaviour was, and always will be, conditioned by environmental factors which differ greatly from one place to another. Unique circumstances produce unique effects and in these terms the Channel Islands Occupation has few rivals. Even the staunchest critic of the Islands' wartime record will have to acknowledge this and admit that their situation was determined by a set of very specific demographic, topographic, social, historical, and strategic factors which bore little relation to other contexts. The fortification work undertaken in the islands was a dossier Hitler was briefed on regularly and in which he took a strong personal interest for extended periods of time. With his attention usually firmly monopolised by the war in the East or his megalomaniac architectural projects, the importance of the top priority status Hitler granted this project should not be underestimated. Testifying to this priority is the fact that, by spring 1944, German fortifications in the Channel Islands boasted eleven heavy batteries with 38 strongpoints, more than along the entire 600-mile stretch of French coastline from Dieppe to St Nazaire.[269] At the height of the fortification programme in May 1943 a little over 66,000 Channel Islanders had to put up with the presence of 42,000 Germans and foreign workers, equivalent to over two-thirds of the civilian population.[270] Whereas the islands had one German soldier to every three islanders, mainland France had one German to every 100 Frenchmen after the Occupation of the Southern Zone,[271] with the German police forces

---

escapees s. Mayne, Richard: 'People who escaped from Jersey during the Occupation', in: *Channel Islands Occupation Review 1975*, 22-24; Thomas, Roy, *Lest we forget. Escapes and attempted escapes from Jersey during the German Occupation 1940-1945*, Jersey, 1992, 128-129.

[269] Toms, Carel, *Hitler's Fortress Islands - Germany's Occupation of the Channel Islands*, London, 1967, 56.

[270] The total civilian population in the Channel Islands stood at about 66,000 during the occupation. 6,600 out of Jersey's population of 50,000 were evacuated to England in 1940. In Guernsey the number of evacuees was considerably higher: 17,000 out of a pre-war population of 42,000. The number of Wehrmacht soldiers rose steadily during the occupation and reached a high of about 26,000 in May 1943, after which it stabilized at around 23,000, a figure that remained stable until the end of the occupation. The peak number of foreign workers (incl. Russian slave labourers) brought into the islands was 16,000, s. Cruickshank, op. cit. 59; 193-94. Of the 11,000 foreign workers in the islands on May 14, 1942, 3,000 were German and 8,000 foreigners, s. BA-MA. RW/49 97. Abwehr Command France (F/IIIc), Channel Islands - Commitment of labour resources, protective security measures 1942-1944. Zollgrenzschutz, Leiter der Befehlsstelle, RV189/42 g, 14 May 1942.

[271] Hæstrup, Jørgen, *European Resistance Movements, 1939-1945. A Complete History*. Westport/London 1981, 135.

concentrated in the urban centres. Not only was the occupier-occupied ratio higher than in any other part of Europe but there was also no place where occupiers and occupied had to coexist on a closer basis. Few people outside the Channel Islands have an idea how small Jersey is and we should recall the dimensions: the area of the island is a mere 45 square miles, with maximum distances of ten miles across and five miles from north to south. Islanders lived cheek by jowl with soldiers waging war on their country, a situation exacerbating tension, discouraging outward signs of resistance and transferring conflict to a more psychological level. There can be little doubt that this promiscuity magnified the variety of other pressures bearing on the population. This is where the Occupation was at its most significant and singular and one wonders indeed why historians have shown so little inclination to deal with the crucial and existential aspect of, what should be called by its proper name, the 'island siege syndrome'. Many observers, now and then, erroneously interpret outward signs of wartime rapprochement as signs of genuine harmony between the occupier and the occupied. Although this was certainly correct in some cases, it cannot obscure the fact that most islanders' attitude had more in common with the 'wait-and-see' approach adopted by Europeans and that as members of a nation at war with Germany the loyalty of the majority of the population for Britain was untarnished.

There are examples of other occupied islands in Europe, but none besides the Channel Islands had been selected as a venue for a gigantic and impregnable fortress. The sense of congestion, the invasion of all spheres of life, the extending tentacles of suspicion, the appalling lack of information that gave rise to the most ludicrous rumours and the absolute impossibility of escaping the reality of occupation all combined to produce an abominable cocktail. Channel Islander Wilfred C Potter was sent to Laufen internment camp in 1942. In a Red-Cross message to a friend in London he described his *'relief from that horrible insular feeling. I can say that I have no regrets in what I have left behind.'* This was no unique display of feeling and the comments of the British Censor in the papers of the Treasury Solicitor show that the messages of many other internees had the same tenor.[272] For the majority of people who remained behind, the Occupation was a stifling and profoundly alienating experience which subjected them to a very peculiar set of pressures, a ubiquitous theme in all diaries and accounts published by islanders who lived through it.

---

[272] PRO. TS 26/89. Wilfred C Potter (Ilag VII) to Mr Jones, London E4.

Then there was the weight of topography. Guerrilla war in Europe was largely restricted to isolated areas such as the Alps or Cevennes, the swamps and forests of Belarus and the mountains of Bosnia. Moreover, in many cases taking up arms against the occupier was conditional on relations between occupier and occupied having reached a critical stage, often in direct consequence of German measures that clearly 'overstepped the line'. The massive growth of the French Resistance in 1943 was partly due to the fact that membership in the Resistance presented the only chance to avoid the German labour draft and that the general conditions were favourable to those wishing to go underground. The Channel Islands in comparison, offered an extremely unfavourable terrain for all clandestine activities; there, anybody on the run or in hiding was well advised to keep as low a profile as possible and attract no attention whatsoever.

The ramifications of Allied strategic planning had an equally important influence. It is fortunate that pragmatism prevailed in the Allied camp, never succumbing to the considerations of prestige which had so captivated Hitler. The minds of Allied leaders were firmly set on winning the war and this priority determined all other commitments. Continental Resistance was encouraged and received extensive Allied aid because keeping alive the spirit of defiance in Europe was considered a vital prerequisite to the opening of the Second Front. In Allied calculations France was the most important country and fuelling its resistance was naturally considered a crucial stepping-stone to final victory. In comparison, the nearby Channel Islands were poor competitors in terms of strategic importance. The recapture of the Channel Islands was by no means a vital necessity to gain victory in Europe and taking action in this theatre of war would have entailed diverting forces, risking heavy losses for questionable returns and, ultimately, prolonging the war. Therefore, quite apart from the difficulties imposed by geographical shortcomings, the marginal importance of the Channel Islands in military terms made it unsuitable for any type of subversive action or encouragement of resistance and the British authorities were well advised not to add fuel to the fire. Revolt in the Channel Islands in the event of an Allied landing would have led to mass reprisals or hostage shootings and such a scenario would have hardly contributed to the cessation of hostilities. In fact, it would have worsened the British position. In the past, Hitler had given sufficient proof of his ability to blackmail governments effectively and the British government may have found itself in a situation vaguely resembling the 1941 French hostage crisis which saw the Vichy government desperately trying to appease his explicit orders to shoot innocent civilians in reprisal for attempts on the lives of German military personnel. Surely, if there was a worst possible scenario that the British wanted to avoid at all costs, then this was it.

Especially in the latter stage of the war the sole British interest with regard to the Channel Islands was for the situation to remain as calm and stable as possible, for in February 1945 the senior German positions in the Channel Islands were taken over by Vice-Admiral Hüffmeyer and the Kriegsmarine.[273] With this appointment the population became a pawn in the hands of buoyant and unpredictable fanatics. Right up to the time of his arrival in the islands in July 1944, Hüffmeyer, known among islanders as the 'mad Admiral', had held the post of National Socialist Education Officer of the Navy, with the task of keeping the Navy in line with official doctrine. According to von Schmettow's ADC, Lieutenant-Colonel von Helldorf, it was perfectly clear to all German officers that this man had been sent to spy on them and slowly to wrest power from the Army.[274] The German Navy was known for its thorough nazification, a fact underlined by Hitler's designation of Admiral Dönitz, the Commander-in-Chief of the German Navy, as his successor at the head of the German government in April 1945. Many of the top Nazis abandoned their Führer in his final days and Hitler sensed betrayal everywhere. After excluding Göring and Himmler from the succession he turned to the German Navy, the last bastion of unconditional loyalty. These were the people in command of the Channel Islands during the last two months of the Occupation and British policy was well advised to avoid anything that might provoke them into taking extreme action. Post-war testimonies of German officers confirm that this fear of extreme action was not unfounded. According to von Helldorf, Hüffmeyer was determined *'to hold the island in a state of siege until 1947, whatsoever might befall the civilian population.'* [275] Hüffmeyer was blunt about what consequences he thought his determination was likely to entail and made frequent statements *'to the effect that he would let the population starve to death and if they revolted he would have them shot.'* [276] Von Helldorf himself - whose uncle (the Berlin police president) was involved in the 1944 bomb plot - was banished to Herm in 1945 and similar action was

---

[273] Cruickshank, op. cit., 120.

[274] PRO, WO 309/192. British War Crimes Investigations. Statement of Lt.-Col. Hans-Werner von Helldorf, 27 Dec. 1945.

[275] PRO. WO 309/192. British War Crimes Investigations. Statement of Lt.-Col. Hans-Werner von Helldorf, 27 Dec. 1945.

[276] PRO. WO 311/677. War crimes in the Channel Islands. Evidence and investigations. Interrogation of Lt.-Col. Hans-Werner von Helldorf by Major A W Neve, The Suffolk Regiment, 19 Nov. 1945.

taken against other military personnel suspected of harbouring rebel tendencies. Therefore, the less the situation in the islands deteriorated, the better the chances of a peaceful take-over on VE-Day became and the more the spectre of futile last-minute bloodshed evaporated.

Another important determinant of successful resistance is the political maturity required to form strong and unified movements of opposition. Channel Islanders did not demonstrate a lack of individual willingness to resist. However, few historical precedents or role models for sustained resistance existed in the history of the Islands, as the short spontaneous outbursts of popular unrest in the 18th and 19th century riots show. The long periods of stability had not favoured tendencies of popular disobedience. A society that had cultivated a natural abhorrence of any kind of public turmoil would have the greatest difficulty in coping with the ambiguities of a situation as presented by the Occupation, especially if things were made to look as though the established and legitimate leaders were still in charge. The traditional lack of political activism in island politics and the non-existence of mass movements or party organisations to translate popular sentiment into action was another serious impediment to those islanders eager to 'do something' during the Occupation.

According to Jacques Semelin's general thesis the degree of social cohesion was one of the factors cementing the capabilities of civil societies to resist the Nazi onslaught. It can be no surprise that the exploitation of inner conflict and an attack on the cohesive forces of civil societies - the feeling of belonging together - were important strategies of German occupation government all over Europe. Jersey chronicler J H L'Amy noted in his diary that German propaganda was geared to sowing dissension. A weighty contribution towards this process of disintegration was made by the recruitment of informers and the hefty remuneration with which the German police rewarded acts of denunciation. In 1943, Jerseywoman Mary Deslandes wrote in her Occupation diary that the Island was *'lousy with despicable Quislings'* who received a reward of £100 for informing on people retaining a wireless and £25 for information leading to the capture of a listener-in.[277] This was only the tip of the iceberg, as many denunciations remained anonymous and were carried out merely for personal reasons.[278]

---

[277] 'The Diary of Mary Winifred Deslandes June 1940 to May 1945', entries of February 13 and July 18, 1943, in: *An Island Trilogy*, op. cit.

[278] Similar attacks on the collective binding forces of society in the Channel Islands were also achieved through German propaganda coups such as the public display of black market goods seized from islanders.

When probing into why resistance in the Channel Islands was so astonishingly piecemeal and lacked the thorough organisation of movements in neighbouring European countries, such elements have to be cited in evidence. Maybe the individualised nature of resistance in the Channel Islands was a vital necessity and natural reaction in order to avoid detection? Surely, the conditions were not conducive for the operation of organised networks or movements which the Secret Field Police would have had little difficulty in dismantling.

Decidedly, most conventional definitions of resistance are difficult to sustain when dealing with the Jersey context. Jersey acts were executed the 'island way': they stemmed from individual decisions and were conditioned by the great potential, but also the drawbacks of life in an island community. This point is fully illustrated by the example of the Jersey offenders portrayed in this book. However, tendencies to risk overt action clearly existed, in particular among the younger generation. On one occasion in June 1943 the Constable of St Ouen received a note from Feldkommandant Knackfuss. The latter instructed him to take measures against the habitual congregation of young people outside the parish hall who were launching 'remarks of disapproval' toward passers-by and Germans, if he wanted to prevent/forestall the FK from proceeding to this mopping-up operation.[279] That this confrontation could also take more violent forms is demonstrated by the street clashes, between German military personnel and Jersey youths, which accompanied the embarkation of the September 1942 deportees. This incident was not taken light-heartedly by the Germans who, while trying to down-play the affair, retaliated with the arrest and imprisonment of Flavian Emile Barbier, a 33 year-old restaurant proprietor, and 18 youths, the youngest of whom was fifteen. While most of these young people received short one or two-months sentences, or were released on two years' probation, Barbier, branded as the 'organizer' of the anti-German demonstration, was severely punished and sent to Germany where he endured a three-year term, similar in conditions to the ones described elsewhere.[280]

The German authorities clearly understood that youth protest could spill over, and young men without 'useful employment' in the German sense therefore became one of the prime groups targeted for the February 1943 deportation. In the latter stage of the War it was again the young generation

---

[279] JAS. D/Z/H5/186. Law Officer's Department. FK Knackfuss to the Constable of St Ouen, 10 June 1943.
[280] JAS. D/Z/H6/4/36. Law Officer's Department. Verdict, Court of FK 515, 12 Oct. 1942.

who took on the occupier by escaping to France by the dozen or by filling up the prison in Jersey to breaking point. Other episodes prove that demonstrations of popular opinion were not always confined to the young: Ogier's return to Jersey after his trial in Paris and the burials of Allied servicemen were events greeted by popular enthusiasm and a mass turnout. While nothing could be done against the crowds and while dead servicemen posed no particular threat, sufficient evidence is available on how tight the supervision of individual displays of popular sentiment was and how swift and rapid German reaction could be in order to 'counter rot'. The 1942 episode on the aborted introduction of death penalties for radio retention, outlined in an earlier section of this book, demonstrates how complacency on the issue of defiance, and on the risks taken by some individuals, was clearly misplaced.

Volatility and deterrence

Fortunately, on the issue of the death penalty the German rulers stuck to their 'velvet glove' approach. But there could be absolutely no guarantee against the iron fist. This volatility of German reaction, much influenced by the constant tug-of-war between Feldkommandantur and divisional commander over occupation policy, was perhaps the one feature which made life most difficult for civilians, as they were given no possibility to gauge their own behaviour on reliable indicators of what the German expected of them in turn for being left undisturbed. This makes even the idea of 'adaptation to the enemy' quite a dysfunctional term to uphold, and impossible to apply with any degree of consistency. How incalculable the situation was is suggested by a constant stream of evidence in the files, all pointing to the fact that one and the same occurrence could elicit very different German responses, depending on circumstances, on who was involved and a variety of other factors such as political events in Germany, a military reversal of fortune on the Eastern front or relations between the Feldkommandantur and the divisional commander. Therefore it was quite possible for some islanders to be deported for listening to the radio, while others were invited to German billets for precisely the same activity - and there is no reason to believe that all Germans were brainwashed to an extent that they were only interested in 'haw-haw' stuff and would not tune in to the revered BBC. German rule had its moments, though it would be foolhardy to reduce the entire occupation experience to those instances of civility. One occasion where the Germans proved surprisingly civil occurred in February 1942: on the 13th of that month two automatic pistols disappeared from the dressing rooms at the football fields used by German soldiers and two teams from the intermediate and 'Beeches' schools. Subsequent inquiries by Feldgendarmerie and Jersey police traced the pistols back to two 'Beeches' boys, Le Cocq and McGarry, who owned up to having the pistols. They were given to understand that if the two pistols were returned, no further action would be taken against them, and the next day the boys handed them over to Seitz, a Feldgendarmerie official.[281] It is impossible to say what caused this resolution, but contrasted with similar cases involving youngsters, such as the Hassall trio or Peter Painter, the treatment was lenient. What can be said, however, is that this German 'fluidity' of making or breaking rules was extremely difficult to accommodate to. The devilish thing about it was precisely that, although some people escaped confrontation virtually unscathed, one could not book on being treated in a civil manner if one got into trouble with the Germans.[282] What looked like a game could turn deadly earnest at any point. There was no consistency in German behaviour and anyone could slip from ordinary citizen 'going about his business' to *persona non grata* in absolutely no time and for virtually no reason. The principle of 'objective enemy' was in full swing here: the ability of the system to reap in any 'bystander'. Volatility made sure that nobody developed any false ideas about exactly who was in control. It was the best German deterrent against 'bad behaviour'.

For those 'unwilling to learn' there was always the appalling example of the mistreatment of slave labourers which emitted an unequivocal signal of absolute obedience to all potential opponents. Seen through this lens, the atmosphere in Jersey was not even that of a giant prison, but of a rather perverse re-education camp, with two universes – benign and malign - coexisting in parallel. These two universes were not hermetically sealed and islanders of all ages witnessed brutalities close up: children came to see people being dragged behind lorries; in fact, such scenes were described as quite commonplace. Drivers working for the OT and other services would find dead bodies strewn about, some with bullet wounds, others badly

---

[281] JAS. D/Z/H5/97. Law Officer's Department. Police report, 13 Feb. 1942, re. complaint from Feldgendarmerie; theft of two automatic pistols from F.B. Fields.
[282] The reader will remember that after the war Mrs Painter stated that Zoltan, the German police officer searching the Painter house, enounced that he would have to 'go hard' with her family over his discovery of a military pistol. Although the present author is not disposed to falling into the habit of using textual exegesis as a method of investigation, one could deduce from this statement that, had the issue been less than a functionable semi-automatic pistol, he might have turned a blind eye. What must be clear, anyway, is that there was more psychological context to the Occupation than is commonly imagined.

bruised. Many were little more than skeletons. Frank Killer, the teenage son of a local vicar, himself on the run from the Germans in 1945, described the labourers as '*starved, weak (with) boils and similar things*'. In a post-war deposition he recounted how, once, when passing a bunker in Five Mile Road he saw an OT man hitting a prisoner on the head with the '*flat of the spade*'. Frank often passed along this stretch of beach where he would catch crabs, and '*cases of hitting the Russians occurred so frequently on the Five Mile Road that no other cases particularly stand out in my memory*'. On another occasion he saw three Russians who had been hanged for stealing bread. How dangerous it was for Jersey families to shelter escapees is demonstrated by another of Frank's remarks, detailing the case of one young Russian who, after his recapture, was taken to the edge of a cliff. There he was threatened and told to reveal the name of the people who had helped him.[283] The 'non-execution' of the death penalty in the Channel Islands was starkly relative and, the way the Germans interpreted it, certainly no token of a model occupation. Another islander, Arthur James Scriven, secretary to the Jersey Evening Post, was assigned to guard duties on the railway construction at St Clements in April 1943. He described the slave labourers as '*clad in anything from sacks to rags, with nothing on (their) feet.*' He witnessed, a few yards away, a demented attack of an OT guard on a boy aged perhaps eighteen: the boy first received a violent fist-blow in the face; this threw off the hat he was wearing; the guard then made him pick it up and put it on again. Another violent blow followed, knocking off the hat again. The guard made the prisoner pick up the hat three times and the same procedure was repeated each time. After the third blow the rules of the 'game' were slightly altered: when the prisoner refused to pick up the hat, the guard picked it up himself, put it on the prisoner's head and carried on with the procedure. Scriven saw this happen about 12 times before turning away in disgust.[284] Scriven was still lucky, for how thin the line between bystander and victim could be, is demonstrated by the case of John Wickings, a young van driver for Jersey Dairy Ltd. People working in transport were frequently confonted with the reality of the slave labourers, and Wickings had made it a habit to throw them his packed lunch whenever he passed work parties in St Brelades or St Aubin. One day in October 1943, while delivering milk at the La Pulente hotel, he chanced upon a slave labourer being knocked about by the OT Lagerführer (head of camp). Wickings went to a bungalow at the back of the hotel, from where he saw a

---

[283] PRO. WO 311/11. Statement, Frank Killer, 26 June 1945.
[284] PRO. WO 311/11. Statement, Arthur James Scriven, 29 June 1945.

young labourer being made to run around the outside of a cider press, while the OT man stood by and hit him as he passed. When the latter discerned Wickings, he shouted at him and Wickings immediately turned away to go, but was beckoned back. Hesitating at first, Wickings finally decided to turn back. When he approached the OT man the latter said something in German, which he followed up by hitting him under the chin. At this point Wickings, as he later deposed, *'lost his temper, hit him back and tried to get away to his milk van.'* The OT man was, however, back on his feet, catching him by his moneybag and grabbing him by the throat. Other OT labourers were called to hold Wickings, who was taken to the bungalow where he was detained for five hours, from one to six. Although the ensuing phone call for the Feldgendarms diverted his attention for a moment, the OT man then recommenced his sadistic routine with his prisoner. Every time the prisoner slowed he was hit, until he was finally stopped and made to run around the other way. Once he fell down and the OT poured water over him, made him get up and pursue. When the Feldgendarms finally arrived to interrogate Wickings, at six o'clock in the evening, he was 'roughed up' and taken to Bagatelle Road, and from there to the prison, where he stayed for one week. His trial took place the following week and he received a two-month sentence. [285]

Was this a 'model occupation'? One has to admit that the differential treatment of islanders on issues such as the death penalty could not have been the mere product of coincidence, or a result of the lack of armed resistance in the islands. A comparison with France - where up to January 1942 two hundred death sentences were executed for similarly trivial offences as those committed in the islands - may suffice to illustrate this point. [286] To infer from this, however, a generic 'velvet glove' policy would be fallacious, as the evidence attesting its reality is circumstantial. No German blueprint for a 'model occupation' has ever been found, and it is unlikely that it ever will be. With so many different blocs competing for power in the Nazi regime – and this is a point on which all historians agree - it would have been a wonder had there been one rock-solid policy. A genuinely unique event in the whole of occupied Europe! Although post-war authors such as Count von Aufsess like to stress the importance of the 'velvet-glove' policy in their reminiscences and published diaries, this was

---

[285] PRO. WO 311/11. Statement, John Wickings, 29 June 1945.

[286] Thomas, Jürgen, *Wehrmachtsjustiz und Widerstandsbekämpfung: das Wirken der ordentlichen deutschen Militärjustiz in den besetzten Westgebieten 1940-45 unter rechtshistorischen Aspekten*, Baden-Baden, 1990, 110.

only one side of the coin.[287] One should not entirely discount the possibility of von Aufsess, a man with more than the usual dose of confidence and an enduring sense of mission, having attempted a very personal propaganda victory, by upholding himself and the other Feldkommandantur men as a minority of shining examples of benign and noble administrators, in a morass of inhumanity. The cultured and politically sophisticated - though anti-Semitic - aristocrat was not alone in influencing policy in the islands, however much he may have dreamt about this being his fiefdom. Others with less enlightened views, the combat troop commanders and OT slave masters, were roaming in his 'garden', shaping policy to an equal, if not greater, extent. It would, no doubt, be fairer to characterize the German stance as 'carrot-and-stick' rather than 'velvet glove' and consign the 'model occupation' paradigm to the dustbin of history.

---

[287] Aufsess, Baron von, *The von Aufsess Occupation Diary*, edited and translated by Kathleen J Nowlan, Worcester, 1985.

3. Offences against the island authorities?

Other reasons for the delay of recognition of acts of defiance were 'home-made' and pertain to the problematic co-operation of the island authorities with the German Feldkommandantur. One allegation we have already come across in this context was that offenders jeopardized the sensitive balance of power in the island, that they were 'rocking the boat' which the island authorities had desperately been trying to steady. The paradox, and the irony, of this claim that offenders were putting an undue burden on the majority of the population is best exposed by contrasting their status with the post-war treatment of escapees. While the latter were celebrated as the heroes of the Occupation, those escapees who failed in their attempts were lumped together with the group of offenders accused of 'rocking the boat'. Had the authorities been consequential in their claim, then they would have needed to abort festivities such as the award of honours to escapees by the Duchess of Kent in 1946. Clearly, 'rocking the boat' could not have been the motivation for denying some offenders their post-war dues while extending the highest honours to others.

Associated with the myth that all offenders had risked German reprisals was the idea that offenders had broken existing law. John Leale gave this idea expression after the war, claiming that it was impossible for his government to honour radio offenders as they had broken existing law, namely the Hague Convention.[288] The Guernsey chief was certainly not alone in this opinion, as many people seemed quite incapable of differentiating between different types of offences, in particular offences which deserved public disapproval and others which had a lot to be commended for. They were helped in as far as some offences looked like regular common law-type offences. This was a strong force in shaping public opinion. The concurrence of the 'criminal' and the 'political' was, of course, exploited by the Germans, who wished nothing more than to lump these categories together, as this greatly facilitated the task of ostracizing offenders and punishing manifestations of opposition. Totalitarian regimes get their name from their proclaimed aim of enforcing total control over society; one of their hallmarks is the frequent confounding of the 'political' and the 'criminal'. Consequently, the borders between political opposition and common law criminal offences are blurred, making it possible for the government to sanction them with the same punishment.

---

[288] cited in Bunting, op.cit., 325.

In the post-war period the authorities in the islands made no reconciling gestures in order to correct possible misgivings. In 1945, during the discussions of an amnesty with the Home Office, the Jersey authorities do not seem to have been overly enthusiastic about the measure, fearing that it might condone anti-social behaviour.[289] Whether common welfare was their sole motivation or whether it was the expression of a creeping sense of guilt – news of the deaths of offenders was meanwhile trickling back to the island - cannot be said. In years thereafter the subject of offenders became a virtual taboo. Frank Falla, the Guernsey journalist sent to Naumburg prison, lived to tell the story of his two colleagues and the other Channel Islanders who died during their incarceration. In the 1960s he wrote a book about his experiences called *The Silent War*.[290] Although Falla never held the opinion that the Guernsey authorities were guilty of active collaboration or fraternisation, he was apprehensive about the lack of subtlety and flexibility they had demonstrated and the categorical interpretation they gave to 'correct relations'. While claiming that this was *'the right impression to give the Nazis'*, he maintained that *'it should not have been practised by authority on its own people'*.[291] Falla was unhappy with the fact that the authorities did not exercise much imagination in feigning compliance with German demands and thought that they could have done more to counter their effects secretly. After the war the authorities' lack of outspokenness on this difficult issue continued and, tellingly, the last chapter of Falla's account, dealing with the postwar memory of Channel Islands offenders, is entitled 'Forgotten people'. The strategy of disengagement continued when victims of Nazi persecution from the Channel Islands, a category including offenders, became eligible for compensation under a scheme negotiated between the British and Federal German governments. His take was that:

> [O]ur treatment in Guernsey left a great deal to be desired. I suppose it all dated back to the days of the German Occupation when we were naughty lads and stepped out of line with the Germans [...] I cannot help feeling that if someone had been nominated officially to help people with their claims, someone who knew those who were really eligible for compensation as against those who just hoped they were, someone perhaps who had access to the

---

[289] s. correspondence between the Home Office and the Attorney-General, JAS. Law Officer's Department. JAS. D/Z/H5/456.
[290] Falla, Frank, *The Silent War,* Guernsey 1994 (reprint).
[291] Ibid., 156.

records which must exist of those who were taken away and imprisoned, then the work of the Foreign Office could have been facilitated. Why, I wonder, was even this small thing not done?[292]

Although Falla wrote mainly from a Guernsey perspective, neither of the island governments was keen on assuming this responsibility and it was Falla who became the Foreign Office's intermediary in the handling of claims applications from Channel Islanders.

Island collaboration?

In order to give perhaps some tentative answers to Frank's puzzled question we have to dig deeper. It was already pertinently clear at the time that few issues brought out the core dilemmas of the occupation better than 'offenders'. The principles of collaboration were endorsed by both parties, and therefore offenders not merely trespassed against German law, but also jeopardized the structure of occupation government. A straight line passed from this dossier to the stratagems adopted by the island authorities. Offenders were a constant reminder that not all was well in the island of Jersey.

The German officials who came into the islands in 1940 were not only well-prepared, but also worldly and adroit. When they arrived in the wake of the invasion force, they commenced a seduction campaign tending toward establishing 'correct relations' between the occupier and the occupied offering the authorities what looked like an honorable 'gentleman's agreement'. This was bolstered by guarantees that no harm would befall the lives and property of Channel Islanders as long as they abstained from acts of hostility. The island authorities were only too relieved to do business not with Nazi brutes, but with rather cultured and reasonable civil servants with whom they had much in common, and accepted. Unsurprisingly, the Channel Islands' bureaucracy, consisting in many cases of locally-trained lawyers whom nothing had prepared for such a situation, was no match for the lawyers of the German military. After the war, the Home Office acknowledged this disparity by suggesting that the standards by which the Channel Islands authorities should be measured were not to be those of Whitehall but rather

---

[292] Ibid., 167

those of a UK county or borough council.[293] Their archaic and naïve understanding of the 'letter of the law' made them an easy target for formalistic duperies. How ill-prepared the Jersey government was for the legal battle is witnessed through the fact that, in October 1940, the Attorney General approached the Jesuit library at Maison St Louis, St Saviour, in order to consult their copy of *Les lois de la guerre sur terre* (The laws of land warfare), a wholly antiquated tome published in Brussels in 1880. Apparently this was still better than what was available at the Jersey Law library and the Public library, which, as the Attorney General readily admitted, were *'very poor in works upon international law'*.[294]

What followed was a 'honeymoon phase' leading many to hope that adversity could be overcome by a common-sense approach on both sides. The idea of an accommodation with the invader was not limited to the governing elite, but widespread among the population. In a September 1941 entry to her Occupation diary Mary Deslandes wrote with great perceptiveness:

> The army of Occupation seems to have settled down to a steady 8,000 now and we have grown quite accustomed to having them around. No one hates the poor wretches individually. They provoke no one and a better behaved, more inoffensive body of men it would be impossible to find. What one does hate, with a bitter, corrosive hatred is the system they represent and the conditions which their presence here imposes. They are very much the dominant autocrats in possession, and only by favour of their much vaunted magnanimity are the natives allowed to live on their own island, on sufferance, shorn of their rights and almost of their liberty.[295]

Mary Deslandes committed these thoughts to paper before the advent of the crash-building programme, but a 'clash of systems' is already preconfigured in her writing. Only a few months later, multiple new pressures brought out the real face of German rule. Repression increased, leading the principles of correct relations *ad absurdum*. Relations between occupier and occupied deteriorated progressively. The process itself was nothing unusual and

---

[293] PRO. HO 45/22399. 'The conduct of the population and the administration of the Channel Islands during the German Occupation', 2.
[294] JAS. Law Officer's Department. D/Z/H5/97. Duret Aubin to Father C Rey S.J., 7 Oct. 1940.
[295] 'The Diary of Mary Winifred Deslandes June 1940 to May 1945', entry of September 3, 1941, in: *An Island Trilogy*, op. cit.

occurred with an astounding uniformity all over occupied Europe. International law was still in its infancy during the Second World War, providing the basis for a fair amount of ambiguity. The Hague Convention, the body of law governing the foundations of occupation government, safeguarded the authority of the local and national administrations, but the occupier could intervene in any area and establish his own jurisdiction on the grounds of 'military necessity'. All over Europe the German occupier took the liberty of exploiting the clauses of the Convention, as in the case of the exorbitant tributes all occupied countries had to grant their German overlords, which were camouflaged as 'occupation costs'. In the Channel Islands the Germans based many of their measures, such as the radio confiscation, on the Convention, while its essential spirit – to ease the burden of war on civilians and find ethical codes of conduct - was continually being violated.

That the island authorities had been seeking to obtain the most favourable terms through negotiations in the beginning of the occupation is not contentious as such; prior to demilitarising the island, the British government instructed the island authorities to continue to perform their duties to the best of their ability and in the best of the island's interests. The error of the island authorities lay not in cooperation – this was inevitable - but in not having correlated the exercise of their duties with the deteriorating state of relations between occupier and occupied. While some countries sought to reconsider their position vis-à-vis the occupier, in the islands the principles of administration were never adapted to new circumstances. Despite a considerable deterioration, the business of administration went on as usual, until the end of the war. Reviewing their relationship with the Germans would have required a combination of courage, shrewdness and foresight.

Successive escalation

The Romans have an old saying: 'Quidquid agis, prudenter agas et respice finem' ('Whatever you do, act with prudence and consider the end'). The island authorities took heed of this truism; but in a one-sided way, interpreting it with regard to caution and mostly pondering what would happen if they quit their posts. But the model also works the other way around: it is not as though the consequences of continuing to function were always merely positive. There were thresholds where the occupier 'overstepped the mark' and where ceasing to function would have minimized harm. The Germans' shipping away of people for trivial offences was one of those moral test cases. There was even a possibility that the entire balance could start becoming negative, with liabilities outweighing assets. A lot depended on what price tag one was willing to put on 'moral principles'. The surrender of moral principles may not seem like a high price to pay if this can save human lives. This forgets, however, that the road to collaboration was a very slippery slope, indeed, and that it proceeded by very small, almost unnoticeable instalments. Many administrations did not start out as outright collaborationist, but became so under the weight of circumstance and incessant German demands, often locking themselves into logics which they had not foreseen and from which there was no escape. Trapping administrations in their own contradictions was one technique of domination where the Germans showed considerable talent. In many places all over Europe, the painful lesson had to be learnt that once a moral principle was 'out of the window', a host of other demands could be derived from the cave-in. The inability to anticipate the inexorable consequences of measures was to be perhaps the gravest failure of the island authorities. Cruickshank already hinted at this in his history, writing:

> If the islanders had refused to register the legislation it would have been promulgated by decree, but at least they would have made a stand. At what cost we cannot tell.[296]

This principle of successive escalation is what sealed Frederick Page's fate discussed in an earlier chapter. Initially, the wireless confiscation was met by protest, but this soon subsided into resigned acceptance: instead of an adamant refusal by the authorities to have anything to do with this measure and its implementation, they took on the task of putting the radios in storage until after the war. Could this not be interpreted as a sign of tacit approval? By not reacting more sternly, the authorities opened the floodgates, as German action on the wireless issue did not end with mere confiscation. Similar to a bad chess player, the authorities had not anticipated the next move and the trap closed in December 1942, when the Germans issued an 'Order for the Protection of the Occupying Authority' compelling the authorities to submit all information relating to offences against German orders. A new crime was born, namely the crime of not reporting offences against German orders, and this placed the knife at the authorities' throat. They thus became an associated party to measures designed to clamp down on 'radio offenders', something they, no doubt, had never intended. It would be too facile to point to their distress without acknowledging that they were partly to blame for this situation. Not only did the authorities not live up to their reputation of 'buffer', but they also failed adequately to assess and foresee the consequences of their action, finally having to abandon citizens to

---

[296] Cruickshank, op. cit., 113.

their own devices. In a game of Crisis Command it is unlikely that they would have scored more than two out of seven. The way out of this quagmire would have consisted of putting up sterner action, of an early refusal; only this would prevented them from being dragged further into the nightmare of doing the occupier's work. Undoubtedly, resistance from the beginning would have entailed risks, but should not considerations of justice lead one to take such risks? The handling of the wireless affair did not make theirs a convincing case of practical wisdom, the necessary condition of moral action according to Aristotle.

Bowing to the new legal norms of the occupier was part of the slippery slope. In February 1944, Captain H. Ballantine was being investigated by the Germans for a wireless offence. Having apparently contacted the island law administration for legal assistance in his impeding trial, it is unlikely that he would have drawn much solace from the curt and non-committal reply he received from the Attorney General on St Valentine's day 1944. Had Ballantine really wanted to be told that there was '*no textbook available dealing specifically with the subject of political prisoners under international law*'? Or that the Hague Convention was silent regarding the position of civilians '*who may be prosecuted before, and convicted by, Military Court in occupied territory*'? Or that it was '*clear in principle and practice that there must be a trial before punishment.*'[297] Punishment for what? Offences which, in the words of R N McKinstry, the island medical officer, '*constituted no offence against our laws*'.[298] There can be no doubt from this 'advice' that Duret Aubin had internalised German legal norms, showing interest in their formal aspects, and scant regard for the 'spirit of law'. Similar to the Page case, the acceptance of the terminology of 'wireless offenders' as 'political prisoners' almost amounted to a retroactive condoning of a measure the authorities had claimed to have opposed. It is unknown whether this was Ballantine's only point of contact with the island administration on this issue, but what we do know is that he was left to fend on his own and sentenced to three months' imprisonment later the same February week. That this was no unique occurrence is documented by another case. On 29 July 1943 Duret Aubin received a visit from the German Secret Field Police who requested him to hand over all anonymous letters received since July 1942. This he promised for the 31 July. The day after the visit, Duret Aubin, ever the

---

[297] JAS. Law Officer's Department. D/Z/H5/348. Duret Aubin to Captain H Ballantine, Red Lodge, Beaumont, 14 Feb. 1944.

[298] JAS. Law Officer's Files. D/Z/H6. R N McKinstry, Medical Officer of Health to A. M. Coutanche, Bailiff, 11 Mar. 1944 (highlight by author).

conscientious civil servant, informed Feldkommandantur judge Seger of his apprehension that the procedure seemed '*irregular*' and that such a request needed the FK *imprimatur*. Naturally, Seger came to the conclusion that the letters in question were better kept in their own hands and instructed Duret Aubin to this effect. The latter followed up on this instruction on 4 August.[299] What is remarkable, again, in this case, is that Duret Aubin does not seem to have questioned the moral implications of transferring denunciation letters, but merely the formal procedures adopted. We do not know whether the letters finally handed over contained any sensitive information or whether Duret Aubin even handed over the complete set letters he had received. And this seems quite irrelevant, for what must be clear is that Duret Aubin never once questioned whether it was legitimate and appropriate for the island authorities to hand over potentially damaging materials. Due to the gratuitous attitude of an important island official and the disregard for taking a principled stand, the Germans had created another precedent, namely that letters of denunciation were to be routinely transferred to themselves. A multitude of other demands could be derived from this cave-in and it could be invoked whenever they chose to do so, and for whatever purpose.

The dangers of consecutive escalation and the importance of principles were probably what was on the mind of the present Bailiff, Sir Philip Bailhache, when he addressed the Jersey Jewish congregation in a 1998 commemorative service. It is a living testimony to his moral leadership that he had the courage to address what would be a painful issue for any public official anywhere in the world. By drawing attention to the need to scrutinize with care legislation which restricts individual freedoms, he demonstrated that Jersey is quite capable of dealing with its past and drawing the right conclusions.

Bargaining and trade-off policy

What drove the island authorities? The authorities' behaviour unravels if we consider that their relationship with the Germans was not static and fixed, but rather fluid. There is ample evidence today that they engaged in a trade-off policy or bargaining strategy, similar (but not identical) in character to the *marchandage* of the Vichy government and other occupation administrations. To the Germans it was quite obvious that keeping in place local administrations, with their special expertise, was essential for the smooth

---

[299] JAS. Law Officer's Department. D/Z/H5/309. Duret Aubin, handwritten notes, 29 July to 4 Aug. 1943.

running of the occupation. In France the Germans succeeded in exploiting pre-war political divisions and winning over those members of the conservative elite who had been dissatisfied with the Third Republic. The Germans clearly knew whom they wanted on the job and that there was absolutely no point in trying to run the country through reliance on the handful of French Nazi enthusiasts and other cranks. To this end they employed a rather astute carrot-and-stick policy, promising a lot, obtaining important French concessions and giving practically nothing of any real substance in return. The French, on their part, often forestalled German wishes; a small price, they thought, to pay for a better place in the 'New European Order'. In particular, Prime Minister Pierre Laval was convinced that he could extract concessions by driving a hard bargain with the Germans. Unfortunately, Vichy myopia became self-destructive after November 1942, when the Germans occupied the South of France. By then the mirage of Vichy sovereignty unmasked itself in its bareness and lack of substance; it should have been clear to most of the men around Petain that no bargains were available and that the Franco-German relationship was entirely one-sided. Many men, such as former French president François Mitterrand, who had a second-tier post in the Laval administration, had the political sense to realize that the Vichy game was up and supported the resistance movement. The logic of the regime itself became based on the self-perpetuation of power and on clinging to indefensible positions. It would be flawed to view bargaining tactics as the mere domain of regimes such as Vichy which had already travelled a long way down the slippery slope of collaboration. Even for a nation as steadfastly self-assertive and fiercely passionate about its independence as Finland, this independence came at a price: recent research by Elina Suominen has revealed that the number of refugees, Soviet POWs (several dozens of them Jews) and, as it appears, even Finnish citizens with the 'wrong' political pedigree handed over to the Gestapo between 1941 and 1944 was much higher than previously admitted.[300] In the words of Max Jakobson, a senior diplomat and prominent member of the Helsinki Jewish community, the findings indicate that they were *made pawns in a cruel diplomatic game*.[301] If even independent national governments with an

---

[300] Unto Hämäläinen, 'More than just eight deportations to Nazi Germany. New book reveals 3,000 foreigners handed over during World War II', *Helsingin Sanomat International Edition*, 4 Nov. 2003, www.helsinki-hs.net/news.asp?id=20031104IE14. The book in question is Elina Suominen's *Luovutetut – Suomen ihmisluovutukset Gestapolle* (*The Extradited – Finland's Deportations to the Gestapo*), published in 2003.

[301] Max Jakobson, 'Wartime refugees made pawns in cruel diplomatic game. Elina Sana book describes history of refugees extradited from Finland to Nazi Germany', *Helsingin Sanomat International Edition*, 4 Nov. 2003, www.helsinki-hs.net/news.asp?id=20031104IE7.

otherwise untarnished record – the exemplary and principled protection accorded to Finnish Jews should be borne in mind - found it hard to maintain leverage over the situation and faltered, what more could have been expected from the Jersey authorities?

An assessment of trade-off policy must, of course, examine whether the authorities had any margin, whether there were grounds for operating such a policy. This they almost certainly did, but it was circumscribed by three factors: firstly their influence was restricted to relatively minor issues; secondly their leverage was proportionate to the degree to which inputs from the island administration were necessary for implementation; thirdly they had to be issues which belonged into the jurisdiction of the Feldkommandantur. One good example of margin was the Freemasons episode of 1941. When Masonic interests were targeted by the Germans in 1941, the Jersey administration put up stiff resistance to protect these, to the point of coordinating action with the Guernsey authorities. The Feldkommandantur men were lucid enough to recognise that they had struck a sensitive nerve and that there was little point in pursuing the dossier without the assistance of the island authorities. The example demonstrates that there were indeed Rubicons which the Feldkommandantur men were unwilling to cross. It quickly became clear to them that taking the action recommended by Berlin or Paris would entail sawing off the very branch of occupation government they were sitting on. It seriously jeopardized their relationship with the authorities, many of whom had close connections with the Masons.

There were, however, also dossiers on which they had no margin and where resignation would have been as futile and pointless as staying on. The 1942 deportation was one of those cases where there was no margin as the order emanated directly from Hitler. The Feldkommandantur already argued during the war (and the island authorities after the war) that in this type of case it did not really matter whether the administration resigned or not; but that it mattered to the island population whether the authorities stayed on to soften the effect of these inevitable measures. In these cases it was not really a question of 'doing' or 'not doing'. Still, there was a feeling that in the process of 'doing' they could have delayed or stalled. On a more general level it must have been felt that the authorities should have tested the water more often, said 'no' as often as possible, taken a firmer stand on elementary questions of conscience and justice, and taken the risk of being deposed and deported. According to the post-war investigators of Force 135, under Major Stopford, '(m)any islanders felt that a stronger line would not, as the States have *argued, have ended in disaster and drastic reprisals, but would have increased the German respect for the people'.*[302]

Bargaining tactics explain the strange and unsettling proactivity of the island government on some dossiers, and their resistance on others, which suggests a relatively high forfeiture of moral integrity. Beneficiaries of this arrangement were 'in-groups' such as British army personnel, Freemasons or the established island Jews who were evacuated in 1940; 'out-groups' such as the Jews who stayed behind, foreigners on the run, escaped slave labourers and deviants from the established path had to foot the bill. The adoption of bargaining tactics led to what one German witness described as the constant *'wangling'* of the administration, *'with its members looking round to see what they could get'*. The post-war investigations saw no reason to contest this view, which was confirmed by other sources.[303] The disposition lay at the heart of a peculiar brand of subservience and gratuitous friendliness on the part of certain officials, who were quite capable of forestalling German demands in order to create a debt. It is as discernible in the implementation of anti-Semitic measures as it is in the authorities' resignation to the 1942-1943 deportations to internment camps. The tendency was also displayed in such a seemingly insignificant act as the surrender to German requests for information on all previous convictions of offenders, up to the late 1920s. Another case where the authorities were clearly bent on ingratiating themselves concerned a dual British-German national by the name of Huyssen. In early 1940 Huyssen, who was English-born, had undertaken steps to volunteer in the British forces, which for the Germans constituted an act of treason. Although it is a principle that the government has no obligation to protect British nationals who are also nationals of another country against the authorities of that country, there was no ruling that officials must support foreign governments in their prosecution of dual nationals. When Huyssen was arrested, he built his defence on denying that he had tried to volunteer, claiming instead that he had received a draft notice. At that time there was no information in the island that could consistently prove or disprove Huyssen's version, apart from the unnecessarily ample information provided by the

---

[302] The passage also read: '*The I(b) Reports state that without hesitation it can be said that the feeling of the people in Jersey and Guernsey is against the States for the policy adopted during the occupation.*', s. PRO. KV4178. Consolidated report: 'The I(b) Reports on the Channel Islands', by Major J.R. Stopford, 8 Aug. 1945, 6. The passage was also adopted for the final report, entitled 'The Channel Islands under German Occupation' and submitted to the Home Secretary on 17 Aug. 1945, s. PRO. HO45/22399.

[303] PRO. KV4178. Consolidated report: 'The I(b) Reports on the Channel Islands', by Major J.R. Stopford, 8 Aug. 1945, 6.

island authorities. And this information proved that he had, indeed, tried to volunteer.[304] Again the authorities had proven rather too forthcoming with their sources of information, abandoning an individual to his fate.

The authorities also covered their flanks by carefully steering around all issues with even the remotest chance of constituting an 'upset potential'. Judging from the paranoid nature of totalitarian regimes, this could be almost anything. At times these attempts at anticipating what might cause German ire and catering to their predilections could go too far. This is in evidence in an appeal by the medical officer R N McKinstry to the Bailiff, in March 1944: by that time food conditions in the public prison had become severe enough for McKinstry to recommend that two political prisoners receive TB rations. At that time the diet consisted of coffee, dry bread, swedes, 'soup', potatoes and 'porridge'. McKinstry considered that speedy action was necessary in order to prevent the situation from getting worse. However, for some time things stalled as nobody was prepared to take any action. To be on the safe side the prison governor, after much initial wavering over whether he should consider the recommendation of the medical officer at all, first wrote to the Feldkommandantur for permission to put the men on TB rations. The Germans, in turn, deferred to the Attorney General who 'passed the chip' back to the prison governor, 'asking him for his opinion'. Exasperated by so much trepidation, McKinstry concluded:

> I consider all this delay unnecessary and even the permission of the German Authorities [sic] need not have been sought. Action could have been taken until such time as the German Authorities [sic] saw fit to interfere.[305]

Obviously, McKinstry had no doubt about where his duties lay.

Trade-off policy in Jersey formed a complex interplay with the utilitarian doctrines of 'greater good' and 'restraint and influence'. The 'greater number' logic came to the fore in the Page case which we have discussed in a preceding chapter. It also appears to have had some bearing on the measures against the island Jews. Bailiff Coutanche himself claimed that the seriousness of its implementation was mitigated because '(t)he *number of persons affected was extremely small*'.[306] 'Restraint and influence' (or 'power and influence') is a popular notion in qualitative business research. The notion

---

[304] For the entire Huyssen affair, s. JAS. Law Officer's Department. D/Z/H5/171.

[305] JAS. Law Officer's Department. D/Z/H6. R N McKinstry, Medical Officer of Health to A. M. Coutanche, Bailiff, 11 Mar. 1944.

[306] PRO. HO 45 22399. Memorandum, Alec Coutanche to Sir Donald Somervell, 3 July 1945.

is based on the principle that leverage over a given situation grows through positive engagement. For the weaker party, restraint, rather than absolute demands indicating positional bargaining, can be beneficial. Coutanche outlined the workings of 'restraint and influence' in a post-war memo:

> I almost invariably found it better to hold myself in readiness to make a final appeal to the Germans for mercy when all other means had failed. Constant intervention by me at an early stage would, it always appeared to me, have weakened my ultimate influence for good.[307]

Both principles were problematic, as they required – similar to a military operation - a conscious selection of ground that was to be defended or abandoned. There is no evidence to support the argument that the Bailiff would use 'restraint and influence' as a matter of principle. He rather appears to have pondered situations warranting a principled intervention, while keeping a low profile in other cases. For if the Bailiff had intervened every time, then his ability to intervene would have been proportionately decreased. Still, 'restraint and influence' seems to have produced some results, notably in the amply documented commuting of a death sentence, in November 1944, which the Bailiff attributed to his personal intervention.[308] The balance sheet for the greater number doctrine is less certain. As noted in a preceding chapter, operating this principle under genuine duress is not unethical. However, situations such as the Page case constituted 'false dilemmas' which the island authorities had brought onto themselves through their lack of prior reflection on the consequences of letting the Germans go ahead with their own law-making. In this context it is necessary to make some very clear distinctions: the confiscation of radios was justifiable under international law, even though it was far-fetched and served other than simply military purposes. There is, however, no clause in the Hague Convention (or in any other body of international law) which could have been invoked to justify the criminal prosecution of offenders against the wireless order, and especially

---

[307] PRO. HO 45 22399. Memorandum, Alec Coutanche to Sir Donald Somervell, 3 July 1945.

[308] This would mark out Coutanche as the most astute Jersey politician, someone able to 'ping-pong' with the Germans on almost even terms. The Germans, as a result, maintained a respectful distance. That Coutanche had scruples where other members of his administration put blind obedience to positivistic law is also attested by a good many other events during the occupation. The ability is also apparent in the run-up to the September 1942 deportations where he can be seen pushing for exemptions with Knackfuss (s. JAS. BA/L33/1. In the matter of German war crimes and in the matter of Alexander Moncrieff Coutanche, statement under oath, 12 June 1945). Without him the wartime record of the island authorities would, no doubt, have looked worse. It was perhaps no mere coincidence that he deservingly received a post-war knighthood.

the clampdown on people spreading the news. This reeked of Nazi law. The authorities failed to see this coming, partly because of their flawed legal tactics of opposing a wireless confiscation through their insistence on the inviolability of private property, guaranteed in 1940.[309] By so doing, they overlooked the fact that there was a clause which could be used to justify the confiscation of the apparatuses. When the confiscation finally occurred they had run out of ammunition and did not shift to defy the Nazi law of prosecuting 'radio offenders'. Thus, with a little more foresight and courage they would never have found themselves in a situation where they had to apply the 'greater good' doctrine. This was a self-inflicted defeat the authorities could and should have known to avoid. Again Aristotle's dictum of practical wisdom as the necessary condition of moral action was not heeded.[310]

One of the other weaknesses of the island administration was their almost slavish adherence to the principle of preventing a German take-over of the whole or parts of the island administration. How high this figured on their agenda is demonstrated by the fact that this is the first idea exposed by the Bailiff in the introductory paragraph of a 25-page memo to the Home Office in June 1945.[311] This firm positioning had a negative impact on the authorities' bargaining ability; it stands in stark contrast to the otherwise rather liberal concession-making on other principles. Throughout Europe, clinging to mere snippets of sovereignty was to damage the legitimacy, and tarnish the record, of many administrations. Robert Paxton, author of the first authoritative account of the Vichy regime, writes that, in November 1942, after the Germans invaded the Southern zone and Vichy's sovereignty became virtual (after having lost its last trump cards of fleet, army and colonial Empire), Pétain held on to power in the belief that he was 'avoiding worse'. A spelling of 'worse' that was starkly relative; and in which the fear of civil disturbances, and of the French political left, counted for more than fear of the Germans.[312] This favouring of the external enemy over the internal enemy

---

[309] Professor Pfeffer, of the University of Berlin, wrote of his sojourn in 1941: '*The permission to listen to the British wireless was exploited so that they placed loudspeakers at the open windows. Often in face of German demands there was an impudent appeal to the Hague land warfare rules or such like*', PRO. HO 45 24756. Report of Professor Karl Heinz Pfeffer on research visit from September 10 to 25, 1941, n.d.

[310] Similarly, the abandonment of the island Jews was not made under duress (at least none that we know of), but a conscious utilitarian decision. In a post-war memorandum to the Home Office Bailiff Countanche stated that '(*t)he number of persons affected was extremely small*' and that '*moderation was shown in the execution of the Order* (sic)', s. PRO. HO 45 22399. Memorandum, Alec Coutanche to Sir Donald Somervell, 3 July 1945.

[311] PRO. HO 45 22399. Memorandum, Alec Coutanche to Sir Donald Somervell, 3 July 1945.

[312] Robert Paxton, *Vichy France, Old Guard and New Order, 1940-1944*, New York, 1972.

was to haunt him for the rest of his life: after liberation he was put on trial for high treason and subsequently banished to the island of Yeu where he died in 1951. Of course such internal divisions were no secret to the Germans who had a field day manipulating them to the best of their ability.

Breaking points

That bringing pressure to bear on the Germans was not wholly inconceivable is attested by examples of cases where European wartime officials decided that there were breaking points beyond which continued co-operation would sap their credibility and jeopardize their position as guarantor of public interest. Not all situations where co-operation with Germany was reconsidered or nullified, ended in direct German rule or take-over by die-hard collaborators. Danish officials knew how far they could go when they refused to comply with a German ultimatum of August 1943, designed to coerce them into rubber-stamping a series of severe measures including suspension of democratic rights, declaration of martial law - making acts of sabotage punishable with death - and the deportation of the Danish Jews. Contrary to a good many other administrations in Europe, the Danish government did not consider itself indispensable and took the calculated risk of resigning. Denmark came under direct German rule in 1943, but this did not spell a worst-case scenario for the population. Although there was an increase in unrest, namely through sabotage and German counter-terror, the situation remained relatively calm. What explains this is the leverage the Danes exercised over the situation, through the heavy German reliance on the Danish economy, especially in agricultural production, combined with the presence of some relatively enlightened German administrators. It is true that, with Hitler and Himmler demanding tougher action and Werner Best, the German high commissioner, trying to steer a middle course, the situation was on razor's edge which required astute political action on the part of the Danes. This is different from saying that all resistance was futile, an apologetic argument often heard in the Channel Islands. In order to come to this conclusion it would have been necessary for the authorities to have tested the water more often and to have seen how far they could go. That they knew how to stand their ground is demonstrated through their opposition to implementing anti-Masonic measures as well as through Bailiff Coutanche's refusal to let the 'yellow star' order pass into Jersey legislation. But they also abandoned ground, choosing to disregard many genuine breaking points. This selectivity in resisting followed a logic replicating the fault lines that were fragmenting the island community. Whether the island authorities would intervene or not was too often conditioned by utilitarianism and sectarian thinking, which did not make theirs a sufficiently moral case. David Feldman, whose parents' business in Jersey had been 'aryanised', perhaps did not know how close he was to the truth when he stated, in a *Sunday Telegraph* article in 2000, that the authorities sought *'to fight only some battles'* and that *'the Jews were a battle they did not fight'*.[313] 'The Jews' were not the only battle the authorities did not fight to the finish. Another case which should have made the island authorities think twice was the prosecution of 'wireless offenders' after the 1942 radio confiscation which affected large swathes of islanders. Considering the many negative windfalls of this measure, Frank Falla's outraged refutation (*'Rubbish!'*) of John Leale's post-war refusal to rehabilitate 'radio offenders' – on the grounds that they had 'broken' the Hague Convention - is justified.[314] Although the island authorities were keen on presenting themselves as the genuine upholders of the interests of the population, there is a troubling lack of consistency in their action: claiming to have resisted the confiscation vigorously, they buckled under the pressure, taking on the task of registering the surrendered sets and putting them into storage. The reason given for this 'cave-in', concerns over the misappropriation of the sets, was too pragmatic to be good. Interestingly, the view that this measure constituted a point of no return in the occupier-occupied relationship was well understood by ordinary people, many of whom were dissatisfied with the 'collapses' of the island authorities in the face of what they considered excessive German demands. W. Gladden, a Jersey building contractor who, as head warden in St Martin was in touch with many people, wrote to Bailiff Coutanche on 9 June 1942. In his letter he said that, as a result of the wireless confiscation order, the temper of the people was rising dangerously high: *'Many are saying that they would be prepared to go to jail rather than comply with the order.'* (And, indeed, they were). He continued to describe that his constituents thought that the order was a *'FLAGRANT BREACH [sic] of the Proclamation of the German Commandant, of the beginning of July 1940'* promising that *'The Lives and Property of the inhabitants will be guaranteed'* [sic]. He also reported that the people thought that the Bailiff and the administration *'should refuse to collaborate in carrying out the order, even to the extent of going to jail.'*[315] Similar feelings of public anger were also voiced in the pamphlets of a group

---

[313] Cited in Frederick Cohen, *The Jews in the Channel Islands during the German Occupation 1940-1945*, 99.

[314] Cited in Bunting, Madeleine, op. cit., p. 325. John Leale was the President of the Guernsey Controlling Committee during the Occupation.

[315] JAS. Law Officer's Department. D/Z/H5/208. W. Gladden, Glencairn, St Martin, Jersey to Bailiff, 9 June 1942.

called the Jersey Patriots. All this indicated that the population did not see things quite the same way as their officials and was prepared to offend *en masse*.

While one can still argue over the radio confiscation, the case was clear in the 1942/43 deportations to internment camps, which were illegal. Post-war investigators were quick to spot a war crime here, under article 50 of the Hague Convention which expressly outlaws collective punishment. An aggravating factor was the differentiation operated by the Germans in establishing the lists of deportees. Other than in the case of men of military age, internment is not sanctioned by international law. The Germans, however, differentiated between several categories such as native Channel Islanders and British-born, politically unreliable and reliable elements, and collected the names of Freemasons, Jews, so-called undesirables and unemployed. As a result, these deportations affected many women and children, and harmless retirees in their 60s and 70s. The measure represented another grave violation of the principle endorsed in 1940 that the life and property of Channel Islanders would remain untouched, if the population remained calm. After the war it was said that the authorities protested '*sharply*' against the September deportation. That the Bailiff was uneasy about the appropriateness of continuing in office can be inferred from the following statement describing his reaction to the deportation order:

> I said that in view of what was proposed I and any member
> of the island government who wished to do so would be
> entitled to resign and that I must have time to consider
> whether that step were not the proper one to be adopted by
> me and the members of the government and to be urged
> upon the Constables.[316]

Ultimately, however, Knackfuss prevailed with his 'buffer argument', peddling the idea that it was in the interest of the people of Jersey that their government stay in office. He and von Aufsess had made it perfectly clear that this order came straight from Hitler and that it could not be aborted or modified. After some time for thought, Coutanche and his government followed suit. There was nothing else they could do. The problem was the farce that followed, as the island authorities associated themselves, indirectly, with this illegal measure: trying to save face, both sides agreed that the evacuation orders would be served by Germans; the Jersey Constables - in the

---

[316] PRO. WO 311/13. In the Matter of War Crimes, Statement by A. Coutanche, Bailiff, 12 June 1945.

interest of humaneness - would only supply the deportees with a 'guide' to finding the addresses of the assembly points. This move could have been motivated by the desire to obtain further exemptions, but it was not the right signal to send out to the Germans. There had to be a point where one called the shots. And even the little sanction the island authorities had announced was not followed through: Clifford Orange, the Aliens Officer, stated after the war that, from September 1942, he refused to supply the Germans with further lists for *'statistical purposes'*.[317] Unfortunately, the reality was less heroic, for the authorities soon fell back into their old ways: in December 1942, when the Germans asked for lists of unemployed men, the administration failed to draw their attention to the fact that they had, in fact, pledged to abide no longer by such requests.[318] Although the subsequent call, which was circulated to the 12 Constables, produced not a single name, the Attorney General had missed one more golden opportunity to make it a principled 'no'. Can it be a surprise that the Germans never took 'resignation threats' seriously, when the authorities had a penchant for defaulting on their own promises?

Another missed opportunity for the Jersey authorities to leave their mark presented itself in early May 1943, when German high command in the Channel Islands (presumably Müller) responded to Allied air attacks on supply ships by ordering Knackfuss to lower the rations of all British subjects. This reprisal constituted another illegal collective penalty, against which the island authorities again protested 'vigorously'. Unfortunately, these protests did not have the desired effect, for, on 3 May, the measure was extended to the entire population of the Channel Islands.[319] It remained in force until August 1943. After what we have heard about the deficient diet of the civilian population, the lowering of the rations warranted more than a simple verbal protest. The only appropriate response of the authorities would have been to translate their sense of protest into relevant political action.

One is often confronted with the argument that the island would have suffered more under direct rule and that it was wise of the authorities to insist on remaining in charge. While this argument is not entirely without justification, it cannot be used to brush aside all reservations. The 'ladder of inference' one is confronted with here is that the proponents of this oft-heard view also want

---

[317] PRO. WO311/13. In the Matter of War Crimes, Statement by Clifford Orange, Aliens Officer, 12 May 1945.

[318] JAS. Law Officer's Department. D/Z/H5/248. Duret Aubin to the 12 Constables of Jersey, 29 Dec. 1943.

[319] PRO. TS 26/431. UN War Crimes Commission, UK charges against German war criminals, Case no. UK-G/B 254, 11 Oct. 1945.

to assert the high moral ground, by claiming an entirely untarnished island record: what we are told is that while the authorities were an effective buffer, the islands' moral virginity was preserved entirely intact. This 'too good to be true' scenario seems to disprove the essential idea that everything comes at a price. It also entirely eclipses the question of moral responsibility. The argument shuns the basic precept that democracy and social justice are not free-riding systems, but based on the sacrifice of preceding generations who fought and died. What this means, is that there was no catch-all solution of the type indicated above; there are risks in assuming a more resolute stance, but considerations of justice should motivate one to take such risks. The entire argument seems to want to make us forget that continued functioning of an administration could make matters worse for a population. And this point is amply documented throughout this chapter.

The other reason why the authorities were not the automatic buffer they claimed to be is that *de facto* the German armed forces ruled the Channel Islands, and not the Feldkommandantur. Many of the measures affecting the Channel Islands were ordered by the military hierarchy or by Hitler himself. And all the Feldkommandantur officals could do was to mitigate. As there was no direct point of contact between the divisional commanders and the island authorities, the island authorities' margin of manoeuvre was rather limited. So how could they always have acted as a buffer? The combat troops were not open to negotiation. We know that they looked upon any dealing with the civilian population as a nuisance, at one point contemplating the complete evacuation of the islands. What they were interested in was a population which obeyed orders; and they could enforce their wishes with brute force if necessary. On several occasions – the wireless confiscation and the deportations - protests pointing to the fact that the civilian population had always acted in the most correct manner fell on deaf ears and were thwarted by the indication that the measures were on the orders of higher authority. On the other hand, despite the sabre rattling, by 1942 nobody was interested in total evacuation of the civilian population. The idea was most clearly resisted by the German Foreign Office who feared that such a measure would harvest retaliation against Germans in Allied or Allied-occupied countries. Therefore it is reasonable to assume that even had the authorities been less forthcoming to the Feldkommandantur, the situation would not have been any worse; simply the masks would have been off earlier.

The Feldkommandantur were not invested in real power to mediate between the Army and the civilians, and when it came to concessions, they had to demand them unilaterally from the islands. In many cases the authorities were to suffer the bitter experience that the Feldkommandantur promises were worthless, often for the simple reason that they were themselves at the end of a long line of command and had virtually no power to abort measures initiated in the higher echelons of the Nazi hierarchy. Above all they had no means of preventing outside intervention; they were in no situation to vouch for their solemn guarantees. Dr Casper, of the Feldkommandantur, wrote after the war - with the benefit of hindsight one is tempted to say - that he had hoped for a time when a corpus of common principles would be created in international law, saving officials and administrators from having to obey 'illegal orders'.[320] As a lawyer, Casper should have known that there can never be a compulsion to obey 'illegal orders'. Such flawed logic only came into play for those who did not want to dent their career by being difficult and who thought themselves above being sent to the Eastern front. Whatever their motivations were, one cannot help but feel that the Feldkommandantur administrators, on their part, were calling a rather cynical game. Up until the 1942 deportations, they did not make the islanders aware of how little independent leverage they actually had. The practical results of this game could be seen when for example Mrs Cohu, who was made believe that the authority of the Feldkommandantur stretched beyond Jersey, followed their advice by sending her husband parcels and letters…which were confiscated on arrival. Naturally, they did not want the situation to deteriorate and some of them would have been, as they claimed, genuine Anglophiles. To conclude that their minds were set on philanthropy, as they would argue in the post-war era, seems somewhat disingenuous. Ironically, more than the island administration needing the Feldkommandantur, it often looked like a case of the Feldkommandantur needing the island administration; without them their job was not feasible. The Feldkommandantur people also had political vision and their relatively benign behaviour as administrators of the Channel Islands helped them build myths paving the way to their post-war rehabilitation. People like Casper very probably already had their minds set on the post-war period, whether this would be a Nazi-dominated Europe or not. Therefore it was in their interest to be seen as benevolent empire builders and benign administrators, and not as war criminals. This partial myth they continued to sell after the war. Can it be a coincidence that Casper left the islands in 1943 to follow a call to Denmark from his one-time superior in the military administration in France, Werner Best, with whom he had been on excellent terms? As a founding father of the Reich Main Security Office who had had the good fortune to fall out with Heydrich in 1939, Best was that rare

---

[320] Aufsess, Baron von/Casper, Wilhelm, *In the Eye of the Hurricane. Remembrances from the Channel Islands 1941-1943,* Jersey, 1991, 123.

combination of a thoroughbred Nazi ideologue and astute political brain. He had enough irons in the fire - not just with the SS - that he was to enjoy an almost uninterrupted career in post-war Germany, right up until the 1980s.[321] Casper or von Aufsess were the career bureaucrats who seconded ideological missionaries such as Best. They would serve any master, but this did not make them entirely devoid of scruples.

The wartime record of the island authorities revealed some very grave errors of judgment; in some individual cases even misconduct: entering into an exploitative Faustian deal with plenty of opportunity for unilateral blackmail; lack of foresight in anticipating the consequences of actions; sweeping application of principles requiring a great deal more finesse as crisis management tools; infatuation with their own position and power. Criticism of the island authorities is not a moot point or a luxury. It is a binding necessity.

But just how far should this criticism go?

Perhaps the most crucial point of defence is that, whatever one may say about the Island authorities, they were not Nazis. There is absolutely no evidence that they were anywhere near the occupier from an ideological perspective. Especially as regards the most contentious issues, there was no intent to assist the new Nazi order in its plans for either world domination or extermination. Although they had travelled some way down the slippery slope of collaboration, they were not a collaborationist government on a par with Quisling, Pétain or Tiso. In the case of the denunciation letters requested of the Attorney General in 1943 – this was mentioned earlier - a hard core collaborationist government would have handed them on the first visit of the Secret Field Police; a resistance government would have pretended that all such correspondence had been routinely destroyed or perhaps even invoked that following up on denunciations was irreconcilable with the principles of justice. The Jersey government was situated somewhere between these two extremes.

There were also cases where they acted with extraordinary professionalism and which mitigated the disaster. Despite initial misgivings over collaboration, this point was also acknowledged by the British investigators who came into the island in summer 1945; their final verdict, throughout,

---

[321] Since the publication of Ulrich Herbert's thoroughly instructive biography *Best-Biographische Studien über Radikalismus, Weltanschauung und Vernunft 1903-1989* (Bonn, 1996), Werner Best is the best documented case of a German civilian administrator in any of the occupied territories.

tended to emphasize the positive in what had been achieved. When the island population was on the brink of starvation in 1944, the authorities showed great resilience in securing supplies through the Red Cross. Getting both war-waging sides to agree to this operation was no mean achievement and nothing short of a miracle. Throughout, the island governments played a constructive role. During the siege period there seems to have been a general boldening or maturing of the attitude of the island authorities toward the Germans; this is also discernible in Bailiff Coutanche's plea to commute the death sentence of Suzanne Malherbe and Lucie Schwob.[322]

At all times the authorities were walking an extremely thin line. Credit should be paid to those officials who kept both eyes shut and who did not discourage resistance within island institutions. As Louise Willmot writes in a recent piece which also touches upon the island assistance network for escaped slave labourers, *'the safety of the participants, especially in the town of St Helier, depended on the willingness of others not to give the game away'.*[323] And these 'others' included many officials. R. N. McKinstry, the medical officer of the Jersey Public Health Department with offices in Royal Square, provided many escaped slave-labourers with false IDs and ration cards. In 1944-45 this type of help was extended to Jersey people on the run. Frank Killer, a teenager who was jailed after a failed escape attempt, injured himself when he broke out of Gloucester Street prison in February 1945. His injuries were tended to by Ray Osmont, the General Hospital doctor who had also provided Ivy Forster with the medical certificate necessary to save her from deportation, while he received false papers from Dr McKinstry.[324] Other diligent Occupation heroes included Pat Tatam of Victoria College and the General Post Office workers who opened countless letters of denunciation and

---

[322] This boldening can also be seen in the attitude of the Jersey prison authorities. Gloucester Street prison was divided into two parts, a German military prison and the Public Jersey prison. When Dora Hacquoil, one of the women arrested with Louisa Gould, was imprisoned in the latter in 1944 the situation for prisoners had changed to an extent that she was able to write later: *'Really, a political prisoner's life in Jersey is a farce. I was amazed to hear that we are all heroes'*, s. 'My Story...Dora Hacquoil - Harbouring Russians', Jersey Evening Post, 2 Feb. 1995. The three women received food from farmers and friends which was duly forwarded to them, and their cell was decorated with flowers. In November 1944 Briard, the prison governor, was finally cautioned with regard to his duty by the German administration because of the negligence shown in connection with an escape from the prison the preceding month (s. correspondance in: JAS. B/A/W/81/4. Bailiff's War Files). It is quite possible that this changed attitude was attributable to the eclipsed fear of deportation, which was stronger than the fear of punishment in the island.
[323] s. Louise Willmot, 'The Channel Islands', in: Bob Moore, ed., *Resistance in Western Europe*, Oxford, 2000, 74.
[324] L'Amy, op. cit.

160

warned the persons in danger.[325] 'Turning a blind eye' extended well into the much-slurred Jersey police force: in February 1945 Jersey policeman Albert Chardine wrote a report in which he refused to execute an order instructing him to patrol the surroundings of the prison, from where escapes were occurring with a frequency that left the Germans breathless. Chardine was a well-known figure to the Germans with whom he had been in trouble on several occasions. In 1942 he served a prison term in Jersey for supplying Gould, Hassall and Audrain with petrol for their escape attempt. Chardine continued to defy the occupier after his release from prison and was on the German blacklist of 'undesirables'. He escaped internment in Germany only through the intervention of his superiors who insisted that he was an essential worker. The report for which Chardine was never reprimanded read as follows:

> Sir, I beg to report that at the above stated time I was instructed by P.Sgt. Griffin to patrol Gloucester St & Newgate St. re. Political Prisoners attempting to escape from prison.
>
> On receiving the instructions I refused to carry them out because I don't think it is the duty of a civilian policeman, and I have friends who have been put in prison by the Germans for very little reason, and I would not like them to know that I was outside waiting to catch them if they tried to escape; and as you know I, and several other policemen have been in prison for the Germans, and I am sure if any of us were in their (sic) today we would not like to know that our own workmates were waiting to try and stop us from escaping.[326]

---

[325] Sinel, op. cit., entry of February 26, 1943

[326] Police Report by Albert Chardine, re. Patrolling of Gloucester St & Newgate St, re. Escaping of Political prisoners, 15 Feb. 1945 (in author's possession). The entire episode casts serious doubt on one of the most enduring mainstream myths of the occupation, the pinnacle of which are the ubiquituous images of British policemen opening the door to Germans or saluting German officers. Uncommented and left to speak for themselves, these photographs allegedly epitomise the Channel Islands Occupation. Having lost none of their haunting fascination, most onlookers fail to question the provenance of these pictures, where exactly, by whom and under what conditions they were shot, and take them at face value. What many publications fail to explain is that they have fallen into a Nazi propaganda trap laid out over fifty years ago, still proving frightfully effective as an instrument of dupery. The power of this myth is particularly annoying for Jersey, as many of these photographs were shot in Guernsey; there was some bearing that the structure of the police forces in the two main islands was by no means identical.

It would have been impossible for the Feldkommandantur not to suspect the involvement of island officials in many of these resistance activities, especially the hiding of escapees.[327] It appears, however, that as long as this did not destabilize occupation government or irk the combat troops, it may have been tolerated by the German administrators. It is even conceivable that they acknowledged the islanders' need to 'let off steam' and made this part of a tacit trade-off. Paradoxically, such tacit tolerance only made matters worse for the island population (I have pointed to this contradiction in the preceding chapter): Army and Organisation Todt had no time for the niceties and political manoeuvring of the Feldkommandantur. They were running a fortress of unparalleled proportions and the only language they knew was the 'iron fist'. Islanders, on their part, perceived the Germans as one monolithic mass, although the reality was that internal German divergences over many vital issues were sending out conflicting messages. This situation gave them little opportunity to gauge their behaviour and it was all too easy for islanders to find themselves stuck between a rock and a hard place.

Recent criticism has gone well beyond the point of according any space to mitigating examples, however. In a recent publication[328] by David Fraser, professor of law at Nottingham University, the island administration is portrayed as an unthinking and inhuman bureaucracy, dedicated only to positivistic law and peopled by closet anti-Semites. This follows a pattern already set in Madeleine Bunting's *Model Occupation*. Fraser must be credited with the discovery of the particular occupation group dynamics which saw some groups benefiting and others not benefiting from protection through the island administration; it was also high time for an academic to dismantle the comfortable historical myth which had tended to deny or belittle Jewish suffering in the island. What damages his cause, however, is his 'holier-than-thou' reverence for a reductionist form of political correctness and his unhealthy obsession with the idea that British officials may have not behaved in line with the 'bulldog spirit'. While there would have been merit in a publication dedicated to a discussion of law, ethics and responsibility during the occupation, as well as in an intricate description of the inner workings of the Channel Islands administration and the individuals involved, this publication - marred as it is by fallacies - cannot measure up to its calling.

---

[327] s. Louise Willmot, 'The Channel Islands', in: Bob Moore, ed., *Resistance in Western Europe*, Oxford, 2000, 74.
[328] Fraser, David, *The Jews of the Channel Islands and the Rule of Law 1940-1945 – 'Quite contrary to the principles of British justice'*, Brigthon, Portland, 2000.

In the end his facile monocausal rationalisation of endemic island anti-Semitism proves counterproductive. David Fraser seems to have overdone it.

The *pièce de résistance* of Fraser's thesis is the (correct) affirmation that the authorities not only failed to protect the island Jews, but that they – in particular the Aliens Officer Clifford Orange - were rather proactive gravediggers, applying over-extensive criteria to the process of registration and participating in the stigmatisation and persecution of island Jews. They forestalled the Germans in their demands and brought mortal danger upon a number of people who could easily have been exempted, even by the exacting standards of German *Erfassung,* resulting in the island administration appearing even more rigorous in its application of anti-Semitic policy than the Germans themselves. This Fraser contrasts with the protection accorded to British forces personnel in 1940 and the prevention of measures against the Freemasons. He concludes that only deep-seated anti-Semitism could have accounted for the difference.

It would be pointless to contest that the remaining Jews did not have the same degree of leverage over the authorities as did, for example, the Freemasons. However, to portray Jews as though they were the only 'out-group' - on which the thrust of Fraser's argument relies - is a step too far. Clifford Orange, the Aliens Officer, was busy compiling lists of many 'categories' of people and some of them were tracked down with a similar gusto as Jews (the example of Huyssen, a German national, springs to mind). Another prominent 'out-group' of the occupation were the slave workers. The Jews who stayed behind – of modest or no wealth, foreign, often too advanced in age to evacuate and, like the authorities themselves, unaware as to what lay in store - were also not the only group with practically no leverage to influence the island establishment in a crisis situation. While offenders were never subject to racist measures, once caught many of them were sitting in the same boat. How sourly their activities' were regarded is demonstrated by the fact that practically no instances are known where they benefited from interventions on the part of the island authorities.[329] The very existence of offenders was an embarrassment to the island authorities, whose bargaining depended on presenting islanders as calm and in no way disposed to opposition. Offences against the Germans invalidated this claim and proved the exact opposite. It is quite possible that their stance was heavily coloured by the very unique brand of Channel Islands paternalism: the island authorities may have been irked by

---

[329] One of the few known instances was the intervention by Jurat Bree on behalf of Emile Paisnel.

the behaviour of people whom they believed that they had fought arduously to protect and who - they may have felt - had compromised their very efforts. Finally, portraying Jews exclusively from the victim perspective fails to recognize that there were Jews who benefited from solidarity, in particularly through asset cloaking. These prominent and established Jews - most of whom seem to have returned after the war - were part of the Jersey 'in-group'.

Fraser's views are not merely shaky from the contents side but also from the methodological and epistemological point of view. In a recent review Donald Bloxham of the University of Southampton criticizes the heavy-handed judgementalism inherent in his exercise and the portrayal of the island authorities as having '*a teleological understanding of their actions as part of a chain leading to Auschwitz*'. There is, indeed, a danger of anachronism in assuming that their relative knowledge can measure up to the sort of extensive knowledge we have today, and which informs our outlook on the Final Solution. This is unsatisfactory not only from the point of view of cognitive psychology. It is all too easy to pass judgment with the 'benefit of hindsight'. Fraser similarly treats the Occupation as a vacuum, not accounting for variation caused by the special conditions in his model. Bloxham hints that for this publication really to have done credit to its subject - rationalising the authorities' behaviour - it would have needed to take account of the psychological and sociological contexts. Although he agrees that a lot more could have been expected from the authorities in protecting the Jews, he also stresses that they would have been subject to German pressures, real and putative. Deplorable as they may be, their failings were '*all too human.*'[330] This is a valid point: Contingent on the pressure exercised by a particular situation, perception rather than reality can determine action, and with it outcomes. And who would want to contest that it was highly likely for the island authorities to have been subject to both actual and putative threats - expressed in innuendos, body language, tone of voice and similarly impenetrable devices - of which we know practically zero? For many decades historians exploring the Third Reich have been both intrigued and troubled by the murky undergrowth of verbal and non-verbal utterances. Therefore one would have assumed that the absence of an elementary interpretive parameter would invite caution and a rigorous application of *in dubio pro reo*. Not so for Fraser, whose epistemological method with regard to the documentary basis is largely that of a prosecutor pleading a case: the essence of the available documents is unidirectional, their content beyond questionable doubt and their

---

[330] Donald Bloxham, Review article 'The Jews of the Channel Islands and the Rule of Law 1940-1945' by David Fraser, *English Historical Review*, CXVII. 470, Feb. 2002, 226-7.

interpretation straightforward. This implies that they can only have the one meaning Fraser assigns them, which in itself is misleading. In addition, what survives in documented form is often the emerged tip of an iceberg. As an example, few documents survive detailing the concrete strategies adopted by the island administrations during the Occupation, while most of the correspondence available in the archives deals with rather routine and mundane matters. What is also missing is the commentary – the subtext to the mundane administrative dealings; wartime officials would have been foolish to commit anything but the barely necessary to paper. Written evidence could be damaging and dangerous, both with regard to the Germans as to the countless malcontents of the Occupation. The island authorities knew that they would be called to provide justification after the war. Consequently, rare is the occurrence where an administrator had to set out his thoughts, such as the Attorney General over the Page case in 1945. Even a document as seemingly incontrovertible as the Alien Officer's diary requires interpretive caution. What is indeed astonishing about Orange is how oblivious he was to the fact that - with the meticulous detail he was going to - he was gathering highly incriminating evidence against himself. Rather than an anti-Semite, Orange appears to have acted like the archetype of the repressed and parsimonious bureaucrat whose understanding of duty was largely limited to obedience and had little regard for human empathy. Orange's forestalling and outperforming of the Germans in bureaucratic zeal carries stark undertones of Adorno's concept of the 'authoritarian personality' and we can be quite certain about how he would have performed in the Milgram experiment.

.Another criticism of Fraser's method is his introduction of 'short cuts' in the interpretation of the documentary basis. Naturally, there still is a trying lack of evidence in documenting the exact inner workings of the Channel Islands governments. Such documentary *lacunae* are extremely unfortunate; they present the sort of problem every historian could write volumes about. Apart from the few weeks in summer 1945 when the heat was turned up by British investigators, the island authorities never really faced tough questioning compelling them to explain their motivations and actions in greater detail. In a reply to a recent *Guardian* article by Madeleine Bunting, Joe Mière rightly criticised that it was a historical mistake not to have staged a post-war judicial inquiry into allegations of island collaboration, as this would have helped set the record straight.[331] Nevertheless, shortfalls in evidence cannot justify

---

[331] Letters to the editor, *JEP*, 21 Feb. 2004. Besides their objective of punishment, the main effects of public judicial inquiries are to expose events to scrutiny and to educate - through the documentation of incontrovertible facts. This was a very clear motivation for all the post-war

interpretive short cuts. Unfortunately, this is what transpires from Fraser's examination of available documents. What Fraser comes up with to demonstrate that the island authorities' action was motivated by deeply engrained anti-Semitism is circumstantial evidence, but not irrefutable historical proof. The best example to demonstrate how he goes about his job is his tendentious interpretation of an occurrence documented in a report written by Professor Karl Heinz Pfeffer, head of the department 'Great Britain' at the Institute for Foreign Affairs in Berlin, on his visit to the Channel Islands in 1941. When Pfeffer meets the Bailiff the conversation centres on a discussion of the Jersey Constitution, soon drifting off to other areas such as the topic of Jewish ritual slaughter. Coutanche uses the pre-war exemption for kosher butchers from a special law introduced in Jersey in 1937, following the visit of a Jewish emissary, to demonstrate how adaptive the island constitution proved:

> As a decent Christian, I instantly came to an agreement with
> this decent Jew and allowed an exception, of which little
> practical use was made. You can see how a decent Christian
> can intercourse with a decent Jew...[332]

Fraser takes issue with the Bailiff's use of the term 'decent Jew' and sees this choice of terminology as proof for the latter's anti-Semitism. What Fraser insinuates is that if the Bailiff used the term 'decent Jew' he must have also had ideas about the 'indecent Jew'. The paragraph following the quotation constitutes nothing short of an incensed rant against anti-Semitism in general, another priming device.[333] The interpretation given to the Pfeffer report is tendentious for three reasons. Firstly, the rendering of the meeting: it is not a direct quotation or even a paraphrasing of the conversation similar to the minutes of an official meeting, but taken from

---

trials in Germany and Japan and it is a principle that informs present day UN International Criminal Tribunals and a body such as the South African Truth and Reconciliation Commission.

[332] Island Archives Service, Guernsey. FK 5-6. *Bericht über Studienreise nach den britischen Kanalinseln vom 10. bis 25. September 1941*, by Professor Karl Heinz Pfeffer (new translation in David Fraser, op.cit., 137). In a post-war translation of this report by the Home Office, the German original *anständig* had been translated with *respectable* (rather than *decent*). If both translations are, in fact, feasible, one does not see why Fraser, who actually concedes that '(*i)n either case, the meaning behind the use of the terminology by the Bailiff remains unchanged*' (Fraser, op.cit., 240), would have needed to change it; save that the pair *decent-indecent* has a stronger connotation and better serves the agenda of exposing the Bailiff's alleged Anti-Semitism than the lamer *respectable-not respectable*. It is typical of Fraser's instrumentalisation of language and fixation on discourse analysis.

[333] Fraser, op.cit., 137.

Pfeffer's memory; as a consequence, there is no guarantee that Pfeffer reported the meeting in an objective manner; context and verbal exchange could have been entirely different. Secondly, Fraser omits giving any indication about the context of the Bailiff's utterance, namely that he was speaking to a German visitor and that - in line with 'restraint and influence' - he may have down-toned disapproval, adapting his verbal expression to suit his visitor, without giving up the effect. Finally, Fraser's interpretation is anachronistic: we cannot expect the Bailiff to have expressed himself in the sort of politically correct vocabulary we have become so accustomed to from public figures over the last twenty years. If we reintegrate the omitted context and take account of the source problem, a contrary interpretation is equally possible, namely that the Bailiff was telling a Nazi that living with Jews is possible. Is it not extraordinary that what started as a discussion of the island constitution would have led to the topic of Jews? Is there not a possibility that the Bailiff may have used the arrival of this high-profile academic to indicate that he disapproved of anti-Jewish policy? It is conceivable that the direction of the Bailiff's remarks was quite similar to that of the Danish foreign minister Scavenius, who is reported to have said to Göring in 1941: *'Es gibt keine Judenfrage in Dänemark'*.[334] Was this not perhaps the Bailiff's 'There is no Jewish question in Jersey'? A less tendentious and more balanced reading of the document would, if not confirm entirely, then at least tend in that direction. However, to give this occurrence the supposedly straightforward reading Fraser assigns it, borders on the neurotic. Such textual criticism is not historical – weighing and corroborating the information contained in every document - but a post-modern text analysis more suitable for literary criticism or Bible exegesis. The entire exercise, with its absence of context and Manichean juxtaposition of good and evil, seriously confuses historiography with the manufacture of myth. This leads, eventually, to a paucity of inquiry.

This type of hair-splitting would be derisible, if its ultimate effect was not so damaging. The entire exercise appears to be guided by an intent to construct a 'guilt by association' fallacy: 'if the authorities were rubbing shoulders with the Germans, some of the evil must have rubbed off onto them.' There is no evidence to support this, however, and for the sake of objectivity and even-handedness such arguments must be fended off with as much resolution as attempts to belittle the suffering of the Jews and other occupation out-groups.

---

[334] Therkel Straede, 'Oktober 1943. Die dänischen Juden-Rettung vor der Vernichtung', <www.um.dk/publikationer/um/deutsch/oktober/oktober.doc>

The current aporia requires new inroads - first and foremost a sociological framework - in order to draw a half-way adequate picture of the group differentiation rightly spotted by Fraser. Although the idea might appear outlandish at first, one has to admit that, as a system, island society reacted to the external shocks in a way very similar to a biological immune system. Therefore, in analogy to Martin Broszat's use of *Resistenz*, the author proposes 'hypothermia' (another medical term) as a paradigm suitable to rationalise the situation. Hypothermia is the condition affecting the human body when exposed to severe cold shocks. The most significant reaction to hypothermia is the phenomenon of vasoconstriction: the brain, having segmented the entire body into consecutive layers, assigns to each a degree of importance, in line with its importance to the system as a whole. When the cold shock starts to take effect, the brain restricts circulation of warmer blood, gradually shutting down the supply to extremities which are not vital to the survival of the organism, such as arms, feet and legs. It does this with the intention of saving the critical core of chest, abdomen and head, where the normal body temperature is maintained as long as possible. Therefore when rewarming an organism exposed to severe hypothermia it is imperative to start warming the body from the 'inside'. If the extremities are rewarmed before the core, colder blood will start circulating back to the core, reducing the temperature in the core and causing the system to fail. The effects are fatal and irreversible.

How can such a model be applied to occupied Jersey? Naturally, one has to be cautious as it is genuinely problematic to uphold a model which upgrades structure at the expense of agency. With the parameters of individual moral responsibility and human free will not accounted for by the model, one might suggest that it should not be used to exculpate or incriminate individuals in their action; that it is an abstraction which should only be applied to the collective. Therefore free will and individual responsibility should be considered on an entirely separate basis (as has been attempted in this chapter). On the other hand, it is evident that the hypothermia paradigm ties in with reflections and evidence along the lines of David Feldman's aphorism that the authorities sought *'to fight only some battles'*.[335] In-groups and out-groups already existed in this society before the war. With the crisis caused by enemy occupation the problem acquires a new magnitude, the invisible pre-war differentiation of Jersey breaks into the open, providing an extremely dynamic backdrop for further differentiation and 'out-group' creation. One

---

[335] Cited in Frederick Cohen, *The Jews in the Channel Islands during the German Occupation 1940-1945*, 99.

could perhaps advance that the war put this society to the test, demonstrating not only how stable it was in terms of cohesion, but, more importantly, which groups were integrated and how far this integration went.

Furthermore, for the analogy of biological model and social organism to function we also need to provide an equivalent to the material trigger – the cold onslaught – which provides an impetus (measurable in temperature degrees) for the brain to stop supplying warm blood to the bodily extremities. Naturally, this issue of measurability of danger to physical substance is more difficult to solve in the case of a society. The human ability for abstraction, especially our highly developed apparatus to register and process threat (whether this be genuine or not), makes this a very fluid concept to uphold. Having a highly developed pre-warning system is not a recipe for altruism and humans do have a tendency to overreact. The ancient world already understood the impact of putative threat scenarios. One of the earliest illustrations is Thucydides' 'Melian Dialogue' which sees the neutral Melians being destroyed because the Athenians, at war with Sparta, do not want to risk taking second chances. The principle holds similarly for the Channel Islands where the threat to the substance did not need to be direct or material, but where already indirect or even highly putative threats could elicit concrete reactions. What helped hot up the cauldron was the ambiance of menace. The principle is at work in the decision of the Superior Council to exclude from its protest against the September 1942 deportations the discriminatory principles operated in the implementation of this measure:

> On the following morning at 10.30 a.m. the Council continued this discussion and it was finally resolved to make no protest on the "Discrimination" question. The ground of the decision was that to make such a Protest might, by enlarging the field of choice, encourage the German Authorities to take a larger number of persons than they then contemplated.[336]

The impact of group differentiation on the authorities' behaviour was reinforced through the pre-war political culture which provided a good environment, not for alternation of power, but for self-perpetuation of power. With its semi-feudal ties, honorary system of appointments, conflicts of

---

[336] JAS. BA/L33/1, In the matter of German war crimes and in the matter of Alexander Moncrieff Coutanche, statement under oath, 12 June 1945.

interest, elitism and only partially realised elective and representative democracy, many of the attributes of a democratic polity were not fully developed in the pre-war States. With the pre-invasion abeyance of democracy through the foundation of the Superior Council and the continuing centralisation of government during the Occupation, it became even less democratic. The political culture had an influence on the attitude of the island authorities who considered themselves indispensable, especially in this crisis situation. While they may have believed that their steadfastness was a *forte*, truth is that it was a weakness which led to their acceptance of questionable moral principles such as 'greater good' and 'trade-offs' as well as encouraging self-delusion; and this was linked to the maintenance of power. To understand the dynamics of power, we need to take a brief sideways glance at organisational behaviour: our blind belief that humans are always progress-oriented is quite reductionist. By no means do organisations always behave in the most rational manner. Business research makes it abundantly clear that resistance to change is an enduring phenomenon in all organisations. Sometimes there is resistance to change, even if it is manifestly clear that this will be for the better. Others miss excellent opportunities to prosper and grow. One of the reasons why organisations may start procrastinating is that power, once acquired, has a tendency to stabilize. It becomes a self-referential means to its own ends. There are a number of reasons for this: power creates commitment and loyalty ties and this can influence current behaviour. Then there is the combined force of bounded rationality, theory perseverance and escalation of commitment: 'What has served us in the past will also serve us in the future. So why change?' All this favours the stabilisation of power. Finally, people have a tendency to follow the strong and successful whose actions are 'sacralised' over time, attaining an almost religious connotation. Accordingly, criticism equals sacrilege. Naturally, the powerful do everything to safeguard and even to extend their position. A vicious circle commences: power engenders power and more power engenders more power. There is excellent reason to believe that the island authorities were married to their jobs and that, compounded by an inflated sense of historical mission, it was impossible for them to imagine being out of power. The above effect was further magnified by the heavier burden of responsibility bestowed upon the authorities, which in turn brought a considerable gain in power. Lord Acton's adage that '*power tends to corrupt, and absolute power corrupts absolutely*' has relevance not only for understanding the wartime behaviour of administrations across Europe, but all governments and administrations. When, in 1940, Britain advised them to remain at their desks, they had done so on the understanding that they were to exercise their duties to the best of their abilities, but not regardless of the situation. One can only congratulate post-war planners to have picked up the ideas of the Jersey Democratic Movement and other groups of disaffected islanders who had realized that the pre-modern constitution of the Channel Islands polity had constituted one of the instrumental flaws. Thus, restructuring through democratic reforms was the main form of drawing consequences from the bitter experience of occupation.

The resistance of the island authorities to a more accurate portrayal of their wartime activities in the post-war era was not the result of a sinister whitewashing plot, but the display of a rather inevitable disposition of the holders of power. Instead of the incessant finger wagging about the island authorities, the more obvious question should really be: What can realistically be expected from politicians, statesmen and power brokers in terms of providing an accurate historical record? Very rare, indeed, are those who are prepared even to consider the less savoury sides of the exercise of power. When former US Secretary of State Robert McNamara apologised about his role in the Vietnam War[337], 25 years after the end of this conflict, he did not do so over the illegal use of napalm by US forces, the establishment of 'free firing zones' or the herding of the civilian population into government-controlled concentration camps. His concerns were rather the strategic fallacies of the war, namely the escalation of US military involvement in an un-winnable war and the appalling strategy blunders. An even more recent example is Henry Kissinger's refusal to consider the moral implications of his Cold War Realpolitik in places such as Cambodia, Chile and Indonesia. Politicians and public figures are definitely concerned about their historical legacy. Is it really so unusual or odd for politicians to try to inflate their successes, portray their role in the best possible light and not be particularly upfront with details on survival stratagems they may have employed in the past? The more they get away with, the more this indicates that the public is not vigilant enough and that the system of checks and balances is not functioning. The politicians are simply being politicians. But people get the governments they deserve. Because power and the exercise of power are such dangerous things, we need to give up our complacency about living in a democracy, which some treat as a free-riding scheme. In order to calibrate the system, it is important to educate the public so that it can fulfil its role as a critical counterweight. George Orwell's configuration of the prototype of the totalitarian citizen in *Nineteen Eighty-Four* included a description of 'crimestop': '*the power of not grasping analogies, of failing to perceive logical errors, of misunderstanding the simplest arguments...protective*

---

[337] Robert McNamara, *In Retrospect: The Tragedy and Lessons of Vietnam*, New York, 1996.

stupidity.'[338] There are no less genuine and potential practitioners of 'crimestop' and 'blackwhite' - the ability to uphold one argument while at the same time also upholding the counterargument - than there were sixty years ago. We must remain alert to the flaws of power and the holders of power, if we do not want to become unable to tell right from wrong, as Orwell's proles. Democracy is not the system of the feeble; it cannot be taken for granted and it is not an eternal *acquis*; it has to be earned daily, and this requires incessant effort.

It is not unusual for humans or human societies to conceal terrible cataclysms under a veil of silence. And this applies to both victims and perpetrators. Daniel Goleman, Harvard psychology professor and best-selling author, reminds us that denial is not the sign of a deficiency, but an elementary and vital part of human nature.[339] Numerous examples exist for unresolved cataclysms: Russia has not come to terms with the perverse ravages of the Stalinist period; China has its Cultural Revolution to contend with; the United States and Australia are still in denial over the destruction of Amero-Indian and Aboriginal tribes; closer to home, the Irish famine is not what one would call a 'popular topic', despite a historical apology by the UK government. Rather than throwing the first stone, we should be immensely grateful to Channel Islanders for inviting historians to explore the fascinating social laboratory of occupation.

On September 29, 1945 an obituary of Canon Cohu, written by a friend, appeared in the *Jersey Evening Post*. He described the Canon as a man who

> persistently refused to be caught by the cheap simplicity of a logic which ignores half of human nature [...] He would not purchase emphasis at the cost of ignoring obvious facts. If life is many-sided, as it certainly is, then faith which is one-sided stands convicted of inadequacy: he knew that the solution of a complicated problem cannot but be complicated itself.[340]

Despite our many advances, 'cheap simplicity of logic' is one of the more sobering facts of modern life. George Orwell prophesised that the battle-grounds of the future would no longer lie in the seas or the skies, but in the minds. In this sense, the above passage is tailor-made for both sides of the enduring contestation surrounding the Channel Islands occupation: the all-

---

[338] George Orwell, *Nineteen Eighty-Four*, London, 1949, 220-21.

[339] Daniel Goleman, *Vital lies, simple truths. The psychology of self-deception*, London, 1998.

[340] 'The Late Canon Cohu – An Appreciation', *Jersey Evening Post*, 29 Sept. 1945.

too-vociferous critics of the island authorities, with their partial denial of human nature and their inability to perceive human fallibility other than through the spectacles of evil intent; and their opposite numbers: the defenders of the indefensible who appeal to emotions and deny reason and inquiry its due place.

There is a lesson in this for us all.

4. Perspectives of Memorialisation

The minefield of controversy that were the wartime choices of the island authorities - and the great potential this presented for journalistic or political misrepresentation - meant that for many decades after the war the only tolerated way of dealing with the Channel Islands Occupation was by focusing on the (seemingly) non-contentious military aspects. This tendency determined the approach Charles Cruickshank chose for his official history of the Occupation written in the 1970s, a text which had a great influence on all subsequent historiography. Despite being mainly a military historian with a special interest in SOE, Cruickshank was nevertheless too accomplished a scholar to ignore social aspects of the Occupation, and his well-crafted study provides numerous details depicting the life of islanders and the garrison. Unfortunately, not all consecutive attempts demonstrated the same academic rigour. Paradoxically, many deployed gigantic efforts on studying military installations and weaponry which were of little historiographical value, as the German fortresses and their fire-power were never put to the test and surrendered without having fired a shot. Apart from helping Germany lose the war (through its diversion of scarce resources) and becoming one of the main attractions of the post-war tourist industry there was practically nothing else of lasting historical impact about the fortress program. The military bias made people ignore the social and economic history of this occupation or the way in which the latter impacted the island consciousness, but it also provided a delay in the treatment of the controversial sides of the Occupation.

A first attempt to bring to public attention other than the military aspects of the war was the Anne Frank Exhibition, organised by the Jersey Museums Service in 1988. That there was a demand for this story was demonstrated through the 5,000 visitors it attracted, making this one of the best-attended exhibitions ever staged. Within this exhibition, organisers dedicated a special section to the fate of Jersey people who had defied German authority. The change in treatment owed much to a widespread new consciousness throughout Europe, which saw each country slowly coming to terms with war, occupation and genocide. In the islands a gradual reappraisal of the occupation years took place in the 1990s, crystallised through the need to identify and remember the unsung heroes of that period. The internal debate clustered around the issue of memorialisation. Many were of the opinion that there already was a memorial; the generic memorial in Howard Davis Park dedicated to all Jersey people who were deported to the Continent and died in prisons, concentration and internment camps.

However, critics advanced that neither did this detail any names nor did it provide an accurate historical record, amalgamating the story of offenders with that of internees who, by no means, shared the same fate.

The 1995 celebrations marking the 50th Anniversary of Liberation, a popular event stimulating the insular binding-forces and instilling a new type of self-assertiveness, provided the ideal setting to address the offenders issue publicly. Fifty years seemed to provide the necessary distance to approach the subject, leading the Jersey Occupation and Liberation Committee, a body set up in 1992, to deliberate several major projects of commemoration, among them a plaque honouring Louisa Gould. With the States' political weight behind these projects, overcoming the last remaining obstacles was a mere matter of time: another plaque, this time to Jersey political prisoners, was unveiled at the site of the former prison in Gloucester Street, on April 27, 1995; exactly fifty years after the execution of Nicolas Schmitz, a young German deserter arrested on the run with his Jersey girlfriend. It is hard to imagine a more symbolic date for such a ceremony which speaks for the organisers' magnanimity, many of whom had suffered at the hands of the occupier.

Plans for a memorial honouring Jersey offenders coincided with a variety of favourable elements. According to Occupation and Liberation Committee President Senator Jean Le Maistre, the memorial project dedicated to Jersey offenders benefited from a positive atmosphere and the fact that a suitable site became available, one of the major obstacles in the past. At the time plans for the restoration of an old warehouse on the New North Quay, to house the Occupation Tapestry Gallery and the Maritime Museum, were progressing, and when Constable Leonard Picot approached the Committee with the idea of a memorial to Jersey offenders, the area outside was seen as the ideal location. The Jersey Museums Service was instrumental in the execution of the project and sculptor Gordon Young created a fitting epitaph by incorporating the memorial around the base of a restored nineteenth century Jersey lighthouse that had been saved for the Maritime Museum. His work has resulted in a striking symbolism of past, present and future of the island and the unveiling ceremony in November 1996 proved a solemn finale to the work of the Committee.

The dearth of public recognition in the face of history has been neutralised by the unveiling of the memorial, a timely gesture which has opened the field for a closer look at the 'missing people', as well as at the motivations of their actions. Sixty years on, the island community no longer feels any uneasiness in addressing the legacy of the offenders; on the contrary, the issue has become a source of pride and reflection. It provides vital reference points to a society in quest of historical role models and examples, and effectively brings a period of strife down to the human dimension.

How will the Channel Islands Occupation be pictured in collective memory, especially when the last of the wartime generation will have taken their testimony to their graves? As the interest of professional historians in the Occupation is increasing, there is much reason to be optimistic. Works such as the recent report into the medical history of the Occupation conducted by Val Garnier at the University of London and Hazel Smith's Ph.D. thesis at the University of Southampton are examples of interesting new research perspectives opened in recent years.[341] This movement heralds the end of the days when the Channel Islands Occupation used to be a mere footnote of history. It should not come as a big surprise if one day in the not too distant future, universities in the UK decide to include the Channel Islands Occupation in their teaching programmes on Modern Britain or the Second World War. A new generation of young and detached historians will foster new approaches to research and introduce an array of methodological skills which should boost further the quality of available publications. Occupation research still needs further boosts, for outside the islands the discussion and image of the period is still captivated by the negative features of denunciation, collaboration and fraternisation. This bias leads to a situation where public opinion on the Continent reacts with relief to the fact that British citizens under German occupation did not behave dramatically differently to their continental counter-parts, whereas mainlanders see their subconscious beliefs about the 'not quite so British' Channel Islanders confirmed. Such conjecture forgets that human behaviour manifests itself in various shades of grey, rather than black and white, especially in an emergency situation where the adoption of unusual strategies becomes unavoidable. The majority have little inclination to end their days as either heroes or traitors and usually prefer survival, above all things. Therefore, rather than oscillating between the two extremes - collaboration and resistance – and trying to fit societies into one of these rigid categories, the entire discussion would be well advised to take account of wartime reality which found expression within the triangular confines of conformism, defiance and self-preservation.

What has created particular consternation is criticism which engages in sweeping assertions about the loyalty and trustworthiness of islanders in

---

[341] Garnier, Val, *Medical History of the Jersey Hospitals and Nursing Homes during the Occupation 1940-1945*, London, 2002.

general, while making little effort to explore the daily routine of features of collaboration such as denunciation or black-marketeering. As in other occupied territories, such behaviour was encouraged by the occupier and adopted by a certain number of Channel Islanders; it would be futile to argue otherwise. The Channel Islands with their short lines of communication and their high density of population provided an ideal terrain for denunciation. In general, denouncers had two motives, both of which were fuelled by self-interest rather than ideology. A tiny minority of islanders had been recruited by the German police force as regular informers and received lump sums for keeping the German authorities up-to-date on public opinion and all movements in the civilian population. That these rewards were too much to resist for certain islanders is hardly surprising if we consider rampant hunger and restrictions. The second group of 'one-off' informers had more personal motives. Their action was usually directed against particular individuals against whom they bore a grudge and, accordingly, most denunciations of this type were anonymous. What can be excluded is that any of the denouncers in the Channel Islands acted out of ideological proximity with Nazi ideology. Many critics tend to forget such realities; even less attention is paid to the fact that denunciation had a positive counterpart in the islands which existed in an almost equal measure: tipping-off in the event of danger.[342]

Transparency provides the most effective antidote to all attempts at exploiting the subject for the mere sake of controversy. But one must also be aware that academic inquiry is a two-edged sword, as there can be no cover from sometimes uncomfortable and penetrating questions. Like other academic disciplines, historiography progresses by stages and is the product

---

[342] A similarly interesting point concerns 'horizontal collaboration'; again the relative figures indicate no abnormal tendencies of fraternisation. One document cites 800 illegitimate births in the Channel Islands, s. PRO. HS 452. Sir Oscar Dowson, Home Office legal adviser to W. E. Beckett, Foreign Office re. children born out of wedlock during the Occupation, 20 June 1945; a second document cites 176 such births in the island of Jersey between July 1940 and May 1945, s. PRO. HS 452. A Le Gros, Superintendent Registrar, Jersey, 10 July 1945. Finally, a third document cites 340 illegitimate births, of which 'it was certain' that 180 were of German fathers. Determining this beyond certainty must have been no mean achievement in the days of pre-DNA sampling, s. PRO. KV4/78/65169. 'Collaborators in the Channel Islands' by J.R. Stopford, 8 Aug. 1945.

of the eternal dialectics of argument and counter-argument. Different opinions are vital prerequisites in the quest for objectivity and any innovative person acquainted with the basic rules of science and capable of exploring a set of salient questions deserves to be treated with respect. There is of course no guarantee for total success, especially in barely researched areas. However, relevant questions can always provide valuable inspiration and serve as a model for future research. In the Channel Islands a research culture of this type, marked by a capacity to discuss controversially, is needed. One of the more painful tasks of every historian is to make a good selection of material from the masses of available information. Historians have a responsibility towards the general public (and in particular their readers) to 'weigh things', to balance their accounts and to establish a guideline that will offer an orientation through history, thus protecting the layman from all fruitlessly quixotic battles with the windmills. In terms of such a systematic approach many publications on the Channel Islands Occupation leave a lot to be desired. All professional history writing establishes its proper 'hierarchy of facts', an intrigue shielded by tight-fitting arguments and designed to withstand any serious criticism. In this account an attempt has been undertaken to weave such a red thread', while avoiding the extremes of an excessively detached and 'dry' narrative and surrender to anecdote.

For this purpose we have argued the case of the recurrent 'macro-elements' of the Occupation, the two abstract categories which, in our opinion, overshadowed most other considerations: the food situation and anything even remotely connected with the fortification programme. Nobody escaped their widespread ramifications and somewhere along the line the fate of all Channel Islands offenders was directly affected by these rather peculiar dispositions.

Occupation historian Charles Cruickshank's dictum that enough material has survived to fill several volumes still remains entirely valid. Considering the abundance of private archives, collections and diaries in the Islands, the location of such material should cause few problems. Other unexplored research resources exist in continental Europe. On the negative side, it must be pointed out that our most important source, oral testimony, is becoming an alarmingly rare commodity and that we are fast running out of time. More than in other countries where German attempts to destroy important documentary evidence was often frustrated by sudden movements of the frontline and a general disintegration of order during the last days of German rule, the services in the islands had many months meticulously to prepare the destruction of their records. In view of the trying lack of data in some areas, oral history is the most important means of obtaining vital complementary information. However, well-informed oral sources are becoming increasingly scarce and with every year that passes, a few more pages of this history are lost forever. Sadly, already today occupation research is highly dependent on the testimonies of those who were youngsters during the Occupation. The elementary problem with this is that youngsters or children shared perceptions of events which deviated largely from those of their parents and that their insight was, by nature, limited. Few islanders who had important responsibilities during the Occupation are still alive today and some of the blanks in our knowledge are indeed disconcerting: Just as the pages of Harold Le Druillenec's splendid manuscript at the BBC archives remained unturned for many years, nobody interviewed personalities such as Pat Tatam of Victoria College or Captain Sowden. Nobody made an attempt to tell the story of the valiant GPO workers who opened letters of denunciation. Similar slips of amnesia, partly based on phobia about addressing the more unpalatable aspects of the Occupation, are frustrating reminders to those interested in the truth of the limitations of the historian's means. Many by now lost vestiges, such as the twenty bundles of records containing names and offences of Channel Islands prisoners which were destroyed when the old prison was dismantled after the war, could have filled some of the gaps in our systematic knowledge of this period. Swift action will have to be taken by the public bodies if further 'memory losses' are to be avoided. It is high time to collect the remaining oral testimonies that are still out there.

The research undertaken for this book shows that it is not too late for the history of the only major occupation of British Isles territory by a foreign force in modern times. It equally demonstrates that a fair amount of archival material is still awaiting its exploitation in the Channel Islands, the UK, France and Germany. There seems to be little need to emphasize that the story has a tremendous potential in offering vital lessons to our society, which is in constant need of reference. This is self-evident. Above all, if there is one thing the author hopes to have achieved, then it is that his collective portrayal of Jersey offenders will help reassess and diversify the debate on occupied Jersey. May it serve as a stepping-stone for increased recognition of acts of defiance against the occupying authority and aid the island in finding its rightful place in the historiography of European resistance in World War II.

ADDENDUM

Edward Peter Muels and John Soyer, by Paula Thelwell

On Holocaust Memorial Day, Monday 27 January 2003, the Bailiff of Jersey, Sir Philip Bailhache, unveiled a plaque on the Lighthouse Memorial to the Islanders who died in Nazi prisons and camps during the Occupation.

The plaque bore the names of two men, Edward Peter Muels and John (Jack) Soyer. Their names were omitted from the original memorial panels because their story did not come to light until after it was unveiled in November 1966.

Muels and Soyer's tragic deaths were finally acknowledged through the unstinting research of Occupation historian Joe Mière.

However, following publication in the Jersey Evening Post of Muel's story his son, David, came forward to finally confirm the details of his father's 'crime,' punishment and death.

Edward Peter Muels

Edward Peter Muels was born on 2 July 1912. He was a lorry driver for the Parish of St Helier, who resided at Sea Breeze, La Rocque, Grouville, with his wife, Olive and their son.

He paid the highest price after being charged in January 1944 with assisting a German soldier – Gefreiter David Hoost - to dessert after he had shot and killed an officer, Alfred König. Muels was sentenced by a German military court to 18 months hard labour and was, until April 2003, believed to have died in June 1944 when the RAF bombed the prison train transporting him to Germany.

In the autumn of 1943 the Muels family - who were studying to become Jehovah Witnesses - formed a friendship with the young German whose family were also Witnesses.

Denied promised home leave to visit his fiancée, Hoost sought comfort on the afternoon of New Year's Eve 1943 at Sea Breeze. He returned that night, confessing to having accidentally killed his commandant as he had tried to regain entry to the barracks, drunk and having forgotten the password. David Muels remembers the Russian Front veteran standing in the cottage doorway, his hands covered in blood. He was carrying a gun.

In an attempt to stop Hoost shooting himself, Mrs Muels gave him some of her husband's old clothes.

Hoost was captured and, under interrogation, named his Good Samaritans. Peter Muels was arrested, tried and sentenced and after a month sent to a German Camp. From June 1944 his wife and son knew nothing of his whereabouts.

When the Liberation came, David Muels spent every Saturday at the harbour scanning the returning faces for his father. He never came home and the family were informed he had died in the bombing of the prison train.

Then, in late 1948, Mrs Muels received a letter though the Austrian Embassy from a fellow inmate of her husband. She invited him to Jersey where he told her and young David that Mr Muels had died in a concentration camp in Germany three weeks before it was liberated. The Red Cross corroborated this version.

David Muels was just seven-years-old when he last saw his father on a prison visit. Now in his late 60s he often remembers happy times playing hide and seek among the vraic stacks, fishing for mackerel off the slip at La Rocque and wading through the sea so full of whiting, father and son had to push the fish away as they walked.

"Those little occasions of being with my father have been with me all my through my life," he said.

He is honoured that his father's act of selfless kindness for his fellow man, no matter what his race, will always be remembered.

Jack Soyer

John (Jack) Soyer was born in St Lawrence on 9 February 1901.

At the time of his arrest he worked as a wood merchant and lived with his wife, Margaret, and children Bernard, Albert and Dorothy, at Belvedere Terrace, Millbrook. They had recently moved from a house in Waterworks Valley.

On 29 August 1943 the German military authorities sentenced him to 12-months in prison for possessing a wireless set and passing on the news. An informer shopped him.

Soyer served the first three-months of his sentence in Jersey before being transferred to Fresnes prison in Paris. The family lost contact with him when the Channel Islands were isolated following the D-Day Landings in June 1944.

After the Island was liberated Soyer's family waited for news. In August 1945 they learned of his fate in a letter from the Justice of the Peace for Granville, Edward Poullain.

Soyer escaped from Fresnes early in 1943, working his way across France to the west coast of Normandy where he ended up in Bréhal on the Granville-Coutances highway. Welcomed by the local community, who nicknamed him 'L'Anglais,' he joined the Resistance taking part in actions against the Germans, usually accompanied by 21-year-old Roger Laubel.

In July 1944, as the Normandy breakout continued and the Americans advanced south, the Germans prepared to mount a last stand and conducted a house-to-house search. Soyer was shot as he made his escape. The next day the American liberated the village.

Two days later villagers and American GIs stood side by side as Soyer's funeral cortege processed to the church. Unbeknown to the mourners there was another tragedy to act out. Laubel climbed the church tower to toll the bell for his friend. As he peered down on the crowd, he caught the eye of a GI who thought he was a sniper and shot him.

The two Resistance fighters lay buried close together in the village cemetery on the Normandy coast, within site of Jersey.

Soyer's memory lives on in Bréhal and his name is carved on the war memorial in St Lô.

APPENDIX

Joe Mière, the former curator of the German War Tunnels in Jersey has compiled a list of islanders deported to German camps and prisons. The original list was included in the first edition of this book as recognition of Joe Mière's determined efforts to record the suffering of his fellow Islanders during the Occupation. It then comprised 300 names, but over the last six years his tireless efforts have resulted in a record comprising over 600 names. The list excludes those deported in September 1942 as part of the general deportation of non indigenous mainland born British Channel Islanders. Included however are those transported to internment camps in February 1943 as part of the deportation of specified categories of individuals in reprisal for an Allied raid on Sark.

Those listed were deported from the Channel Islands for a variety of reasons, some had committed acts of sabotage against the German regime, others had sheltered slave workers. A number were deported because they were Jews or because they were felt likely to exert an unduly anti-German influence or had generally offended the German administration. The deportees were sent to a number of prisons, work camps, internment camps and concentration camps. All suffered, a number died through ill-treatment, many were scarred for life by their experiences, but happily the majority survived.

The list is now too extensive for inclusion in this work but can be viewed at www.occupationmemorial.com.

SOURCES

I. ARCHIVAL SOURCES

BBC Written Archives
BBC talk by Harold Le Druillenec, 25 September 1945
BBC feature programme 'The Man from Belsen', based on the experiences of Harold Le Druillenec, 12 April 1946

Bundesarchiv (BA)
- Military Archives (MA), Freiburg
RH 26/319. 7th Army High Command
RW 4/624 and 625. OKW/Wehrmacht HQ
RW 5/243. OKW/Foreign Section/Abwehr
RW 35/537. Military Government in France (Militärbefehlshaber in Frankreich): reception of enemy broadcasts
RW 49/97. Abwehr Command France (F/IIIc): Channel Islands - Commitment of labour resources, protective security measures, 1942-1944
- Reich Documents Section (R), Berlin
R 22/1341 to 1342. Reich Ministry of Justice (RMJ)
- Zentrale Nachweisstelle (ZNS), Aachen
W 11/104 to 107. Court Martials-General correspondence
Z 726. Court of the 319th Infantry Division (ID), Jersey branch:
Investigations into the case against William Marsh
Investigations into the case against Walter Dauny

Government House, Jersey
50/4. Lieutenant Governors' files

Jersey Archives Service (JAS)
- Bailiff's War Files
B/A/W/30/94. Papers relating to the order to surrender wireless sets, 1942-43
B/A/W/80. List of persons evacuated from Jersey
B/A/W/85/5. War graves-Civilians in enemy and enemy occupied territory
- Bailiff's Liberation Files
B/A/L/15. Liberation files-Inquiries for relatives
- C/C/L. Occupation and Liberation Committee Files
- D/S/A. Occupation Registration cards, Registration and Identification of Persons (Jersey) Order, 1940
- D/Z. Law Officers Files. Sentences and prosecutions by Field Command and Troop Courts
- L/C/24. Joe Mière Collection
A 5. List of political prisoners in the Channel Islands, 1940-1945
D 2. Death and birth certificates of Frank Le Villio

Island Archives Service, Guernsey
FK 23-3. *Feldkommandantur* papers

Musée de la résistance et de la déportation, Besançon
de la Martinière documents concerning NN prisoners

Public Record Office (PRO), London
- Home Office (HO)
45/22399. The conduct of the population and the administration of the Channel Islands during the German Occupation
- Foreign Office (FO)

741. UK-Federal Republic of Germany agreement on compensation for victims of Nazi persecution
765. Questions of compensation for servicemen
766. Index to names of British subjects in enemy concentration camps and statistical survey of camps
950. Claims Department
- War Office (WO)
11. German Occupation of the Channel Islands: death and ill-treatment of slave labourers and transportation of civilians to Germany
192. Channel Islands deportation and ill-treatment of civilians
235. Ravensbrück Trial, Hamburg, 1946
309. War of 1939-1945: HQ BAOR, War Crimes Group (NWE)
311. War of 1939-1945: Military Deputy, Judge Advocate General - War Crimes Files
317. Ravensbrück Trial. Depositions of Johann Schwarzhuber and Ruth Closius Neudeck
677. War crimes in the Channel Islands: evidence and investigations
- Treasury Solicitor's Papers (TS)
26. UN War Crimes Commission
89. Channel Islands
- Records of SOE (HS)
452. Channel Islands
- Records of the Security Service (KV)
4/78. Production of 1(b) brief by Security Service for the Channel Islands, Dec. 1943 to Oct. 1945.

State Archives of Hessen, Wiesbaden
46/18893. Prosecutor's Office at District Court Frankfurt
409/4. Preungesheim prison records

State Archives of Saxony-Anhalt, Merseburg
Rep. C 131 II. Naumburg Death Register

II. ORAL SOURCES
Chapter One - Advocate Valpy
Chapter Two - (an anonymous relative of William Marsh)
Chapter Three - 'Birdie' Paisnel, George Sty
Chapter Four - Roy Mourant, John Painter, Vernon Cavey
Chapter Five - Phyllis Le Druillenec, Rex Forster, Robert Le Sueur, Raymonde Martel, Daphne Syvret, Madeleine Breslin
Chapter Six - Helen Ogier
Chapter Seven - Douglas Tanguy

III. OTHER SOURCE MATERIAL

Lists
French Ministry of Veterans and War Victims, Paris. List of Jersey prisoners
Archives de Paris. List of Channel Islands prisoners in French penitentiaries, 1943

Private Papers
Ogier Papers (in possession of Helen Ogier, Paris)
Painter papers (in possession of John Painter, Jersey)

BIBLIOGRAPHY

1. PUBLISHED WORKS

Aufsess, Baron von/Casper, Wilhelm, *In the Eye of the Hurricane. Rememberances from the Channel Islands 1941-1943*. Jersey, 1991.

Aufsess, Baron von, *The von Aufsess Occupation Diary*, edited and translated by Kathleen J Nowlan, Worcester, 1985.

Broszat, Martin/Fröhlich, Elke/Wiesemann, Falk, eds., *Alltag und Widerstand. Bayern im Nationalsozialismus*, Munich, 1987, 6 vols.

Bunting, Madeleine, *The Model Occupation - The Channel Islands under German Rule 1940-1945*, London, 1995.

Cajani, Luigi, 'Die italienischen Militärinternierten im nationalsozialistischen Deutschland', in: Herbert, Ulrich, ed., *Europa und der Reichseinsatz. Ausländische Zivilarbeiter, Kriegsgefangene und KZ-Häftlinge in Deutschland 1938-45,* Klartext, 1991.

Cohen, Frederick, *The Jews in the Channel Islands during the German Occupation 1940-1945*, Jersey Heritage Trust (in association with the Institute of Contemporary History and Wiener Library), 2000.

Cruickshank, Charles, *The German Occupation of the Channel Islands*, London, 1975.

Davies, Peter, *Dangerous Liaisons. Collaboration and World War Two*, London, 2004.

De Carteret, Basil/Deslandes, Mary/Robin, Mary, *An Island Trilogy. Memories of Jersey and the Occupation,* Jersey, n.d.

Falla, Francis, *The Silent War. The Inside Story of the Channel Islands under the Nazi Jackboot,* Guernsey, 1994 (reprint).

Foot, M R D, *Resistance. An Analysis of European Resistance to Nazism 1940-1945*, London, 1976.

Fraser, David, *The Jews of the Channel Islands and the Rule of Law 1940-1945 – 'Quite contrary to the principles of British justice'*, Brigthon/Portland, 2000.

Garnier, Val, *Medical History of the Jersey Hospitals and Nursing Homes during the Occupation 1940-1945*, London, 2002.

Gellately, Robert, *The Gestapo and German Society. Enforcing Racial Policy 1933-1945, Oxford, 1990.*

Ginns, Michael, *The Organisation Todt and the Fortress Engineers in the Channel Islands* (Channel Islands Occupation Society, Archive Book No. 8), Jersey, 1994.

Gutman, Israel, ed.,*Encyclopedia of the Holocaust,* New York, 1989,4 vols.

Haestrup, Jørgen, *European Resistance Movements, 1939-1945. A Complete History,* Westport/London, 1981.

Harris, Roger E., *Islanders Deported. Part 1: The Complete History of those British Subjects who were deported from the Channel Islands during the German Occupation of 1940-45 and imprisoned in Europe*, Illford, 1980.

Hawes, Stephen/White, Ralph, eds., *Resistance in Europe 1939-1945* (based on the proceedings of a symposium held at the University of Salford, March 1973), London, 1975.

Hensle, Michael, *Rundfunkverbrechen. Das Hören von 'Feindsendern' im Nationalsozialismus*, Berlin 2003.

Herbert, Ulrich, *Fremdarbeiter-Politik und Praxis des Ausländer-Einsatzes in der Kriegswirtschaft des Dritten Reiches*, Berlin/ Bonn, 1985.

Hillsdon, Sonia, *Jersey-Occupation remembered*, Norwich, 1986.

Journeaux, Donald, *Raise the White Flag - A Life in Occupied Jersey*, Leatherhead (Surrey), 1995.

King, Peter, *The Channel Islands War 1940-45*, London, 1991.

Kogon, Eugen/Langbein, Hermann/Rückerl, Adalbert et al., *Nationalsozialistische Massentötungen durch Giftgas*, Frankfurt, 1983.

Kosthorst, Erich/Walter, Bernd, *Konzentrations- und Strafgefangenenlager im Dritten Reich. Beispiel Emsland. Dokumentation und Analyse zum Verhältnis von NS-Regime und Justiz,* Düsseldorf, 1983.

Lasker-Wallfisch, Anita, *Inherit the Truth 1939-1945. The documented Experiences of a Survivor of Auschwitz and Belsen*, London, 1996.

Lean, Tangye, *Voices in the Darkness. The Story of the European Radio War,* London, 1943.

MacAuslan, Alan, *Darling, Darling Meg. Belsen? Where's that?,* Edinburgh/Cambridge/Durham, 1996.

Martinière, Joseph (de la), *Le décret et la procédure 'Nacht und Nebel' ('Nuit et Brouillard')*, Orleans, 1981.

Martinière, Joseph (de la), *Nuit et brouillard à Hinzert. Les déportés NN en camp spécial SS*, n.d.

Mallmann, Klaus-Michael/Paul, Gerhard, eds., *Die Gestapo - Mythos und Realität*, Darmstadt, 1995.

Moore, Bob, ed., *Resistance in Western Europe*, Oxford/New York, 2000.

Phillips, Raymond, ed., *Trial of Josef Kramer and forty-four others (The Belsen Trial),* London, n.d.

Schwarz, Gudrun, *Nationalsozialistische Lager*, Frankfurt, 1991.

Semelin, Jacques, *Unarmed against Hitler. Civilian Resistance in Europe 1939-1943,* Westport/London, 1993.

Sinel, Leslie, *The German Occupation of Jersey: A Complete Diary of Events, June 1940-June 1945*, Jersey, 1984 (reprint).

Streit, Christian, *Keine Kameraden. Die Wehrmacht und die sowjetischen Kriegsgefangenen 1941-1945*, Stuttgart, 1978.

Taylor, James/Shaw, Warren, *A Dictionary of the Third Reich*, London, 1987.

Thomas, Jürgen, *Wehrmachtsjustiz und Widerstandsbekömpfung: das Wirken der ordentlichen deutschen Militärjustiz in den besetzten Westgebieten 1940-45 unter rechtshistorischen Aspekten*, Baden-Baden, 1990.

Thomas, Roy, *Lest We Forget. Escapes and attempted Escapes from Jersey during the German Occupation 1940-1945,* Jersey, 1992.

Tillion, Germaine, *Ravensbrück*, Paris, 1988.

Toms, Carel, *Hitler's Fortress Islands - Germany's Occupation of the Channel Islands,* London, 1967.

2. UNPUBLISHED WORKS

L'Amy, J.H., *The German Occupation of Jersey*, unpublished memoirs, n.d. (custody of the Société Jersiaise).

Hassall, Peter, *Night and Fog Prisoners*, memoirs published online at:
<http://www.jerseyheritagetrust.org/occupation_memorial/pdfs/hassallbookcomplete.pdf.>

3. PERIODICALS, NEWSPAPER ARTICLES, BROCHURES

Ginns, Michael, 'The Commandant', in: *Channel Islands Occupation Review 1981*, 6-11.

Grossmann, Anton J., 'Fremd-und Zwangsarbeiter in Bayern 1939-45', in: *Vierteljahreshefte für Zeitgeschichte,* 34 (1986).

Hassall, Peter, Synopsis of *Night and Fog Prisoners*

Mayne, Richard, 'People who escaped from Jersey during the Occupation', in: *Channel Islands Occupation Review 1975*, 22-24.

Mayne, Richard, 'Forgotten Islanders', in: *Channel Islands Occupation Review 1974*, 15-18

SPD Preungesheim, *8. Mai 1945 - 8. Mai 1985. Preungesheim* 40 Jahre danach- *Erinnern oder vergessen?,* 1985.

The Evening Post, Jersey

'Well-known Jerseyman's Death in Action - Brilliant Scholar and Sportsman', 15 July 1941.

'A Russian Officer's Story - His Escape from Jersey P.O.W. Camp - How He Was Hidden and Fed for 2 1/2 Years', 10 May 1945.

'Tragic News for Jersey Family - Father and Son Die in German Prison Camp', 2 June 1945.

'Definite News of Canon Cohu - Died in German Prison Camp', 25 September 1945.

'Russian presentations', 29 March 1966.

'My Story...Dora Hacquoil - Harbouring Russians', 2 February 1995.

'In Memory of Those who Never Came Back', 8 November 1996

'Fighting to Lay the Past to Rest', 9 December 1996.

'Obituary: Ivy Forster', 7 July 1997.

The Sunday Island Times

'Canon Clifford John Cohu: A Victim of the Occupation', three-part article by Alex Glendinning, 27 February, 6 March, 13 March 1994.

Index